CHRIST

in the

HOLY LAND

Edited by
Michael Prior and William Taylor

THE WORLD OF ISLAM FESTIVAL TRUST

Front cover: the publishers gratefully acknowledge permission to reproduce a positive image of a breadmould belonging to the collection of the late Dr Tawfiq Canaan, given by his daughter Mrs Leila Mantoura.

Second printing 1995

First published in 1994 by
World of Islam Festival Trust
33 Thurloe Place
London SW7 2HQ

ISBN 0-905035-32-1

British Library Cataloguing–in–Publication Data
A catalogue record of this book is
available from the British Library

Produced and distributed by
Scorpion Publishing Ltd
Victoria House
Victoria Road
Buckhurst Hill
Essex IG9 5ES
UK

General editor: Leonard Harrow

Printed in Malta for Amon-Re Ltd

Contents

Obligations and Expectations

Participants in the seminar, Cumberland Lodge, May 1993

Contributors

ABU EL-ASSAL, Archdeacon Riah
Representative: Protestant/Anglican Bishopric in Jerusalem

AGHAZARIAN, Dr Albert
Director of Public Relations, Bir Zeit University

ALI, Rt Revd Bishop Michael Nazir
Secretary General CMS London (Bishop of Rochester 1994)

BARAMKI, Dr Gabriel
Vice President, Bir Zeit University

CRAGG, Rt Revd Bishop Kenneth
Honorary Asstistant Bishop (Oxford)

GERAISY, Dr Sami
Chairman, International Christian Committee of Israel

HAGOPIAN, Dr Harry
Middle East Council of Churches (UK),
Seminar Steering Committee

HANANIA, Agnes D
Professor of Education and Psychology,
Bir Zeit University

KATTAN, Dr Jeanne
Assistant Professor of English, Bethlehem University

LAHHAM, Revd Maroun
Rector of the Latin Catholic Seminary, Beit Jala

MOXON, Canon Michael A
Canon of St Georges', Windsor Castle,
Chaplain to Cumberland Lodge

MUNAYER, Mr Salim
Dean of Bethlehem Bible College

O'MAHONY, Dr Anthony
SOAS/London University

PRIOR, Revd Dr Michael CM
Head of Department of Theology and Religious Studies,
St Mary's University College, University of Surrey,
Seminar Steering Committee

RAHEB, Revd Dr Mitri
Minister of the Lutheran Christmas Church, Bethlehem

SABELLA, Dr Bernard
Professor of Sociology, Bethlehem University

AL-SARRAF, Mr Faraj
Lawyer. Author of *Christianity in Gaza*

SFEIR, Dr Jacqueline
Assistant Professor of Early Childhood Education,
Bethlehem University

TAYLOR, Revd Dr William
Vicar of St Peter's Church, Ealing, former priest
in the Diocese of Jerusalem

WYBREW, Canon Hugh
Former Canon of St George's Cathedral, Jerusalem

ZARU, Mrs Jean
Religious Society of Friends, Ramallah

Foreword

Within living memory, Christians in the Holy Land have existed as a religious and social minority on the edge of the Arab heartland under Turkish, British, Arab and Israeli rule. Their status and well-being have been determined by the government of the day, but they find sympathy and support from the churches outside the Holy Land, whose membership spreads around the world.

For the past twenty-one years the World of Islam Festival Trust has sought to encourage understanding and appreciation of the multifaceted contributions of Islamic culture to the development of global civilization in terms of academia, the sciences, art and architecture. That much of this cultural expression has, as its mainspring, the concept of faith in One God, prompted the Trust to concern itself with the present welfare of Christians in the Holy Land, who share, with Muslims and Jews alike the Abrahamic tradition.

The Trust therefore decided that it should use its initiative and resources for the benefit of all concerned by offering the churches of Jerusalem an occasion and a platform outside their own area in which they could present a resumé of their historic role to a concerned audience and to discuss, in relative privacy, their present circumstances, aspirations and the opportunities in which they could assist in the immediate and elusive search for peace. It was hoped, too, that the seminar would also contribute to the growing links between the churches.

We also hoped that this ecumenical experience for both clergy and laity would find some practical expression in Jerusalem. There were surely matters and projects concerned with education, health, housing and other aspects of social welfare which could benefit from a joint approach or sponsorship by all the churches, which need not infringe upon doctrinal or mutually recognized theological differences between them.

Such experience could, hopefully, lead to extending this co-ordinated and cordial activity with the Muslim authorities. We would like to think that such an example by the Mother Church could not only have a beneficial effect upon the interests shared by all congregations and communities, but would help to inhibit the opportunities for mischievous exploitation by extremists from any quarter.

In order to assist in the organization of the seminar, a Steering Committee was set up under the chairmanship of Sir John Moberly, which worked hard and imaginatively. Two of its members, the Revd Dr Michael Prior and the Revd Dr William Taylor volunteered to act as joint rapporteurs of the subsequent publication and we offer our unreserved gratitude to them for all their expert work and enthusiasm.

Aided by Dr Bernard Sabella of Bethlehem University, the Steering Committee offered the churches an outline programme, whose headings covered their historic and traditional bases and a spectrum of their present circumstances. The patriarchs and heads of churches in Jerusalem were invited to select those scholars who would present papers, and to nominate the members of the official delegation, which would come to Cumberland Lodge.

We record our gratitude to the Archbishop of Canterbury, the Most Reverend and Rt Honourable Dr George Carey, and the Cardinal Archbishop of Westminster, His Eminence Cardinal Basil Hume OSB, whose warm letters of support were of great value in stimulating the prosecution of the project.

It was indeed most fortunate that the King George VI and Queen Elizabeth Foundation of St Catherine's (often referred to by the name of its home, 'Cumberland Lodge') was able to accommodate us at the time of the Pentecost festival. We record our special appreciation of the friendly efficiency of their officers and all their staff, which greatly contributed to the smooth running of the seminar.

We express profound gratitude to Muslim and Christian sponsors recorded here, without whose generosity this seminar project would not have been realised.

Finally we hope that all who participated, and all who will now read this account of the seminar will understand that we, with our Christian and Muslim sponsors, tried to offer the churches in the Holy Land a place and a time in which to consider their circumstances with Christian friends from outside their own immediate area, and to explore constructive ideas for the future welfare of all who dwell therein. With God's Grace, we hope these will influence and aid the prospects for peace in the Holy Land.

Alistair Duncan
September 1994   *Director, World of Islam Festival Trust*

Sponsors

Letters of Support to the Trust

During the preparations for the Cumberland Lodge meeting, the organisers received many letters and expressions of support and encouragement, a number of which are reproduced below.

From the Rt Revd and Rt Hon George Carey, Archbishop of Canterbury

It was with much encouragement that I have heard of the advanced state of your plans for the seminar *Christians in the Holy Land*. My own knowledge of the Holy Land and particularly my visit there in early 1992 made me realise how important it is that we tackle the problem of the dwindling Christian population in that part of the world.

Your seminar will gather together participants from all the main churches of the Holy Land and it has the clear support of the Patriarchates and of our own Bishop in Jerusalem. I very much hope that it will help us to see ways in which the problems of Christians in the Holy Land can be tackled. I am sure that it will also be a positive contribution to better ecumenical understanding between Christians working together there. I wish the seminar every success.

From His Eminence, the Cardinal Basil Hume, Archbishop of Westminster

I warmly welcome the initiative to mount a seminar in England in May this year about Christians in the Holy Land. This event will bring together participants from all the main Churches of the Holy Land and it has the active support of the Patriarchates of Jerusalem. I hope it will do much to further knowledge and ecumenical understanding between the Churches in this country and those of the Holy Land.

I wish this important event every success.

From Jerusalem, a Message of Greeting from Their Beatitudes, Diodorus I, Greek Orthodox Patriarch, Michael Sabbah, Latin Patriarch, and Torkom Manoogian, Armenian Patriarch

If I forget thee, O Jerusalem, let my right hand forget her cunning
(Psalm 137:5)

We, the Patriarchs of the Holy city of Jerusalem, greet this gathering with the words of St Paul: ' . . . Grace to you, and peace, from God our Father and the Lord Jesus Christ' (Romans 1:7)

We extend to you all, Our blessings from the Holy City where the Holy church was first established on the Day of Pentecost. We are blessed by Our Lord, Jesus Christ, to be His servants and Archpastors in this Holy Land where He Himself planted and nourished the Church with His Blood. Jerusalem is the place where Christianity was born, and from which God's Word and Love was carried by His disciples to all corners of the world.

The Church had to endure persecution and suffering for centuries and Her fate could not be different from that of Her Founder. She, too, had to walk along Her own Way of the Cross. Her mission has always been, despite trials and tribulations, to lead humankind to salvation in the Resurrected Christ. This is indeed an extremely difficult mission, if We take into consideration the culture and religious diversities of Our context.

The Church of Jerusalem has been nourished by the blood of Her martyrs, Patriarchs, Bishops, priests and lay people. Her spiritual heritage is deeply rooted in the Holy Land while She firmly abides in the hearts of Christian souls everywhere. Through these sacrifices, the Church obtained for Her survival certain rights and privileges which are inviolable and internationally recognized. These guaranteed, also, the continuation of Her vital universal mission.

Today, the Church in Jerusalem is profoundly concerned over the continuation of Her presence and witness because of unfavourable conditions, both internal and external. We believe this is also the basis of your concern for the Christians in the Holy Land and the purpose of your highly appreciated initiative.

The Life of Our Lord, Jesus Christ, in the Holy Land, left traces marking His Divine Presence on earth such as Bethlehem, the Calvary where the Great Sacrifice took place, and the Tomb where He was buried and resurrected. These Holy Places retain a spiritual significance for all Christians in the world who feel a need to visit and venerate Them. As the sole legal custodians of the Holy Places, entrusted with the responsibility of maintaining and guarding Them, the Patriarchates have through long years and heavy cost, fulfilled this task on behalf of all Christians in the Holy Land and all over the world.

But the Holy Land has not only those stones which bear witness to the passage of Christ, but the Living Stones, the faithful, who constitute the Body of Christ. These Living Stones are standing firmly in the Holy Land, prepared to witness to Christ by truth, justice and peace.

In these modern times, We hope that the Holy Places will continue to be central in Our Faith and that Christians in the Holy Land will be the living link between the Church of Jerusalem and the Church in the whole world, as they are part of the Living Chain that connects the present Church with Jesus, the Saviour.

· Therefore, the Church in the Holy Land is entitled to enjoy all legitimate rights, including the freedom of exercising Her pastoral activity, performing religious ceremonies, the freedom of worship and access to the Holy Places by all Her members wherever they come from. All rulers of Jerusalem, throughout the centuries, have recognized these rights of the Christian communities in the Holy Land.

With these thoughts, We joyfully greet you and pray that the Holy Spirit, Who always guides the Church, may enlighten you and grant you Divine Wisdom in your deliberations and success in your endeavours.

With Our Patriarchal blessings.

From His Eminence, Archibishop Loutfi,
Greek Catholic Patriarchal Vicar in Jerusalem

Greetings from Jerusalem, the Mother Church!

I thank you very much for your letter of 3 July 1992, and for your initiative to organise a conference or a seminar about the present situation of the Christian communities in the Holy Land and especially in Jerusalem.

I agree with this project and I bless it. It is a sign of your interest and love for the church of the Holy Land and for the whole of the inhabitants of this country. Because a Christian concern must be always a human concern, and not a ghetto concern or a coven of a group or club. Because the Christian like Christ cannot live for himself, but always with others and for others: this is our faith, this is our experience and this is the meaning of our presence in the Holy Land and in the Arab world. This is our mission!

God bless you and the initiative you are leading!

From the Rt Revd Samir Kafity, President Bishop, the Episcopal Church in Jerusalem and the Middle East

I want to affirm my own support to this historic occasion that brings together the leaders of the churches in Jerusalem with the many churches in Britain in discussion and consultation over the serious issues that Christians in the Holy Land face.

From Bishop Naim Nassar, the Evangelical Lutheran Church

Thank you for your fax dated July 16th with regard to your request for the preparations for the imminent seminar on 'Christians in the Holy Land'. I can herewith assure you that I personally encourage such a seminar. I am also sure that my colleagues from the other churches in Jerusalem will do the same. I think that they will also write to you and endorse your enterprise as soon as the summer vacations are over, since most of them are out of the country during this period.

I do really hope and pray that God will provide all the necessary need for such a programme, since it is a very important issue. We also feel that there has been too little done in this regard. May God bless your efforts.

With our warm wishes and regards.

From His Eminence, Archbishop Luigi Barbarito, Apostolic Pro-Nuncio in London

I much appreciate the purpose of the seminar you are organising and I feel convinced that it will be beneficial through concentrating on the problems of Christians in Palestine. . . . I do hope that the arrangements can be made for what promises to be an important meeting.

Introduction
Michael Prior and William Taylor

International concern for the conditions of Christians in the land of
Jesus has reflected the dire circumstances of that community.
Already in 1974, Pope Paul VI decried the fact of the diminishing
number of Christians in the Holy Land. He predicted that, if their
presence in the Holy Land were to cease, 'The shrines would be without
the warmth of the living witness of the Holy Places of Jerusalem and the
Holy Land would become like a museum' (Apostolic Exhortation,
'Concerning the increased needs of the Church in the Holy Land').

Paul VI put the deteriorating condition of Christians in a moral
framework, combining concern for the Jews, the victims of the
Holocaust, and the plight of Palestinians, the victims of the victims of
the Holocaust: 'Although we are conscious of the still very recent
tragedies which led the Jewish people to search for safe protection in a
state of its own, sovereign and independent, and in fact precisely because
we are aware of this, we would like to ask the sons of this people to
recognize the rights and legitimate aspirations of another people, which
have also suffered for a long time, the Palestinian people' (*Acta
Apostolicae Sedis*, January–March 1976, p. 134). This was the first time
that any Pope had recognized the rights and legitimate aspirations of the
Jews to a sovereign and independent state of their own, and
concomitantly, appealed to the victors to recognize the corresponding
rights of the vanquished.

More recently, after he had visited the Holy Land and Jordan

1

(3-8 January 1992), Archbishop George Carey expressed his fear that, 'In fifteen years' time Jerusalem and Bethlehem, once centres of strong Christian presence might become a kind of Walt Disney theme park' (*MECC News Report*, January 1992, p. 2). We must not allow that to happen, he insisted.

The establishment of the State of Israel and the expulsion and displacement of 714,000 Palestinian Arabs, including some 50,000 Christians – 35 per cent of all Christians who lived in Palestine prior to May 15, 1948 – was a major disaster for the Christian community, the effects of which are experienced to this day. The International Church's reaction at the time scarcely went beyond the expression of anguish at the general conditions of refugees, and the reiteration of predictable, broad moral and religious principles, with no explicit political implications.[1] Such was the international support for Zionism in the wake of the virtual annihilation of mainland European Jewry that it was virtually impossible for the leaders of the Christian churches to challenge Zionism publicly. Moreover, it would not have been wise for them to offend the USA in its support of the State of Israel, since the West needed its alliance in the face of Soviet expansionism. Nevertheless, Monsignor Thomas McMahon, representing Roman Catholic and other Christian interests in Palestine before the United Nations, insisted in several meetings with Israeli and American officials that the return of the Christian exiles was 'basic to an Israeli-Church rapprochement'.[2] However, the Palestinian issue was not mentioned publicly in Vatican circles for the twenty years after the establishment of the State of Israel.

One of the abiding results of the influence of Liberation Theologies from several developing nations throughout the Christian world is the conviction that issues of justice and peace are at the heart of any authentic interpretation of the gospel. Translated to the Middle East, two seemingly conflicting tendencies have developed: a greater respect for the Jews, and a growing sympathy for the plight of the Palestinians. Since the military might of the State of Israel, unequivocally and energetically supported by massive government aid from the United States, assured its security, attention was directed to contributing towards a just solution to the Palestinian problem. This should include the establishment of a Palestinian homeland; an internationally guaranteed special status for Jerusalem, with access to, and equality for Christians, Jews and Muslims, making Jerusalem a real centre of spiritual and fraternal development; and an improvement in the legal

[1] E.g., Pope Pius XII's Encyclical Letter, *In Multiplicibus* of October 1948, and six months later, *Redemptoris Nostri*.
[2] Kreutz, A. 1992. 'The Vatican and the Palestinians: A Historical Overview', *Islamochristiana* 18: 109-125, p. 117.

rights and social situations of the Christian communities living under Israeli control.

Concern for the Christian communities of the Holy Land could never have exhausted the Church's interest in a region which had by now become a focus of global interest, and a potential flash-point for conflict between the great powers. More than the future of a Jewish homeland, or the recovery of the dignity of the downtrodden Palestinians, was at stake. Future regional, and even world peace, would depend on the establishment of a lasting peace in the region. Contemporary theology, with its recovery of the sense of the Church as the People of God, could not allow its interests in the people of the region to be swallowed up by a parochial interest in the antiquities of a vibrant past. The Church is a building composed of living stones.

One of the results of the Palestinian *Intifada* was the increased politicization of the Christian churches in the Holy Land, and a new awareness within the churches in the West of the situation of the Palestinians. The report of the visit to Israel and the Occupied Territories by the official Delegation of the British Council of Churches in March 1989, impressed upon its readers the extent of the oppression of the Christian community, and the urgent need for a lasting peace.[3] An Arab priest said, 'Occupation is always a corrupting situation both for occupier and occupied. A wooden cage or a golden cage is still a cage' (p. 2). The Middle East Council of Churches sent a delegation to Britain in November-December 1989, and it emphasized that Christians in Britain 'should come to understand the reality, and the seriousness of the situation in the Holy Land, and that they should pray for true peace, peace based on justice.'[4]

Since then several Palestinian Christians have reflected theologically on life under military occupation within the Occupied Territories, or as third-, fourth-, or fifth-class citizens of the Jewish State of Israel.[5] Their theological reflections are distinctive in that they are quarried out of the sad memory of expulsion from their own homes and land, and the ongoing tragedy of living under occupation or oppression. Some forty years after the establishment of the State of Israel, the spirit of these Christian leaders and theologians has not been devoured by hatred or despair. Together with other colleagues they have established a

---

[3] *Impressions of Intifada. Report of a British Council of Churches Delegation to Israel and the Occupied Territories, March 1989*, (p. 1). Available from BCC, Inter-Church House, 35-41 Lower Marsh, London SE1 7RL, price £3.95.

[4] From the interview with Revd Audeh Rantisi, the leader of the Delegation on the *Sunday* programme, BBC Radio 4, December 3, 1989.

[5] Elias Chacour, 1985, *Blood Brothers*, Eastbourne: Kingsway. Naim Stifan Ateek, 1989, *Justice and Only Justice. A Palestinian Theology of Liberation*, New York, Maryknoll: Orbis. Audeh Rantisi, 1990, *Blessed are the Peacemakers. The Story of a Palestinian Christian*, Guildford: Eagle.

Committee of Palestinian Liberation Theology.[6]

Palestinian Liberation theologians have to contend with a number of very sensitive issues. Firstly, they are themselves all victims of oppression. Secondly, some Christians see in the establishment of the State of Israel the fulfilment of God's promises to the Children of Israel. Thirdly, some fundamentalist Christians share with some fundamentalist Jews views about the resettlement of Jews in Palestine as a stage preliminary to the Coming of the Messiah's End-Time Kingdom (Jews), or the Second Coming (Christians). Such proponents of biblical fundamentalism read the Pentateuch as providing the guarantee of God's unconditional gift of the land to the Israelites, without any regard to those who were living in the land already. Fourthly, even when there is abundant evidence of Israeli oppression, there is a deep unease within Western Christian circles about even the most tame criticism of Israeli policies. Fifthly, in Western circles the revulsion which one expects to surface at any form of wicked behaviour is muted in the case of the State of Israel. It is one of the great anomalies of recent church history that while Christians throughout the world have engaged energetically in favour of the oppressed in all kinds of areas, there has been almost total silence on the state terrorism of Israel, and its persistent abuse of human rights. Sixthly, some influential members of organisations committed to the noble ideal of Jewish-Christian dialogue remain silent on the oppression of the Palestinians, in spite of the presence of overwhelming, embarrassing evidence. They create a climate in which good relations between Jews and Christians appear to exact a condoning by silence of Israeli brutality.

The international seminar on Christians in the Holy Land at Cumberland Lodge developed from a concern to provide a dialogue between Christian scholars and Church people in the Holy Land and abroad. The mood in which the dialogue took place reflected the prevailing political context of the time. The planned date was May 1993, to coincide with the Christian celebration of Pentecost, which marks the outpouring of the Holy Spirit on the Jerusalem Church. For several months already, access to the Holy City of Jerusalem had been severely restricted to West Bankers, and this gross deprivation of freedom was the source of much inconvenience in the planning stage. It was not possible for all the delegates to meet together in the Holy Land prior to travelling to England, nor was it possible for any reasonable number to meet in Jerusalem, which left Bethlehem as the next choice for preliminary meetings.

The delegation of eighteen Jerusalem church leaders and academics

---

[6] *Faith and the Intifada. Palestinian Christian Voices*, ed. N S Ateek, M H Ellis, and R R Ruether, New York: Maryknoll (Orbis Books) 1992.

engaged with British and international academics on the subject. There was ample time for the participants to share their insights, in the general lectures, in groups, at table, and while relaxing together. This volume presents their contributions, adapted for publication. They describe aspects of the situation of the Christian Church in Israel and the Occupied Territories, and some reflections from Christians from other parts of world.

Anthony O'Mahony provides an historical survey of Christianity in the region since the first Muslim conquest of Jerusalem in 638, down to the present day, concentrating on developments in the 19th and 20th centuries. Dr Sami Geraisy and Professor Bernard Sabella discuss the socio-economic and demographic characteristics of the Christian community in Israel and the Occupied Territories, respectively. Dr Geraisy (Chairman of the International Christian Committee in Israel, and of the Department of Services to Palestine Refugees) describes some of the particular qualities of Israeli Arab village life, and how the establishment of the State of Israel has affected it. As a community which has lost its home, its land, its work, and its faith in justice, it looks to the establishment of peace as the only hope for a future. He stresses the role the churches can play, particularly in education and social services.

Professor Sabella (Bethlehem University), the major researcher in the field, considers the impact of emigration on the Christian community. The haemorrhage of the community will continue as long as there is no peace, and emigration will slow down dramatically when there is peace. The survival of Christians in the Land of Jesus, he insists, is contingent upon the establishment of tolerable political and social conditions.

Faraj al-Sarraf situates Christianity in Gaza in an historical and contemporary context. The distinguished Quaker, Jean Zaru, reflects on the issues of justice and peace, deriving her perspectives from the noble tradition of the biblical prophets.

Dr Jacqueline Sfeir (Bethlehem University) examines the place of education in Palestine, with particular reference to the Christian schools. They can play an important role in helping to bring about a process of educational change in Palestine, rather than insisting on retaining their sectarian nature. The local church should make itself available to the wider national and cultural context of the Church in Palestine.

The results of the investigation of Dr Jeanne Kattan (Bethlehem University) explode several of the myths, propagated by some Western propagandists, concerning the relations between Muslims and Christians. Dr Albert Aghazarian (Bir Zeit University) outlines the multi-cultural nature of Jerusalem, and stresses its significance for Christians. He traces the patchwork of Jerusalem's history and the significance for indigenous Christians of the repeated and successive occupation of Jerusalem by foreign forces.[7] Salim Munayer tackles the difficulty of Christians relating with Jews from within the experience of oppression and occupation.

Five representatives of different churches reflect on their ecclesial communities – the Greek (Dr Gabriel Baramki), the Latin, (Fr Maroun Lahham), the Anglican (Archdeacon Riah Abu El-Assal), the Lutheran (Dr Mitri Rahab) and the Armenian (Dr Harry Hagopian).

Fr Maroun Lahham includes Jordan in his perspective. He stresses the significance of Jerusalem as the Holy City for all the sons and daughters of Abraham, Jews, Muslims and Christians. It is the cradle of Christianity, and the spiritual home for all Christians. Jerusalem is a mosaic, wherein each church has its place, and where the whole forms a beautiful image of Jesus Christ Lord and Saviour. The Roman Catholic Church has its place in that mosaic. Like all other churches in Jerusalem, it strives to give back to Jerusalem its essential characteristic of openness and universality, and to act as a bridge between the Christian and Muslim worlds.

Archdeacon Abu al-Assal draws on the early history of the Anglican/ Lutheran bishopric of Jerusalem, and focuses on an issue which vexes many of the Christian communities of the Holy Land – how to be authentically Arab and indigenous when Christianity is often (erroneously) portrayed as a Western import.[8] This is true for Latins, Anglicans and Lutherans who have their 'centres of power' elsewhere, and also for the autocephalous Orthodox patriarchate of Jerusalem with its hellenistic hierarchy.

Similarly, Dr Mitri Raheb draws attention to the Germanic roots of the Anglo-Prussian bishopric of Jerusalem, and points out the contemporary vitality of the Lutheran diaconal presence in schools, social work, and in contextualized theological work.

Dr Harry Hagopian recalls the historic connections of Armenians with Jerusalem, and the significance of the Armenian Quarter for the demography of the city. He draws attention to the importance of pilgrimage in the Armenian tradition, as well as its economic and social effects for the indigenous Christian community. The Armenian experience of suffering and tragedy is recalled, and is an important reminder that 'holocaust theology' applies to more than one people.

Views from outside the Holy Land are expressed by Bishop Kenneth Cragg, Bishop Michael Nazir Ali, and Dr Michael Prior. Bishop Kenneth Cragg reflects theologically on the origins of the Christian Church in Jerusalem. Jerusalem is seen as central to the earliest Christian

---

[7] See also *Jerusalem in History*, ed. K J Asali, Buckhurst Hill, Essex: Scorpion 1989.
[8] See also Gerald Butt, *A Rock and a Hard Place, Origins of Arab-Western Conflict in the Middle East*, Harper Collins, 1994.

self-identity, and reveals for Cragg much of the nature of God himself. Contemporary Christian identity must always be aware of its deepest roots, whatever its geographical location.

Similarly, for Bishop Michael Nazir Ali, the world-wide characteristics of the universal church are strengthened by intimate knowledge of its roots – both place and people. He draws on this universal characteristic of the church to make a plea for justice and peace. His model for this is the ideal future settlement of the deep-rooted conflicts of the region – 'a non-confessional homeland for all Palestinians, and the recognition of the right of Israel to secure borders . . . the necessity for a comprehensive peace settlement is central to this.'

Dr Michael Prior (St Mary's University College) surveys the different attitudes of world-wide Christians to the Holy Land, both in history and today. He examines four models of traditional patterns of pilgrimage and highlights that which interacts with the social, political and cultural life of the region. Pilgrimage should interrogate the pilgrim, rather than merely fulfil her/his expectations, or even confirm her/his prejudices.

Finally Dr Agnes Hanania (Bir Zeit University) and Canon Hugh Wybrew issue a challenge to the international community of Christians to concern itself with the affairs of the Mother Church.

All of this, of course, was before the Oslo Accord, the September 9 handshake on the grounds of the White House, and the December 31 accord between Israel and the Vatican. As events since the conference have demonstrated, the road to a settlement based on justice and peace for all the people of the region is as hard and stony as it is fraught with danger. But the risks for peace must be taken by all sides, that Jerusalem may once again be 'a vision of peace' for all people.

A HISTORICAL SURVEY

I

Church, State and the
Christian Communities
and the
Holy Places
of Palestine

Anthony O'Mahony

Christianity in the Holy Land:
The Historical Background

The Christian Church was, in its earliest days, one undivided church. However, well before the time of the first Muslim conquest of Jerusalem in 638 AD the process of fission had commenced and a number of communities had come into being. There was, however, as yet only one patriarch of Jerusalem and he it was who negotiated with the Muslim conquerors on behalf of all Christians resident in the area. Available records indicate that from this date until the establishment of the Crusading kingdoms there was harmony among the various Christian communities in Jerusalem, in spite of the growing estrangement between Rome and Constantinople. However, with the capture of Jerusalem and the setting up of the Latin kingdoms, the cleavage between the Latin and the Eastern wings of the church became more pronounced, and the Latins, under a Latin patriarch, enjoyed paramountcy in all the Holy Places. Since there was some doubt in Eastern eyes about the validity of the appointment of the Latin patriarch, the Eastern churches also elected a patriarch, but he returned to Constantinople for the duration of tenure of the Crusading kingdoms. From about 1250 until about 1675 the Orthodox patriarch returned to Jerusalem but then retired once more until the middle of the 19th century. After the demise of the Crusading kingdoms the Latin patriarchate was based in Rome until its revival in 1847.[1]

From the capture of Jerusalem by Saladin until its absorption into the Ottoman empire, Jerusalem was governed by the Ayyubids and the Mamluks of Egypt. The supremacy enjoyed by the Latins was maintained for almost a century after the fall of the city, although this period also saw the fall of the Latins from their prominent position and the true beginning of the constant struggle between the Latin Church and the Orthodox Church for supremacy, particularly in connection with the ownership of and rights over the Holy Places. The struggle was largely confined to the three main rites recognised by the authorities, namely the Gregorian Armenians, the Orthodox Church and the Latins. The other rites, although represented in the Holy Places, were generally too poor to be able to take any significant part in the struggle for authority. Nevertheless in 1384 it was reported that seven different communities (Copts, Ethiopians, Armenians, Nubians, Orthodox, Latins, and Georgians) were represented in the Holy Places. However, throughout the Mamluk period and the subsequent Ottoman period, the history of Jerusalem is primarily a history of continual change of status, of rights of ownership and of position among the various Christian communities in the Holy Places. It should be noted that the majority of the Christian inhabitants of Jerusalem were Eastern Christians, whatever happened in the Holy Places. The struggle for position arose not only out of the basic rivalry between the faiths, but also out of the Muslim concept of legal ownership of religious buildings and institutions.[2]

Muslim rulers held themselves to be the legal owners of all religious buildings and institutions within their dominions, no matter the faith to which they were devoted. They therefore claimed the right to allocate them, confiscate them or close them at will. Such buildings could not be repaired or rebuilt without permission, while the building of new churches was for obvious reasons forbidden. Thus Saladin closed the Church of the Holy Sepulchre when he captured Jerusalem in 1187 until he had decided under whose jurisdiction he would place it. Similarly,

[1] Peters, P E. 1985. *Jerusalem: the Holy City in the Eyes of Chroniclers, Visitors, Pilgrims and Prophets from the Days of Abraham to the Beginnings of Modern Times.* Princeton: Princeton University Press.
[2] Gil, Moshe. 1992. *A History of Palestine, 643-1099.* Cambridge: Cambridge University Press.

the Franciscans, who had become established as official representatives of the Holy See in Jerusalem, with the official title of Custodia Terrae Sanctae, were expelled by imperial decree from their headquarters in the Cenaculum on Mount Zion in 1552. They finally settled in the Convent of St Saviour which they acquired from the Orthodox patriarchate, which had itself acquired the convent from the Armenians.[3]

From about beginning of the 16th century onwards the influence of the Orthodox church was generally greater than of the Latin, despite periods of reversion. This was a logical outcome of the conquest of Constantinople by the Ottoman Turks in 1453 and their subsequent capture of Jerusalem in late 1516, since the Orthodox and the Armenian Churches were the first recognised Christian *millets*, while the Latins were usually supported by foreign states with which the Ottoman authorities were at war. The Ottoman period also saw the introduction of international politics into the controversies surrounding Jerusalem and the Holy Places. Thus France claimed the right to protect not only foreigners of Latin persuasion resident in the empire, but also Ottoman subjects who were members of the Latin or Eastern Catholic communions. The Russians claimed a similar position in respect of Ottoman subjects with Orthodox beliefs following the Treaty of Kuchuk Kainarja in 1774 as a direct result of French intrigues and opposition to Russian ambitions.[4]

The Christians of Palestine during the Ottoman Empire

For administrative purposes the non-Muslim subjects of the Ottoman empire were organised into autonomous religious communities known as *millets*. The heads, both central (i.e., in Istanbul) and local, of the *millets* were chosen by the *millet* but the choice was subject to the sultan's

[3] Braude, B and B Lewis (eds). 1982. *Christians and Jews in the Ottoman Empire*, 2 vols. New York: Holmes and Meier; Cohen, Ammon and B Lewis. 1978. *Population and Revenue in the Towns of Palestine in the Sixteenth Century*. Princeton: Princeton University Press; Cohen, A. 1989. *Economic Life in Ottoman Jerusalem*. Cambridge: Cambridge University Press; Cohen, A. 1984. *Jewish Life under Islam, Jerusalem in the Sixteenth Century*. Harvard: Harvard University Press; Cohen, A. 1986. 'The Expulsion of the Franciscans from Mount Zion, old documents and new interpretations', *Turica* XVIII: 147-158.

[4] Cohen, A. 1973. *Palestine in the Eighteenth Century*. Jerusalem: the Magnes Press; Issa, Anton Odeh. 1976. *Les minorités chrétiennes de Palestine à travers les siècles, étude historico-juridique et développement moderne international*. Jerusalem: Franciscan Printing Press; and Heyer, Friedrich. 1984. *Kirchengeschichte des Heiligen Landes*. Stuttgart: Verlag Kohlhammer.

approval, communicated in the form of an imperial *berat*, which alone enabled the nominees to assume their offices and take possession of their temporalities. The heads, both local and central, of the *millets* had a high place in the official hierarchy of the state, of which they were regarded as functionaries. In the provinces they were *ex officio* members of the provincial administrative councils, while those in the capital had the right of audience with the sultan. The heads of *millets* represented their flocks in their general and personal affairs *vis-à-vis* the Sublime Porte. The autonomy of the *millets* was based on ancient custom, which was reinforced in the 19th century by specific edicts whose general spirit is incorporated in the Khatt-i Humayun. Their affairs were conducted by the head of the *millet*, generally assisted by a council composed of both lay and clerical members. The *millets* were autonomous in spiritual matters and in certain administrative and judicial matters. Their jurisdiction embraced, in the religious sphere, clerical discipline; in the administrative sphere, the control of their properties, including cemeteries, educational institutions and churches; in the judicial sphere, marriage, dowries, divorce and alimony, civil rights. Sentences pronounced by *millet* courts, if within their competence, were executed on their behalf by the state. In the case of *millets* composed of Christians whose spiritual heads resided outside the Ottoman empire which principally concerned the Catholic and Armenian communities, the spiritual head recognised by the authorities had to be an Ottoman subject in the possession of the imperial *berat*.

For a few years following the Ottoman conquest of Constantinople, the head of the Orthodox *millet* was more than the spiritual and temporal head of the Orthodox subjects of the empire only. The sultan's original *berat* gave the patriarch jurisdiction over all Christians in the empire, whatever their church or rite. Eight years later, however, the Armenian church under an Armenian patriarch of Constantinople, was recognised as a separate community, comprising not only the Armenian Christians, but also the Latins, the Eastern Catholics, the Jacobites, the Nestorians and the Copts. By the end of the 19th century, the number of Christian *millets* recognised by the Ottoman authorities had risen and these may be grouped as follows:

A The Eastern Orthodox Church 1 The Greek Orthodox *millet* (the four Eastern Orthodox patriarchates of Constantinople, Jerusalem, Alexandria and Antioch) 2 The various Orthodox churches in the Balkans which had removed themselves from the jurisdiction of the Orthodox *millet* in the 19th century.

B The Oriental Orthodox Churches	3 The Armenian Orthodox 4 The Nestorians/Assyrians 5 The Syrian Orthodox (Jacobites)
C Latin, Eastern and Oriental Catholic Churches	6 Roman Catholics (Latin Rite) 7 Greek Catholics (Melkites) 8 The Maronites 9 The Syrian Catholics 10 The Armenian Catholics 11 The Chaldeans
D Protestants	12 The Protestants. In 1850 the sultan recognised the Protestants as a separate *millet*. However, no special jurisdiction was conferred.

Most of these communities would have had a presence in Jerusalem at some level from the beginning of the 19th century onwards if not before. It is noteworthy that most of these *millets* were of comparatively recent origin. Only the Orthodox *millet*, the Armenians and the Latins had any real standing before the 19th century, and the Latins were almost entirely foreign (until the latter part of the 19th century).

A number of points should be noted concerning the jurisdiction and rights of the *millets* and their members. Firstly, the *millet* organisation applied only to Ottoman subjects, and where a particular community included foreigners, these foreigners were treated under the terms of the Capitulations. which accorded a number of privileges including that of a consular jurisdiction. Again, no community was recognised as a *millet*, unless specific formal acknowledgement was given, in the shape of an imperial decree or other statutory instrument, and the rights and privileges accorded to each *millet* were closely defined in various decrees, *firmans* (decrees or edicts issued by the Ottoman government under the sultan's cipher), etc. Ottoman members of other religious communities were either treated in accordance with the Ottoman civil code or were regarded as coming under the jurisdiction of one of the religious *millets*. Foreign members of religious communities not recognised as *millets* were normally treated in accordance with the terms of the Capitulations. Again, the rights and jurisdiction accorded to the *millets* did not include jurisdiction in the matter of *waqf*, or religious and charitable trust endowment constituted under Muslim law. A *waqf* trust, no matter the religious persuasion of the person making the endowment or its purpose, could only be constituted and administered through the Muslim courts.

A further restriction was applied by the Ottoman laws which forbade

15

the succession of a foreigner to the estate of an Ottoman subject or of a non-Muslim to the estate of a Muslim, and which provided for the question of succession to be dealt with in the civil courts of the Ottoman empire. An Ottoman interdiction on the owning of immovable property by foreigners or foreign corporate bodies had led to a system under which such property actually owned by foreign charitable or religious organisations was registered in the name of an Ottoman subject, with separate and unofficial registers kept recording the actual state of affairs in respect of such property. It should be noted, however, that this interdiction appears to have been circumvented in some cases. Finally, certain of the religious and charitable organisations operating within the Ottoman empire had been accorded certain privileges and exemptions from various taxes and duties.[5]

The 'Rediscovery' of the Holy Land in the 19th Century

The 19th century witnessed a worldwide religious revival which quickly manifested a revival of interest in the Holy Land by all Christian Churches. At the beginning of the century, the Franciscans were the only representatives of western Christianity to be found in Jerusalem, although strictly speaking no foreigner was permitted to reside within the walls of the city. The various Eastern Churches were represented as they had been for centuries, but with the exception of the Orthodox Church and the Armenians, their following in Jerusalem was insignificant, apart from the inhabitants of the various convents and monasteries. This is, however, hardly surprising since the population of Jerusalem at the beginning of the century was estimated to be more than 10,000.[6]

The first stirrings of interest in the area were shown by the Anglican church. Proposals for the establishment of a permanent post in Jerusalem by the Church Missionary Society (an Anglican foundation) was under consideration as early as 1821 and the London Jewish Society

---

[5] See the various articles in B Braude and B Lewis (eds): *Christians and Jews in Ottoman Empire, op. cit.*

[6] Scholch, Alexander. 1992. *Palestine in Transformation, 1856-1882: Studies in Social, Economic and Political Development.* Washington, DC: Institute for Palestine Studies; Gilbar, Gad (ed). 1990. *Ottoman Palestine 1800-1914; Studies in Economic and Social History.* Leiden: E J Brill; Kushner, David (ed). 1986. *Palestine in the Late Ottoman Period.* Leiden: E J Brill; Ma'oz, Moshe (ed). 1975. *Studies on Palestine during the Ottoman Period.* Jerusalem: The Magnes Press; and for an important overview see, Doumani, Beshara B. 1992. 'Rediscovering Ottoman Palestine, Writing Palestinians into History.' *Journal of Palestine Studies*, vol XXI, no 2: 5-28.

(LJS), which had as its aim the conversion of Jewry, also took an interest in the city. However, it was not until after the capture of the city by Muhammad 'Ali of Egypt in 1831 that much progress was made, and the LJS established the first permanent mission station in Jerusalem in 1833. It was not until 1845, however, that the first Anglican church of the city was dedicated. Following the establishment in the city for the first time of a British consul in 1838 (the first foreign consul to be appointed to that city) a Protestant bishopric under joint British and Prussian auspices was established in 1841. In 1881, the dual arrangement lapsed and the bishopric became exclusively Anglican, and centred on the Cathedral Church of St George and the related schools in Jerusalem and elsewhere. Many of the educational and medical foundations under the auspices of the combined bishopric were founded by the second bishop between 1846 and 1879, although many of the schools were later taken over by the CMS, who had begun their educational work in the region in 1851.[7]

Since most of the various mission societies also provided educational facilities for all and sundry, there were by 1880 over a hundred schools scattered throughout Palestine run by various societies and representing different churches and countries. The fact that such educational work tended to foster a desire to join the church of the teachers led to complications later in relations with the Orthodox Church. In this connection it should be noted that the Ottoman authorities refused to countenance mission work among Muslims.[8]

In 1847, the Roman Catholics revived the Latin patriarchate, which had fallen into desuetude since the Crusades, and at the same time there was some attempt to bring order and conformity into the various Eastern Catholic churches. Thus a Greek Catholic patriarchate was established in Damascus in 1848, and in 1865 a seminary for Greek Catholics was established in Jerusalem in the ancient Crusader Church of St Anne, which had been presented to France at the end of the Crimean War. Some difficulty arose over the position of the new Latin patriarch, who was both much poorer and possessed of greater responsibilities than the Franciscan Custos, who remained firmly

[7] Cragg, Kenneth. 1969. 'The Anglican Church,' in A J Arberry (ed), *Religion in the Middle East: Three Religions in Concord and Conflict*, vol 1, pp. 570–595. Cambridge: Cambridge University Press; Hornus, J-M. 1962. 'Les missions anglicanes au Proche-Orient avant la création de l'évêché de Jérusalem.' *Proche-Orient Chrétien*, vol XII: 255-269; Hornus, J-M. 'L'évêché anglo-prussien de Jérusalem (1841-1881), controverses autour de sa création (1841)'. *Proche-Orient Chrétien*, vol XIII (1963): 130-149, and 234-258, vol XIV (1964): 184-201 and 307-334; Hornus, J-M. 1969. 'La fondation effective de l'évêché anglican de Jérusalem et son premier titulaire (5 oct 1841-23 nov 1845)'. *Proche-Orient Chrétien*, vol XIX: 194-219.

[8] Tibwai, A L. 1961. *British Interests in Palestine 1800-1901, A Study of Religious and Educational Enterprise*. Oxford: Oxford University Press.

outside the patriarchal jurisdiction.[9]

During the first half of the century Russian interest in the Holy Land also increased, although Russian influence was not felt until after the Crimean War, when the year 1860 saw the beginning of the building of a Russian cathedral and a vast complex of hostels, offices and hospitals to house and care for Russian pilgrims on a plot of ground near the Jaffa Gate.[10]

During the period between the end of the Crimean War and the beginning of the First World War, there was a general extension of all religious interests. The increase of Russian influence among the Orthodox was paralleled by a steady increase of French influence among the Latins and Eastern Catholics. In this connection the establishment of consuls in Jerusalem helped considerably, the first in the field being, as already stated, the British in 1838, followed by the French, Prussian and Sardinian consuls in 1843, the Americans in 1844, and the Austrians replacing the Sardinians in 1849. The Russians, however, were content to be represented by an agent in Jerusalem dependent on their consulate general in Beirut, which had been there since 1839, until 1858. The Catholics established such foundations as the Ratisbonne Institute, the houses of the Sisters of Our Lady of Sion, the seminary in the Church of St Anne, and by the end of the century had established throughout Palestine 30 orders, brotherhoods and associations, with 29 convents, 18 hospices, 6 higher schools, 16 orphanages, 4 industrials schools and 5 hospitals. The Anglican church, in addition to the cathedral, founded the associated schools in Jerusalem; the Ophthalmic Hospital of the Order of St John was established; and the German Evangelical church administered the hospital of the German deaconesses, the Syrian Protestant Orphanage, the Leper Hospital in the German colony and the Lutheran church which was built on the site of the hospice of the Knights of St John. Similar work was undertaken by other Protestant churches both during the 19th century and after. Thus a Church of Scotland mission operated, mainly outside Jerusalem, with its main emphasis on medical and educational services.

---

[9] On the Latin patriarchate of Jerusalem see: Manna, S. 1972. *Chiesa Latina e Chiese Orientali all'epoca del patriarca Giuseppe Valerga (1813-1872)*. Naples; Duvignau, Pierre. 1972. *Une vie au service de l'Eglise: S B Mgr Joseph Valerga, Patriarche Latin de Jrusalem 1813-1872*. Jerusalem: Imprimerie du Patriarcat Latin. For the development of the Greek Catholic church in the Holy Land see, Frazee, Charles. 1983. *Catholics and Sultans, The Church and the Ottoman Empire 1453-1923*. Cambridge: Cambridge University Press, and for the history of the Franciscans see, Roncaglia, Martiniano P. 1957. *St Francis of Assisi and the Middle East*. Cairo.

[10] Hopwood, Derek. 1969. *The Russian Presence in Syria and Palestine, 1843-1914: Church and Politics in the Near East*. Oxford: Clarendon Press; Stavrou, Theodore. 1963. *Russian Interests in Palestine 1882-1914: A Study of Religious and Educational Enterprise*. Thessaloniki: Institute for Balkan Studies.

The organization of the various church communities under the Ottomans in Jerusalem seems to have been complicated. For most practical purposes the authorities recognised only the three leading communities, namely the Orthodox, the Armenian and the Latin communities. Also, many of the smaller communions were unable to compete with the older and richer communities in vying for tenure of religious buildings and institutions. It should be noted that the Franciscan Order, which was the official representative of the Holy See for some centuries, and was formally headed by a Custodian of the Holy Places, was able to gain control of almost all the Catholic holy sites. However, although the Ottoman authorities would only recognise the three main communions in all matters relating to the Holy Places, the Maronite and Melkite communities in addition were recognised as having jurisdiction over their members.[11]

The Christian Communities and Holy Places during the British Mandate for Palestine

Before the Islamic conquest of Palestine, Christians were the overwhelming majority of the population, divided between the Greek Orthodox, who were predominant in the urban world and the Syriac Christians in the countryside. It was members of the Greek Orthodox community which formed the majority Christians in Palestine until the latter part of the 19th century. At the beginning of the mandate the Christian population in Palestine comprised 9.6 per cent of the total population. In the 1931 census it was reduced to 8.8 per cent, although its absolute number increased. The decline of the Arab Christian percentage of both the Arab and the total population was a continuous process.

	Palestine		Jerusalem
1922	81,361	9%	14,699
1931	92,802	8%	19,894
1944	148,910	8%	29,350

The reduction of the Christian proportion of the Arab population was the outcome of their lower birthrate and continuous low level emigration abroad. Migration in search of economic opportunities was more remarkable among Christians than among Muslims. Emigration

[11] Carmel, Alex. 1985. 'The Activities of the European Powers in Palestine, 1799-1914'. *Asian and African Studies*, vol 19: 43-91.

of Christians abroad had started in the late 19th-early 20th centuries, mainly from Jerusalem, Bethlehem, and Ramallah.

The centres of Christian settlement was naturally close to the Holy Places, notably in Jerusalem, which attracted members of nearly every denomination. The other large area of Christian settlement was in the north, including Haifa, Acre, Nazareth, Tiberias, Safad and surrounding villages.[12]

In order to provide a basis for a consideration of subsequent developments, it is necessary to summarise the position of the Christian communities under the Mandate. The Mandate for Palestine was allotted by the League of Nations to the United Kingdom in 1920, the text of the Mandate document was finally approved by the League in July 1922 and it came formally into effect in September 1923, two months after the signature of the Treaty of Lausanne. This document, together with the Palestine Order in Council 1922, as subsequently amended and modified by later Orders in Council and enactments of the government of Palestine provided the framework within which the Christian communities in Jerusalem and in Palestine as a whole functioned.

Article 13 of the Mandate vested in the Mandatory 'all responsibility in connection with the Holy Places and religious buildings or sites in Palestine, including that of preserving existing rights and securing free access to the Holy Places', while Article 14 provided for the appointment of a Special Commission to 'study, define and determine' rights and claims in connection with the Holy Places and the different religious communities in Palestine. Article 9 charged the Mandatory with responsibility for ensuring a complete guarantee of their rights to all inhabitants of Palestine, whether nationals or foreigners, under the judicial system to be established in Palestine, and states: 'Respect for the personal status of the various peoples and communities and for their religious interests shall be fully guaranteed. In particular, the control and administration of *waqfs* shall be exercised in accordance with religious law and the dispositions of the founders.' Articles 15 and 16 enjoined the Mandatory to ensure freedom of worship, the right of individual religious communities to maintain schools for the education of race, religion or language, while allowing for such supervision of religious and charitable bodies of all faiths as was required for the maintenance of public order and good government. Finally, Article 8 decreed that the privileges and immunities, including the benefits of consular jurisdiction and protection, formerly enjoyed under the terms of the Capitulations would not apply in Palestine during the period of the Mandate.

[12] McCarthy, Justin. 1991. *The Population of Palestine: Population History and Statistics of the Late Ottoman Period and the Mandate*. New York: Columbia University Press.

These general provisions were further defined and clarified in the 'Palestine Order in Council 1922' which was promulgated in August 1922. The preamble to the Order stated that although His Majesty's government were committed to implementing the Balfour Declaration, this was subject to the understanding that 'nothing should be done which might prejudice the civil and religious rights of existing non-Jewish communities in Palestine'. Article 46 of the Order laid down that the jurisdiction of the civil courts as defined in the Order should be exercised in conformity with the Ottoman law in force in Palestine on 1 November 1914, such later Ottoman laws as had been or might be declared in force by public notice, and such Orders in Council, ordinances and regulations as were in force when the Order took effect, or might subsequently be applied or enacted. Matters not governed by such legislation would be treated according to English common law. Article 51 provided that the courts of religious communities which were established and exercising jurisdiction at the date of the Order would continue to exercise jurisdiction in matters of personal status, defined as suits regarding marriage, divorce, alimony, maintenance, guardianship, legitimation and adoption of minors, inhibition from dealing with property of persons who were legally incompetents, successions, wills and legacies, and the administration of the property of absent persons. Article 54 further defined the jurisdiction of the courts of the Christian communities as:

i Exclusive jurisdiction in matters of marriage and divorce, alimony and confirmation of wills of members of the community other than foreigners as defined in the Order.

ii Jurisdiction in any other matters of personal status of such persons, where all parties to the action consented to their jurisdiction.

iii Exclusive jurisdiction over any case concerning the constitution or internal administration of a *waqf* or religious endowment constituted before a religious court according to the religious law of the community concerned.

The judgements of the religious courts would be executed by the civil court procedures (Article 56). It should be noted that the above provisions applied only to Palestinian members of the communities, and that jurisdiction over foreigners who might be members of a community was exercised by the civil courts, although, in matters of personal status, a foreigner could agree to such matters being tried by the religious court applicable, then the Muslim religious courts could not grant divorce to foreigners. The Order provided that the term foreigner would include corporations constituted under the law of a foreign state, and religious or charitable bodies or institutions wholly or mainly composed of foreigners. The Order also provided that no ordinance should be passed which restricted complete freedom of conscience, the free exercise of forms of worship, which discriminated in any way between inhabitants of Palestine on grounds of race, religion or language, and which were in any way inconsistent with the terms of the Mandate (Article 18).

Although the position of the Christian communities was fairly closely defined by the Mandate and the 1922 Order in Council, there was no legal provision for the continuation of the network of privileges and immunities which had accrued to the communities in general, or to certain members of the communities in particular, under Ottoman rule. Subject to the provisions of the Mandate and the Order in Council, these privileges and immunities were generally maintained by the Mandatory administration. It was, however, found necessary from time to time to enact ordinances to validate the continued enjoyment of the privileges, to provide further definition of rights and jurisdiction and to deal with anomalies which arose. The necessity for such legislation arose because the rights, privileges and immunities enjoyed by the religious communities were of two types. The several rights and privileges in connection with the Holy Places, as defined by Ottoman statutes, had been laid down in the Status Quo of 1757, and confirmed in 1852. During the Mandate these rights and privileges were regulated by the 1757 and 1852 statutes, as extend by later decisions of the secular power based on the Status Quo principles. However, other rights, privileges and immunities enjoyed by some or all of the Christian communities and their charitable, educational and medical institutions had never been satisfactorily defined or codified. To some extent they were covered by various Ottoman *firmans* and decrees, but in some cases the relevant *firmans* were contradictory, and in others an oral grant of a privilege was never confirmed in writing. The Palestine government, therefore, took the view that any community or organisation could claim the right to enjoy a particular privilege it could prove that it had enjoyed the privilege under the Ottomans.[13]

History and Conflict over the Holy Places of Palestine

Disputes about the Christian Holy Places have played a major part in the

[13] Wasserstein, Bernard. 1979. *The British in Palestine, the Mandatory Government and the Arab-Jewish Conflict, 1917-1929.* London: Royal Historical Society; McTague, John J. 1984. *British Policy in Palestine 1917-1922.* University Press of America; and Laurens, Henry. 1993. 'Genèse de la Palestine Mandataire'. *Maghreb-Machrek*, no 140: 3-34.

history of the Middle East and indeed of Europe for many centuries. The disputes about the Holy Places are essentially disputes among Christian communities, and not controversies between Christians on one side and members of other religions – Judaism or Islam – or the government of the country, on the other.

On December 9 1917, British troops occupied Jerusalem, and the Holy City passed into Christian hands for the first time since the rule of Frederick II. Jerusalem now lay with the Western powers, and was, to all intents and purposes, bound up with the question of harmonizing their interests in Palestine as a whole. Over the long centuries of European involvement in Palestine many of them acquired certain rights and obligations not only to the Holy Places, but also to the various Christian communities. In the course of time after 1535 France had acquired the position of protector of the Catholics in the Ottoman empire, while Russia had assented the right to protect Orthodox Christians. Protection, however, had often meant protection of the Latins against the Orthodox or the Orthodox against the Latins, rather than protection against the Ottoman authorities.

An Attempt at Reconciliation: the Holy Places Commission

On August 31 1922 Lord Balfour submitted to the League of Nations Council a memorandum outlining a proposal for the commission on the Holy Places. In essence, it provided for a commission divided into three sub-commissions, one Christian, one Muslim and one Jewish. It proposed that the Christian sub-commission be composed of a French president, three Roman Catholic representatives (Italian, Spanish and Belgian), three Orthodox representatives (one of whom should be Greek and one Russian), one Armenian, and one or possibly two representatives of the Ethiopians and the Copts. The Muslim sub-commission was to consist of an Italian president, a Palestinian Muslim, a French Muslim and an Indian Muslim. The Jewish sub-commission was to consist of an American president, a Palestinian Jew, a British Jew, and a Portuguese or Spanish Jew to represent the Sephardis. The chairman of the whole commission was to be an American Protestant. According to the proposal, the duties of the commission were to be confined to settling claims or disputes and were not to include any administrative responsibilities. Where there was no unanimity the matter was to be referred to the chairman of the whole commission for a decision.

The British proposal was discussed outside the League Council for almost five weeks. The Vatican objected to the proposal. It objected that in the whole commission, the Christian members would be drowned in a majority composed of Muslims and Jews and that in the Christian sub-commission, the Latins would be outnumbered by Christians not in communion with Rome. In addition, the Vatican thought the American Protestant chairman of the whole commission would have undue power of decision. As an alternative, the French suggested three autonomous commissions: one Christian, one Muslim and one Jewish. The Christian commission would be divided in two sub-commissions: a four-man sub-commission for the Latins, and a four-man sub-commission for the Orthodox and the Armenians. The two Christian sub-commissions would meet separately on their own problems, but they would consider jointly matters that concerned both – for example, matters related to the Church of the Holy Sepulchre or the Church of the Nativity. In addition, the Christian commission would have a ninth Latin member who would be its president and would preside over joint meetings of the two sub-commissions. Thus, the Latins would be assured of a majority of one on the Christian commission. The French said that, of course, the presidency of the commission would be occupied by a Frenchman, in view of France's historic role as protector of the Holy Places. The Italian delegate to the Council of the League of Nations, Marquis Imperiali, thought highly of the French proposal, but in view of the fact that the Latin patriarch in Jerusalem was Italian, and of the fact that the preponderance of those who cared for the Holy Places had been Italian, the presidency of the commission should naturally go to an Italian. A deadlock ensued.

It was against this background that Balfour addressed himself to the matter of the Holy Places Commission in the Council of the League of Nations on October 4, 1922. He said Great Britain was in no position to settle a dispute between the Catholic powers over the presidency of the Christian commission, and that before any further progress could be made on the appointment of the Holy Places Commission, the Catholic powers would have to resolve their own differences. He then noted that there were no Orthodox powers on the League Council. Great Britain, as the Mandatory, was responsible for seeing that all the religious groups in Palestine, including the Orthodox, were dealt with fairly. Therefore, no scheme could be accepted that did not guarantee justice for the Orthodox. In the absence of agreement on the implementation of article 14, the responsibility for settling difficulties and disputes in the Holy Places devolved entirely upon the Mandatory. Thus, in the arrangements made for Palestine following the First World War, the Catholic powers acquiesced in a situation not consonant with their desires but at least not unsatisfactory to them. Control of Jerusalem and the Holy Places went with control of Palestine, and British control in their view was better than Turkish control. If they had been unable to improve the position of the Latins in the Holy Places, they had at least prevented it from deteriorating further. The Orthodox were satisfied with British control of Jerusalem and Bethlehem as long as the Status Quo of 1852 was adhered to. Since Jerusalem was in the hands of a Protestant power, Protestants found little of a religious nature to complain about.[14]

United Nations Proposals and the Future of Palestine and Jerusalem

At its final session in 1946 the Assembly of the League of Nations adopted unanimously, with Egypt abstaining, a resolution which recognised that, 'on the termination of the League's existence, its functions with respect to the mandated territories will come to an end, but notes that Chapters XI, XII and XIII of the Charter of the United Nations embody principles similar to those declared in Article 22 of the Covenant of the League.' These chapters provided for the establishment of an international trusteeship system for certain categories of territories, including territories held under Mandate, but provided that the terms of individual trusteeship would be subject to individual agreement by the states concerned. In 1946, the United Kingdom agreed to concluded trusteeship agreements for all territories which it administered under the mandate system, with the exception of Palestine. Transjordan was also excepted on grounds that the United Kingdom intended to recognise her independence. Transjordan's independence was subsequently recognised in the Treaty of Alliance signed on 22 March 1946.

With regard to Palestine, the British government advised the United Nations in April 1947 that they intended to place the question of Palestine on the agenda of the next session of the General Assembly, and to ask the Assembly to make recommendations concerning the future government of Palestine, on the grounds that the Mandate had become unworkable and they had no powers to alter its terms. In May, therefore, the United Nations set up a Special Committee on Palestine (UNSCOP) to examine the position and make recommendations. The UNSCOP report, submitted at the end of August 1947, was unanimous on a number of general points, and the majority report recommended the partition of Palestine into an Arab and a Jewish State, and the placing of Jerusalem under a special regime. The two states were to become fully

---

[14] Zander, Walter. 1971. *Israel and the Holy Places of Christendom*. London: Weidenfeld & Nicolson; Minerbi, Sergei. 1990. *The Vatican and Zionism: Conflict in the Holy Land, 1895-1925*. Oxford: Oxford University Press, and Bovis, H Eugene. 1971. *The Jerusalem Question, 1917-1968*. Jerusalem: Hoover Institution Press.

independent, though bound together by an economic union, after a transitional period of two years under special arrangements. The UNSCOP proposals were adopted by the General Assembly on 29 November 1947. The proposals provided for freedom of conscience and worship, the continuance of existing provisions for the status of the various religious communities, and religious or charitable bodies, the continuance of the right enjoyed by each religious community to maintain its own schools and other educational establishments, including those run by foreign bodies, of the nature the state might impose, and for the maintenance of existing rights in respect of Holy Places and religious buildings or sites, including exemption from taxation. The proposals for Jerusalem provided for the establishment of a *corpus separatum* under an international regime and laid down in some detail its administration. The UNSCOP proposals were accepted by the Jewish Agency, but rejected by the Arab states.

Fighting broke out in Palestine shortly after the United Nations had accepted the plans. This was to continue sporadically until armistice agreements had been signed early in 1949. In the meantime the Mandate ended on 14 May 1948, the State of Israel was proclaimed, and Arab forces entered Palestine. In the course of the fighting Israeli forces occupied West Jerusalem (the New City) and Transjordanian forces occupied East Jerusalem including the Old City. The *de facto* control exercised by the opposing forces formed the basis for the demarcation lines laid down in the armistice agreements. By the end of 1948, it was clear that both sides had completely rejected the idea of an international regime for the city of Jerusalem, and the Israelis told the United Nations that they would assume sovereignty over West Jerusalem and the strip connecting it with the Jewish state. The Transjordanian response was to state their intention to annex the West Bank, to appoint a new Mufti of Jerusalem and to announce the intention of claiming East Jerusalem for Transjordan. In January 1950, Jerusalem was formally proclaimed the capital of Israel, and in April 1950, the West Bank, including East Jerusalem, was officially annexed to Jordan.[15]

Conclusion

The division of Jerusalem into Jordanian and Israeli sectors was of considerable importance to the Christian communities in the city, since

[15] Smith, Charles D. 1988, revised edition 1992. *Palestine and the Arab-Israeli Conflict*. New York and London: St Martin's Press ; Pappe, Ilan. 1988. *Britain and the Arab-Israeli Conflict 1948-1951*. London: Macmillan; Morris, Benny. 1988. *The Birth of the Palestinian Refugee Problem, 1947-1949*. Cambridge: Cambridge University Press; and Morris, Benny. 1990. *1948 and After: Israel and the Palestinians*. Oxford: Oxford University Press.

the Arab quarters of West Jerusalem which had been taken by the Israelis were almost entirely Christian Arab quarters, and much of the centre of West Jerusalem was Christian church property on which the shrines and monasteries of East Jerusalem depended for their maintenance. In additions, the heads of the various communities lived and worked, almost without exception, in places which fell under Jordanian control. The war of 1948 saw some 714,000 Palestinians become refugees, of whom some 50,000 would have been Christians, or some thirty-five per cent of all Christians within what was British Mandatory Palestine.[16]

[16] Sabella, Bernard. 1991. 'Palestinian Christian Emigration from the Holy Land', *Proche-Orient Chrétien*, vol XLI: 74-85.

SOCIO-ECONOMIC,
SOCIO-DEMOGRAPHIC CHARACTERISTICS

2

Socio-Economic Characteristics and the Challenges to Palestinian Christians in the Holy Land

Bernard Sabella

The Land and Its Population

The West Bank including East Jerusalem has a total land area of 5,800 square kilometres. It is a hilly region with four distinct geographic areas: the Coastal Plain in the north which is known for its fruits, vegetables and melons. The Uplands which span the Nablus, Jerusalem and Hebron mountain ranges. This is a good agricultural region as it receives sufficient rainfall and its topography includes low-lying valleys and plains. It is in this region that most of the 430 Palestinian villages are found, with agriculture being one of major preoccupations of their inhabitants. The Eastern Foothills comprise the third geographic region, and it is located between the Central Uplands and the Jordan Valley. The foothills are mostly dry with scarce rainfall which explains the limited population. The Jordan Valley possesses a tropical climate, and like the Eastern Foothills is sparsely populated, with Jericho (10,000 inhabitants) the major population point.[1]

---

[1] Sabella 1990: *The Diocese of the Latin Patriarchate, Introductory Study of the Social, Political, Economical and Religious Situation (West Bank and Gaza Strip, Jordan, Israel and Cyprus)*, by Dr Bernard Sabella, Patriarchatus Latinus, Jerusalem, April 1990, p. 4.

The Gaza Strip is an area of 363 square kilometres which lies in the southern part of the Palestinian Coastal Plain. The Strip is 45 kilometres in length and only 8 kilometres in width. Historically, the territory served as a main communication link between Egypt and Syria, and was an active sea port during the period of the British Mandate of Palestine, 1919-1948. At present, Gaza is known for its citrus plantations and for other agricultural produce. However, because of increasing salinization of the soil and the high population density, agricultural activity has suffered. Other constraints, mostly Israeli settlements and the regulations imposed by the military authorities, also limit the agricultural potential and activity of Gaza (Sabella 1990: 5).

The Population

In 1991, the population of the West Bank reached 1,156,600, of whom 151,000 lived in East Jerusalem. The population of the Gaza Strip was 676,100 inhabitants. The population density of the West Bank was 199 inhabitants per square kilometre. That of the Gaza Strip was 1,863 inhabitants per square kilometre, which gives an indication of the living conditions in which 36.5 per cent of the Palestinians of the Occupied Territories find themselves.[2] Another indication of these conditions is the average number of persons per household, which in 1990 was 6.2 for both the West Bank and the Gaza Strip. Moreover, the Palestinian population has a high annual growth rate, which is 3.6 per cent and 3.8 per cent for the West Bank and the Gaza Strip respectively.[3] As a result of this growth rate, the population below 14 years makes up over 47.8 per cent of the population of the West Bank, and over 50.4 per cent of that of the Gaza Strip. The percentage of Palestinians born after 1967 is 66.3 per cent, and 69.5 per cent, for the West Bank and Gaza Strip, respectively. This is dramatic, in that the majority of Palestinians are under 25, and have known no form of government other than Israeli military occupation of their land, and all that that implies.

One cannot envision peace and future prosperity without considering these figures. Although demographic characteristics of Palestinian Christians differ somewhat from those for the general population, as will become clear in this paper, the general conditions which effect the Palestinian population in general operate in an equal manner on Palestinian Christians. The majority of those Palestinians, estimated at over 400,000, arrested by the Israeli authorities since 1967 are

---

[2] Central Bureau of Statistics, *Statistical Abstract of Israel 1992*, no. 43, Jerusalem, p. 732.

[3] *Ibid.*, p. 733.

youngsters below the age of 25 years. The fact that Palestinian society is a young one, undergoing occupation, has left no choice for its youth other than either to confront the occupation or leave the country in search of their future. The society suffers as the great potential of its youngsters is engaged in development in an atmosphere best characterized as one of siege, and it continues.

Palestinian Christians

Palestinian Christians have roots which strike deep in the land and society of Palestine. They are an indigenous group, some of whom trace their descent from the early church, while others trace it from the events and historical developments which made modern Palestine what it is. World-wide, Palestinian Christians number 400,000, or 6.7 per cent of a total Palestinian population of 6 million. 51,000 of these 400,000 Palestinian Christians live in the West Bank and Gaza, while there are 114,000 Palestinian Christians in Israel. The indigenous Christian population of the Holy Land numbers 165,000, or 41.3 per cent of all Palestinian Christians world-wide. The Christians of the West Bank and the Gaza Strip are only 2.9 per cent of the entire Palestinian population in the Occupied Territories.[4]

Palestinian Christians contribute far more to the national community than their numbers would at first suggest. In part their contribution is tied to the relatively high level of education, and to their preference for liberal professions and white collar occupations.

The national identity of Palestinian Christians is rooted in the same experience which befell the entire Palestinian society: In 1948, as a result of the creation of the State of Israel, over 714,000 Palestinians became refugees. 7 per cent, or 50,000 of these refugees were Christians, and they made up 35 per cent of all Christians who lived in Palestine prior to May 15, 1948.[5] During the period of the British Mandate, 1920-1948, Palestinian Christians, like other Palestinians were engaged in activities to affirm the national Arab identity of Palestine. They participated in Palestinian political congresses in the twenties, which sought to change or modify the implementation of the Balfour Declaration, and they also played an active role in the Palestinian delegations which set out to argue

---

[4] Figures for Christians in Israel are derived from the *Statistical Abstracts of Israel*, while those figures for the West Bank and Gaza Strip are derived from various surveys on the Christian community and from individual reports of parish priests and other clergy.

[5] Kossaibi, George. 'Demographic Characteristics of the Arab Palestine People', in Khalil Nakleh and Elia Zureik, *The Sociology of the Palestinians*, Croom Helm, London, 1980, p. 18.

the Palestinian case in London and other international capitals.

At present, Palestinian Christians have undergone the same measures and processes which arise from the occupation. The *Intifada*, as a popular uprising, saw Christians and Muslims engaged in an effort to end the occupation and achieve independence. The Beit Sahour Tax Revolt of 1989 was but one example of Palestinian Christian grassroots participation in challenging occupation. The records of young Christians imprisoned and martyred are other indications of the attachment to, and identity with, Palestine and its cause.[6] In addition, the active involvement and participation of Palestinian Christians in all aspects of life in the country is itself a testimony to the love they harbour for their country and their fellow Palestinians.

A Good Tradition of Christian-Muslim Relations

The involvement and participation of Christians in the affairs of their national community is not surprising, given the good relations which obtain between Christians and Muslims, and the fact that Palestinian Christians are indigenous to the land and society. A number of factors have contributed to good Christian-Muslim relations:

1 The modern history of Palestine with the Arab-Israeli conflict affecting the entire population equally, with the experience of dispersal and loss of homeland

2 The contribution which Christian institutions, mostly Western, have made since the 19th century to the education, health and other needs of the population irrespective of religion

3 The presence of the Holy Places, and the recognition by Islam of the centrality of Jerusalem, Bethlehem and Nazareth to Christianity. This recognition is best crystallized in Caliph 'Umar's *al-'Uhda al-'Umariyya*, which was his guarantee of the safety of Christians and their holy places in 638 when Islam entered the country.[7]

---

[6] Exact numbers on imprisoned and martyred Palestinian Christians are not available, since records are not kept on a religious basis. However, it is estimated that hundreds of Christians were imprisoned since 1967, particularly in the last few years, and that at least twenty Christians have been martyred during the *Intifada*. Christians are usually active in centre, and left-of-centre Palestinian political groups and organisations.

[7] For the text and an in-depth analysis and discussion of *al-'Uhda al-'Umariyya* or *Firman d'Omar*, see Anton Odeh Issa's *Les Minorités chrétiennes de Palestine à travers les siècles*, Franciscan Printing Press, Jerusalem, 1976, pp. 110-124.

4 The urban nature of the Christian population and its living in religiously mixed neighbourhoods, thus emphasising openness and neighbourly relations between Christians and Muslims. In those instances where the Christians lived in villages and rural areas, relations were always characterized by friendly co-operation and communal sharing.

5 Christians take equal pride in their national and religious roots. Being a good Christian has never detracted from being a good nationalist Palestinian, and *vice versa*.

6 The Ottoman *millet* system which recognized the autonomy of the Christian communities to run their own internal affairs, especially those related to religious and civil matters. The system allowed Christians of the Ottoman empire to assume important positions, especially in certain areas, such as commerce and finance, which were previously frowned upon by Muslims (Sabella 1990: 7).

Socio-Economic Characteristics of Christians

Education

Palestinians pride themselves on their educational achievements. Older Palestinians reminisce how, in the aftermath of the 1948 exodus, education served them as capital wherever they went, and it was through their educational achievement that they were able to rehabilitate their lives and bring up their families. Education once acquired, as Palestinian popular wisdom puts it, cannot be taken away, short of inactivating or silencing a person forever. It is this wisdom which has sustained the value of education in our society. At present, 541,000 Palestinian students are engaged in over 1,700 educational institutions in the West Bank and Gaza Strip, i.e., 30.7 per cent of the entire population are at school, which compares favourably with other societies of the region and abroad.[8]

Among Palestinian Christians, education has been valued for the sense of security which it imparted to the educated, through acquiring foreign languages and qualifications for employment. The Christian missionary schools which were set up in Jerusalem, Bethlehem and Nazareth in the mid-19th century started the indigenous Christians on this course. While these schools were not restricted to Christians their presence encouraged Christians to stress education for their children. This spread to other strata of society as the advantages of education in these schools became known to the general population. As a

[8] *Statistical Abstract of Israel*, no. 43, p. 782.

consequence of this tradition of private education, Palestinian Christians have on average 11.2 years of education per person.[9] This figure was confirmed by three different surveys on the Christians of the West Bank, which have been conducted by the author since 1986.[10]

The percentage of Christians with a secondary certificate, or higher qualification, is almost twice the percentage in the general population, while the percentage of Christians with an academic degree is close to three times the general percentage.[11] This clearly points to the preference among Palestinian Christians for an academic career culminating in a university degree. With the spread of university education in the West Bank and Gaza Strip, more of our student population, not only Christians, is channelled through this academic course. While this a blessing in a society undergoing a long military occupation, this particular direction in education trends poses a great challenge to the Christian community and to the society in general. At present, our university graduates have a record unemployment rate reaching 50 per cent. As our graduates get discouraged with not finding employment, they begin to think seriously of leaving the country in search of employment, or in pursuance of higher education. In other words, the academic course of education is a recipe for the emigration of young Palestinian people. The emigration survey has indicated that the group most likely to leave the country is that with a first university degree. Within this context, there is a need to reorder our educational system, so that more technical and practical careers would be considered by our young people. This is important at a time when the academic orientation of our educational system lags behind developments in the economic and market conditions of the society and the region. Given the prevalent political conditions, it is unlikely that a major overhauling of the educational system will be undertaken. This has to await achieving our freedom and independence.

Employment and Occupational Prospects

Understandably, Palestinian Christians tend to predominate in the

---

[9] Bigelman, Shimon (ed.). 1988. *Statistical Yearbook of Jerusalem*, Municipality of Jerusalem and Jerusalem Institute for Israel Studies, Jerusalem, p. 10.

[10] In 1986, a Jerusalem survey, sponsored by the Palestinian Christian National Association, gathered descriptive information on 826 Christian families in the greater Jerusalem area. In 1988, a youth survey, sponsored by the Knights of the Holy Sepulchre, interviewed 1192 Palestinian youths in order to gain knowledge on occupational expectations and future plans of the younger generation. In 1990, an emigration survey, sponsored by Al-Liqa Center, interviewed 550 household heads in the central part of the West Bank to study the intent to emigrate and actual emigration in these households.

[11] Central Bureau of Statistics, Population and Households' Provisional Results, 1983. Census of Population and Housing Publications, vol. 5, pp. 116–117.

sector of public services, which includes such areas as education, health, and tourism. This is particularly so in the central area of the West Bank where over 47.4 per cent of employed Christians work in public services, in comparison to 26.3 per cent of the general population.[12] While this employment picture reflects the educational background of Christians, it also points to a limited employment path, which renders the majority of Christians employees. In a society where employee status does not ensure economic security, nor guarantee long term prospects of personal and family prosperity, being an employee becomes a precarious state which, unfortunately, encourages emigration.

Almost 55 per cent of employed Palestinian Christians work in academic, technical, managerial and clerical jobs. By way of contrast, only 20 per cent of employed Palestinians work in these occupations. In industry, the percentages of the employed are 37 per cent for the general population and 21 per cent for the Christians.[13] The Jerusalem survey shows that a majority of Christians, 57 per cent, are employed in non-church institutions, while church-related institutions employ at least 30 per cent of employed Christians. The churches continue to be a source of employment for indigenous Christians, but the skills and qualifications of Christians make them sought after in the society at large, thus reinforcing their integration and interdependence with the national community, especially in the Jerusalem-Bethlehem-Ramallah area.

Unemployment is a challenge to the Christian community, especially in view of the indications that the unemployment rate reaches close to 30 per cent in the community. Unemployment is blamed on the ageing nature of the Christian community, with more than 10 per cent of the community aged 65 years and above. Some blame this on the emigration of younger members, which leaves the community with the older and less mobile members. It was clear in the emigration survey, that those who look for employment have the highest percentage of those wanting to leave the country, while those with secure jobs have the lowest percentage. Thus employment status is rather deterministic on the emigration pattern of Palestinian Christians.

Employment in academic and related fields remains limited and often unrewarding, especially in the sector of the public services. But in spite of these limitations, our young people continue to shun blue-collar occupations which can secure a comfortable income. Judging by the occupations of fathers in the Jerusalem survey, and the occupational aspirations of children in the youth survey, the community at large

---

[12] *Ibid.*, pp. 128-129.
[13] *Ibid.*, pp. 128-129.

inclines less and less towards manual occupations, and tends instead towards academic and white-collar occupations. This situation would certainly not help in checking emigration tendencies within the population, especially at a time when the Occupied Territories are closed to Palestinian workers and labourers. One continues to hope, however, that political arrangements in the next two to three years will enable Palestinian society and its economy to absorb the great majority of those with academic and technical training, in addition to the skilled and unskilled workers whose livelihood has been disrupted by the recent closure of the Occupied Territories.

Christians: Geography, Denomination and Demography

The geographic distribution of Palestinian Christians in the West Bank and Gaza finds them in fifteen different localities, with concentrations in the urban centres of Bethlehem, Jerusalem and Ramallah. The following table shows the localities and numbers of Christians by denomination in each place.[14]

	Aboud	Bethlehem	Beit Jala	Beit Sahour
Greek Orthodox	536	2133	4733	5749
Latins	443	2934	1116	919
Greek Catholics	10	480	134	528
Syriacs	–	902	120	44
Protestants	28	110	240	95
Total	1017	6559	6343	7335

	Bir Zeit	Ein Arik	Gaza	Jenin
Greek Orthodox	918	211	2207	169
Latins	1104	117	210	327
Greek Catholics	39	–	22	41
Syriacs	17	–	–	–
Protestants	80	–	40	–
Total	2158	328	2479	537

[14] Figures of Christian population were compiled from Bethlehem University's Socio-Economic Survey of the Bethlehem area conducted in 1989 and funded by the European Community, in addition to the socio-economic survey conducted by the Latin patriarchate in 1990 in ten different localities in the West Bank and Gaza city. For a couple of localities, estimates were given by parish priests and other clergy.

	Jericho	Jerusalem	Jifna	Nablus
Greek Orthodox	256	3500	272	436
Latins	164	3900	369	291
Greek Catholics	81	500	8	64
Syriacs	22	250	–	–
Protestants	12	850	–	250
Armenians★	–	1500	–	–
Copts★	–	250	–	–
Ethiopians★	–	60	–	–
Maronites★	–	100	–	–
Total	535	10910	649	1041

★ The figures are inclusive of the West Bank, but the major concentration is in Jerusalem.

	Ramallah	Taybeh	Zababdeh
Greek Orthodox	4000	72	631
Latins	1100	872	1302
Greek Catholics	650	166	125
Syriacs	100	–	43
Protestants	600	–	150
Total	6450	1760	2251

The total number of Palestinian Christians is 50,352, distributed as follows:

Greek Orthodox	26473	52.6%
Latins	15168	30.1%
Greek Catholics	2848	5.7%
Protestants	2443	4.8%
Syriacs	1498	3.0%
Armenians	1500	3.0%
Copts	250	0.5%
Ethiopians	60	0.1%
Maronites	100	0.2%

The richness of these communities lies in their perseverance in a land which needs their presence. It is heartening to know that over 40 per cent of marriages among Palestinian Christians are interdenominational. The spirit of ecumenism is felt among Palestinians also, as Orthodox, Latin, Catholic and Protestant institutions offer their services to Palestinians, irrespective of religion or denomination. The heads of churches in Jerusalem follow events and developments in the land, and express their concern, or act to ease the difficult conditions imposed upon their faithful and others in the society. The kaleidoscope of Christian denominations in the Holy Land must be viewed in a positive and integrative light. It reflects the colour-rich traditions which derive from Christ and his teachings, and offers the promise of unity in a spirit of Christian love and compassion.

This promise is badly needed in a community which has witnessed close to 40 per cent of its members leaving the country since 1967, with dire consequences for those left behind, and for the national community in general. The median age of Christians is now 31.9 years in Jerusalem, and slightly lower in the rest of the country. In Jerusalem, males comprise 45.5 per cent of the Christian population, and females 54.5 per cent. Put another way, for each 1,000 female Christians there are 833 male Christians.[15] The situation is similar in the other localities where Christians are found. This has a negative effect on the dynamics of the community, as more of the younger male members opt to leave the country, thus upsetting, among other things, the marriage market which is so essential to the continuity and vitality of the community. At the same time, young people below 14 years of age number 13,260, i.e., 26 per cent of the Christian population. The prospects for these youngsters are indeed gloomy as the gap between them and the older members of the community grows ever wider. Moreover, the lure of the drug culture, audio-visual distractions, and the beginning of consumerism all challenge the traditions and culture of the community which were its mainstay in years past. As families and clans break down into the nuclear type, the whole world-view based on the group disappears, and is replaced by the world-view of individuals seeking to maximise interest, pleasure and a variety of egotistic pursuits.

These social changes make it imperative that the Christian community draw strength and wisdom from its rich traditions. The Church must gather its children and take them under its wing. We Palestinian Christians are invited to examine the malaise in our midst, and to call upon the hope offered us by Christ and his teachings. The churches of the Holy Land are the embodiment of this hope, each and every one of them. When Christians leave, there is a feeling of a failure of community, a certain disintegration, or, a transition for the purpose of rebuilding community somewhere else. Bethlehem and Jerusalem, the beginnings of Christian community – the mother churches – are being abandoned by their children. As we examine the specificities of emigration, both national and communal, we are also reminded of the

[15] *Statistical Yearbook of Jerusalem*, no. 10, 1991. Municipality of Jerusalem and Jerusalem Institute for Israel Studies, 1993, p. 33.

promise that the community in Christ in the Holy Land can offer the wider society and national community.

Why Palestinians Leave

Since 1967, close to 290,000 Palestinians have left the West Bank and the Gaza Strip: 170,000 and 120,000 respectively.[16] The groups most likely to emigrate are refugees who reside outside the refugee camps, and the middle class, including Christians and urban dwellers. The percentage of those who have left is 15.8 per cent of the overall population. Among the Christians, estimates place the number of those who have left at 18,000, i.e., 35.3 per cent of the entire Christian community, which is over twice the national average. Reasons given for the 8,500 Christians who have left since 1967 are: employment and permanent emigration (43.4 per cent); family and marriage (28.6 per cent), and study (18.8 per cent). In other surveys of 2,505 emigrants conducted in 1989 and 1990, the reasons given for emigration were employment and permanent emigration (44.8 per cent), family and marriage (34.1 per cent), study (14.9 per cent), and other reasons (4.4 per cent).[17]

It is clear that Palestinians leave because they do not have proper economic and occupational opportunities and prospects in their own land. Palestinian Christians, who, because of their educational and occupational backgrounds, follow a middle-class style of life, are in a particular predicament. The Palestinian Christian community fits well the definition of a migrant community as proposed by migration experts. 'A community with a high educational achievement and a relatively good standard of living but with no real prospects for economic security or advancement will most probably become a migrant community.'[18]

When asked what conditions might halt emigration, 60.4 per cent in the emigration survey placed work opportunities, education and economic conditions as an important condition. When the political situation is added, the percentage becomes an overwhelming 82.7 per cent. Given the reasons cited for emigration, one can definitely conclude that those who leave, or think of leaving, undertake the step for concrete reasons, and not because of an unspecified general malaise. People with a good and secure job will think twice before deciding to leave the

---

[16] *Statistical Abstract of Israel*, no. 43, p. 732.

[17] Emigration Survey, Bethlehem University and Latin Patriarchate's Socio-Economic Surveys.

[18] Danilov, Stavro. 1981. 'Dilemmas of Jerusalem's Christians', in *Middle East Review*, vol. XIII, No. 3-4.

country. Palestinians, including Christians, do not leave simply out of political or social frustration – they seem to have grown accustomed to these. They leave if they do not have opportunities to gain a livelihood, and in order to ensure some sense of stability in their own lives, and in those of their children.

Effects of Emigration

Aside from the ageing of the community as evidenced by the relatively high median age (30 years+), and the male-female ratio (833 male to 1000 female), emigration also affects the pool of human resources in the society, as well as the quality of services rendered to the general population. As more qualified and potentially qualified members leave, the society suffers, as a significant part of its human capital is transferred to other societies. In addition, Christian emigration weakens the role of the churches in the community and in society as a whole. At a time when political, economic and social transformations are taking place in our society, there is need for each and every Palestinian to stay on his/her land. The choice is not easy, and places a heavy burden on those who are discouraged, and who choose to leave the country. Leaving one's own country is not an easy undertaking, since it involves a real uprooting. The factors which push people to undertake it nevertheless point clearly to the political and economic instability in the land. For many emigrants and potential emigrants staying put under difficult conditions is equivalent to forgoing better prospects for their children.

Christian emigration robs the churches of their vitality, and restricts their communal and social activities, which could respond to the needs of the individual and the family, at a time of great personal and communal stress and strain. Emigrants who have settled down in their country of adoption maintain contact with members of their immediate families in their country of origin but, apart from an occasional visit, most probably they will not be involved in the life of their original community. While one wishes the Palestinian communities of the diaspora well, it is the separation which denies the country of origin of their talents, skills and dedication. Their leaving makes it more difficult still for those who have opted to stay put in their homeland.

Emigration: Religion and Politics

At a time when Israel has received over half-a-million immigrants, mostly Russian Jews, in the last three years, there are some in Israel who like to disclaim any direct or indirect blame for the emigration of Palestinians from the Holy Land. Others, in an attempt to confuse issues, point to the rise of Islamic fundamentalism as a cause for the emigration of Christians. As outlined in this paper, it is clear that the characteristics of the Christian community make emigration a feasible alternative, especially since the political situation does not offer prospects for stability and economic advancement. The factors which encourage Christians to leave probably function in a similar manner among other Palestinians with the same economic, educational and social characteristics. It goes without saying that a government which runs a military occupation will not put as one of its priorities the halting of emigration among the occupied population.

The argument that Islamic fundamentalism has led to Christian emigration from the Holy Land is not supported either by the findings of various surveys, or of the social reality of the West Bank and the Gaza Strip. The reasons cited for emigration among hundreds of respondents do not include reference to Islamic fundamentalism, and while some of the respondents have expressed concern over the rise of Islamic fundamentalism on future prospects of coexistence, this was not, of itself, a sufficient cause to think seriously of leaving the country. Those who argue that Islamic fundamentalism is the cause of Palestinian Christian emigration wish to obscure the fact that interrelated political and economic factors are the primary reasons for the departure of Palestinians, Christians and others, from their homeland.

The Situation in Israel

There are 114,000 Christians in Israel, or close to 2.3 per cent of the overall population, and 14.0 per cent of all Arabs in Israel. In 1990, Dr Hatem Khoury conducted an emigration survey in Haifa which covered 487 respondents, of whom 142 were Muslims and 345 Christians. The survey found that the intention to emigrate was three times higher among Christians than among Muslims. The reasons given for wanting to leave revolved around employment (38.6 per cent), and permanent emigration and family reasons (with 13.5 per cent each). As in the West Bank survey, the intention to emigrate was found in all denominations, even though smaller Christian denominations, such as the Haifa Maronites, showed a higher percentage of intention to emigrate. The highest level of actual emigration from Haifa took place between 1984 and 1989. This could be related to lower employment opportunities and the absence of real prospects for advancement. When asked of conditions which must prevail to stop or limit emigration, the Haifa respondents cited better employment opportunities (31.3 per cent), improvement of the political situation (17.7 per cent), opportunities for higher education (15.1 per cent), and improvement of the overall economic conditions (9.9 per cent).[19]

Demography and the Future

Lest these figures provide some with comfort or lead to political misconceptions, it must be stated that the population balance between Israelis and Palestinians will not be changed dramatically, in the long run, even if Palestinian emigration continues at its present rate, and Jewish immigration increases drastically. In fact, Israeli demographic experts regard the year 2015 as the 'parity date', when there will be an equal number of Jews and Arabs in Israel/Palestine. Each additional 100,000 Jewish immigrants to Israel pushes the parity date back one year. It is expected that by the year 2010, there will be 6.5 million Jews in the country, out of 12 million Jews world-wide.[20] From a demographic perspective, time is no comfort to either Israel or the Palestinians. Demography, in our case, is the essence of politics. There is no point, on either side, in adopting a position of demographic determinism, and magically making the rival national population disappear. Emigration of Palestinians will slow down dramatically when there is peace. But peace is not dependent on one side only. It needs both sides to agree to produce political and administrative arrangements which would guarantee the rights of both national groups in the Holy Land. Continued control and hegemony by one side over the other does not promise an improvement in economic and social conditions, and therefore continues to contribute to the haemorrhage of Palestinian emigration. It is only with the coming of a just and lasting peace that the potential and integrity of our religious and national communities will be guaranteed.

[19] Khoury, Hatem. 1991. 'The Emigration of Arab Christians from Haifa' in *Al-Hijra* [Emigration], Al-Liqa Center, Jerusalem (in Arabic). Recently Al-Liqa published a series of original articles on emigration (in English), mostly by Palestinian authors.

[20] Interview with Professor Sergio Della Pergola, Head of Jewish Demography and Statistics at Hebrew University, Jerusalem, *The Jerusalem Post*, February 5, 1992.

3

Socio-Demographic Characteristics: Reality, Problems and Aspirations within Israel

Sami F Geraisy*

The Arabs in Israel

Main Social Characteristics of the Arab Community in Israel

The Arab family has been characterized as being patrilineal, patriarchal, extended, patrilocal, endogamous, and occasionally polygamous. Several patrilineally extended families form a larger social and power unit called the *hamula*. A village may consist of only one *hamula*, though usually it consists of two or more. Members of a single *hamula* generally live in a common quarter (*hara*). The *hamula* sometimes is named after the location of the *hara* in the village (*hara gharbiyya*, 'western locality,' or *hara sharqiyya*, 'eastern locality'), or after the ancestral name.

Usually members of the same *hamula* cooperate and share responsibilities in different matters and on a number of occasions. They cooperate in building, in marriage expenses and celebrations, or in harvesting. They are mutually and collectively responsible for the

* This paper devolves from a comprehensive monograph written by Dr Geraisy earlier, under the title 'The Holy Land: Home of Christianity'.

protection and security of each other, for sharing the consequences of blood feuds and other wrongs inflicted by them on others, or by others on them.

Males have rights in marriage to their parallel patrilineal cousins. Endogamy is not prescribed, but is preferred. It is the men who control marriage rights; they can, and often do, relinquish such rights to marry a cousin. The fact remains that a cousin is by custom the most eligible bridegroom. It is alluded to in several proverbs: e.g., *ibn al-'amm bitayih 'an thahr al-faras*, which means, a cousin can take her down off the horse.

Often there is a traditional state of enmity between different *hamulas* of a single village which is periodically kindled by disputes over land, water rights, women, legacies, status, or appointment of a *mukhtar*. In elections to heads of a village council a neutral *hamula* volunteers to mediate between the conflicting parties. Some *hamulas*, for protection or other purposes, often make pacts. Some make connections with government officials or city notables. Often the *hamula* has its party political ties. Sometimes villagers join a party or other social group only by virtue of their *hamula* membership.

Politically, the government often supports patriarchal leadership and *hamula* factionalism, and it promotes young men who are prepared to support 'traditional' relationships both in the village and with the outside. The historical and social conditions that produced these forms of leadership might have changed, but the possibilities of using them for new needs are exploited and encouraged.

Some Arabs attribute the encouragement of the *hamula* leadership and structure to certain intended or unintended politics of the Jewish authorities, as a part of a general policy of 'divide and rule.' Yet many villagers who advance such arguments have acted in a number of situations in maximum adherence to *hamula* loyalties. In the parliamentary elections thousands of villagers who gave their votes to the Communist Party voted at the same time for their *hamula* leaders in the village council.

The *hamula* leader (*mukhtar, shaikh*, or *za'im*) emerges spontaneously from among the elders of the *hamula*. He is consulted on several *hamula* matters and takes the initiative in settling disputes among its members. Or he may compete with other leaders for power, wealth, or status, and thus drag his kinsfolk into controversies and hostilities. The success in the attainment of power depends on wealth, the successful manipulation of relatives, and on gaining recognition from the government.

Another characteristic of the village social structure is the existence of the patriarchal rule. The father is master and head of the nuclear family. He is the sole owner of land, house, and property. During the last decade, due to the increasing independence of children in earning money in the out-of-village labour market, and due to the limitation on land ownership for eligibility to social insurance, this patriarchal power is being challenged.

Polygamy, which was practised on a very limited scale by some Muslim males, was outlawed during the first years of the state.

The traditional ways of life of the village community began to undergo change some generations ago. This included the growth of towns and cities, the decline of agriculture as the main source of income, the assumption of more social, economic, and judicial responsibilities by modern governments, the introduction of Western ideas by means of schools, universities, missionaries, and mass media, the rule of the British for thirty years, and, lately, the establishment of the State of Israel.

While Israel's Jewish population consists of several communities with different traditions and cultural backgrounds, its main character is predominantly Western and industrial. There is no doubt that this modern state has speeded up change in the Arab village community.

The Israeli government has introduced into the Arab villages modern concepts of local government, health and welfare services, free compulsory elementary education for boys and girls, national insurance schemes, political parties, trade unions and social benefits. It is assumed that these services and institutions will gradually replace the functions of traditional *hamula*, and thus change the social structure.

This is a country claimed by two peoples: one is modern, mostly urban and industrial; the other is traditional, mostly rural and wage-earner. The Arab rural community is becoming less self-sufficient and more dependent on the Jewish economy. Jewish political and social institutions are penetrating the Arab rural life and are gradually taking the place of the traditional Arab familial social functions.

The Arab-Israeli war of 1948 interrupted the continuity of the social, economic, and political development of the Arab population. This continuity was challenged by changing circumstances and new patterns following the establishment of the State of Israel. The Arabs in the new state were reduced in number and changed in a very short time from a majority to a minority stripped of political leadership and power. Most of the economic and political elite fled; economic institutions were dissolved; and the ties with the Arab countries were severed when the government passed into Jewish hands.

The Arab Population in Israel

The Arab population is concentrated in four areas:
1 Galilee, with an Arab population of 570,000, of whom ninety thousand are Christian.
2 The Triangle with a population of 120,000, all Muslim.

3 The Mixed Cities (Acre, Haifa, Lod, Ramla, Jaffa), with an Arab population of about 65,000, of whom 16,000 are Christian.
4 The Negev with a total population of 80,000, all Muslim Bedouins.

Population of Israel in thousands, at the end of the year

	Druze & others		Christians		Muslims		Jews		Total
	%	1000s	%	1000s	%	1000s	%	1000s	1000s
1949	1.2	14.5	2.9	34.0	9.5	111.5	86.4	1013.9	1173.9
1950	1.1	15.0	2.6	36.0	8.5	116.1	87.8	1203.0	1370.1
1955	1.1	19.0	3.4	43.3	7.6	136.3	88.9	1590.5	1789.1
1960	1.1	23.3	2.3	49.6	7.7	166.3	88.9	1911.3	2150.4
1965	1.2	29.8	2.2	57.1	8.2	212.4	88.5	2299.1	2598.4
1970	1.2	35.9	2.5	75.5	10.9	328.6	85.4	2582.0	3022.1
1975	1.2	42.2	2.3	80.2	11.8	411.4	84.7	2959.4	3493.2
1980	1.3	50.7	2.3	89.9	12.7	498.3	83.7	3282.7	3921.7
1985	1.7	72.0	2.3	99.4	13.5	577.6	82.4	3517.2	4266.2
1989	1.8	80.3	2.3	107.0	14.4	655.2	81.5	3717.1	4559.6

(*Government Statistical Year Book 1990*, p.38, table 1)

Distribution of the non-Jewish population and their percentage

Year	Druze & Others %	Christian %	Muslim %	Total Numbers
1949	9.0	21.3	69.7	160000
1950	9.0	21.5	69.5	167100
1955	9.5	21.8	68.7	198600
1960	9.8	20.7	69.5	239200
1965	9.9	19.1	71.0	299300
1970	8.1	17.2	74.7	440000
1975	7.9	15.0	77.1	533800
1980	8.0	14.0	78.0	639000
1985	9.6	13.3	77.1	749000
1987	9.6	13.0	77.4	793600
1989	9.5	12.7	77.8	842500

(*Government Statistical Year Book 1990*, p.38, table 2)

60 per cent of the Arab population are villagers (in 101 villages), while 87 per cent of the Jewish population is urban. The Arab urban population constitutes 3.6 per cent of the total urban population, while their rural proportion is 41 per cent of the total rural population.

In the State of Israel the Arab minority not only remembers vividly that it had been a majority in the recent past with national aims and aspirations, but also feels keenly that, in the confrontation with the

Jews, it is facing a victor, more advanced in material civilization and speaking a different language.

Christians and Muslims equally together went through the same process of uprootedness and change. Tens of thousands of Christians either ran away from their villages in order to escape, or avoid the consequences of military occupation. Rumours, and also facts, spoke of massacres by the Israeli occupiers against the Arab civil population, such as in the case of Deir Yasin near Jerusalem, or Ailaboun, and others in Galilee. Others stayed in their towns and villages but were later driven out to a neighbouring village or town, or were ordered to leave the country and cross to Lebanon (in the case of Ailaboun) or Jordan. The inhabitants of two villages in northern Galilee, totally Christian (Ikrit and Bir-Im), chose to stay in their villages. They even offered the Israeli soldiers bread and food, but two or three days later, the army commander ordered them to leave for another two villages (Jish and Rama), and promised to let them return upon the cessation of the military operations. For the last forty-four years they remain refugees, not allowed to return. In spite of their continuous struggle and their willingness to share their limited land with the settlers, they are refused any reconciliation. They tried all legal, political and diplomatic means, but to not avail. They appealed to the Knesset (the Israeli parliament), but the majority of members continue to deprive them of the right to return, on the assumption that there are tens, if not hundreds of thousands, who are refugees inside Israel, and any resolution which might allow refugees of one village to return may serve as a legal precedent to allow others.

The peoples of Ikrit and Bir-Im appealed to the Israeli High Court of Justice, to embassies of countries that are friends of Israel, to the United Nations, but to no avail. They have not given up. They continue to struggle and to be hopeful. Tens of churches in villages and towns, which are abandoned stand lonely, and are in terrible neglect. Some are surrounded by filth and garbage, while others are used as stores and cowsheds. These churches cry to heaven seeking justice. They have no bells to call their believers. In the graveyards the gravestones are broken and covered with thistles and thorny bushes. The ancestors inside them cannot raise their voices in protest. Christians have lost home, land, job, and faith in justice. To an extent, they have lost faith in their own churches and church leadership because the leaders have not done enough to support them.

The Arabs in Israel are debarred from certain opportunities, economic, social and political, which deprivations circumscribe the individual's freedom of choice and self-development. Their subordinate position became manifest in their unequal access to educational opportunities, and in their restricted scope for occupational and professional advancement. They suffer more than the ordinary amount of social and economic insecurity. This is especially so because they are less than equal in wealth, in education, in technical experience and in political power, in addition to enjoying minority status.

For the individual member of a minority, the most onerous condition under which one has to labour is that one is treated as a member of a preconceived category, irrespective of one's individual merits. Lack of intimate contact with others tends in the course of time to generate incapacity for mutual understanding, allowing mental stereotypes to arise on both sides.

One of the more disturbing problems resulting from the Arab-Israeli war was the imposition of the military administration on the Arabs, which enabled the military governor in each administrative area to arrest or deport 'troublesome elements', to define closed areas, and to compel the Arab inhabitants to obtain travel permits when wishing to leave or enter the militarily-administered zones. Legally, the military administration was based on the British Emergency Regulations of 1945-1946. Although its authority and scope were restricted, it remained a subject of controversy among both the Arab and Jewish population until it was abolished in 1966. It was substituted by a policy aiming at converting the Galilee from a predominantly Arab region into a predominantly Jewish one. Examples of this policy were the establishment of 'Upper Nazareth' on the hills of Arab Nazareth, and also the establishment of 'Carmeil' in the heart of western Galilee, etc. Steps also were taken to settle the Bedouins. This had succeeded already in Galilee as well as in the Negev.

Another feature of change was that most of the Arab villages lost a great proportion of their agricultural and village land. Some villages lost relatively little, while others like Ul el-Fahm lost considerable areas. When the villagers demanded their land back, they were offered compensation at the 1948 government assessment of value, which was regarded by the owners as unjustly low, and consequently many peasants refused to accept it. The expropriation of certain Arab village land, for purposes of 'vital development, settlement and security,' increases the need for employment outside the village.

The land issue is 'replete with political and national feelings', and of central importance to the status of the Arabs in Israel. The process of expropriation of land has culminated in almost 93 per cent of all land in Israel being brought under state control and administered by the Israel Lands Administration (ILA). Of this, 13 per cent is owned by the Jewish National Fund (JNF), and, according to the fund's own constitution, is 'national' land, the inalienable property of the Jewish people, and may not be leased to non-Jews. Even the other 80 per cent (owned by the state, or the Israel Development Authority) is often treated also as 'national' land, the inalienable property of the Jewish people, and may not be leased to non-Jews. Even the other 80 per cent (owned by the state, or the Israel Development Authority) is often treated also as 'national' land, and, significantly, six of the thirteen members of the ILA, which is responsible for leasing land, are Jewish Fund nominees.

It is impossible to calculate precisely the effects of land expropriation, but there is little doubt that it is considerable, even though compensation has been paid or offered, and the Arab population has benefited from the general progress of the State of Israel.

After the establishment of the state, immigration of the Jews to Israel was encouraged and facilitated. They came in relatively great numbers, so that the population tripled in the first seventeen years. In 1991 about 400,000 Russian Jews, and 70,000 Ethiopian Jews immigrated to Israel. In order to accommodate this increase in population, there was a rapid development of new towns, moshavim, kibbutzim, and expansion and growth of all the already existing towns, settlements and cities. Roads, railways, and public buildings were built. New industries were established, others were expanded, while agriculture was developed and mechanized.

Such enterprises were financed and fostered by a steady inflow of substantial capital. The supply of Jewish labour could not cope with the demands of the different branches of the expanding economy, and Arab labour was available to fill the gap. Tens of thousands of Arab villagers were employed in the Jewish urban centres and in the expanding agricultural settlements. However, while Arab labour was recruited mainly to fill construction, service, and agricultural jobs, certain segments of the Jewish economy continued to be closed to them for security reasons.

Another important feature of change in the life of the Arab villagers was their transformation from a village peasantry to becoming wage-earners outside, whilst living in the villages. The majority of male Arab villagers have become wage-earners in urban centres and Jewish settlements, whilst others have become wage-earners in their own villages.

As compared with other countries in the Middle East, ownership of land in the Arab villages in Palestine was much more equal than in other countries in the region, and retained traces of a communal village organization. One of these was the division of cultivable land into two areas, a winter crop zone, and a summer crop zone. Another institution was the periodic re-allotment of *Masha'a* land, which was a system of joint ownership. Taking into consideration the crop rotation, the elders periodically re-allotted the shares (*asham*) among the village households.

Though the methods of farming have changed tremendously, they continue to lag behind, compared with the highly-developed co-operative farming in the Jewish sector. The use of machinery is quite prevalent. With the exception of a few villagers with irrigated areas,

51

most villages continue to sow traditional summer and winter crops, by using traditional extensive methods of cultivation.

Hopes That Could Be Fulfilled

1 The majority of Arabs and Jews need peace and wish for peace. Palestinians in Israel have this wish twofold. They need it as citizens of the Jewish state on the one hand, and as being part of the Palestinian people on the other. We ask our Christian brothers and sisters, and all people of goodwill to support us in our endeavours. We seek peace in the Holy Land, for each community in its own way.

Recent developments have raised expectations and hopes in our region. The accession to power of a Labour-led government in Israel, committed to a peace between Israel and its Arab and Palestinian neighbours based on territorial compromises, gives reason for optimism. The present peace talks, both between Israel and Syria, and between Israel and the Palestinians, may lead to a peaceful resolution of the conflict and a negotiated settlement.

Governmental goodwill alone will not be sufficient in making significant progress toward peace. Indeed, the Israeli government will have to convince its voters that the concessions it proposes are indeed necessary and vital, and that without them Israel cannot hope to achieve a lasting peace. It will have to persuade Israelis that in ceding territory Israel is not compromising its security. The government will also have to engage in a strongly competitive information campaign in the battle to win over public opinion, against the claims of Israeli ultra-nationalists, religious fundamentalists and vested interest groups, such as settlers on the Golan Heights, the West Bank, and Gaza, who have made their home in these territories for the last 25 years.

Even as negotiations in Washington were in progress, a poll conducted in mid-October 1992 indicated that 50 per cent of Israelis are opposed to any territorial concessions on the Golan. Public opinion in Israel is very volatile, and much depends on the conviction of citizens that peace is really possible. The fragile nature of the present government coalition means that it will have to demonstrate massive public support in order to be able to make the concessions necessary in any peace settlement.

There has never been a moment of greater opportunity or consequence for Israel and the peace camp within it. The challenge is to prepare a positive public response to new developments in the face of ignorance, stereotypes, hostility, and the fear of change. This means extensive and systematic educational work through an information

campaign that targets diverse constituencies, and attempts to speak to
each in its own language.

2 Education is a basic right for any person. Arabs in Israel, as a national
minority struggling for equality, have to equip themselves first and
foremost with education and skills, in order to be able to provide
services for their community in all the social, professional, and
educational fields. The community needs teachers, social workers,
physicians, agronomists, politicians, legal advisors, etc.

University tuition fees have been rising all the time, as the following
table shows.

Year	Tuition in Israeli Shekels	Increase
1982	1648	−2.7%
1983	2591	57.2%
1984	2429	−6.3%
1985	4787	97.1%
1987	4286	−12.2%
1990	4677	9.1%

The increase in school fees, coupled with increasing unemployment
and increasing inflation, make it hard for parents to be able to afford the
increasing financial burden. Moreover, universities in Israel are located
in cities, a situation which necessitates Arab students to travel daily and
pay bus fares, or live in the city where there is a university, which also
means more money for food and rent.

The Jewish students enjoy several funding resources, for loans and
grants which are not available to the non-Jewish student.

Arab students are only 5 per cent of the university student body in the
Israeli universities. Others who are not accepted seek higher education
in Europe and the USA. Most of them do not return because of better
employment opportunities outside, and difficulties involved in
obtaining suitable employment in Israel.

The establishment of a university in Galilee with diversified courses of
academic learning can offer an alternative to the drift of young educated
people leaving their country.

3 Although Israel is an industrial country, only 15 per cent of Arab
pupils benefit from technological education, while 60 per cent of the
Jewish pupils attend technological schools which offer courses and
training in about sixty different skills.

In Nazareth, Haifa, Jaffa and Ramla the majority of both elementary
and secondary schools are church schools, mainly Catholic, and some

Orthodox or Protestant. These schools are open to all pupils without any discrimination or privilege. It is important to encourage and assist the Christian schools to include technical education. There is an excellent example: the School of Jesus the Adolescent, a Catholic (Salesian) school offers good technical education in Nazareth.

4 The youth have very limited opportunities for sports, arts, music, and all that they need, and can enjoy, helping them to have a good, clean and useful life.

There are very few churches, schools, or local authorities that have community centres or youth and community clubs that can serve as places of social education for any age group, but especially the youth. We believe that this is a basic service, which is of the utmost importance, and which can offer an alternative to the streets and street corners, and can offer happiness and hope, as well as develop abilities. The Christian churches and organisations can be very helpful in developing this service.

5 Israel, a small country that has absorbed millions of Jewish immigrants, has done little or nothing to ease the problem of housing for the Arabs, in towns as well as in villages. The Arab church and lay leadership should continue to pressure the government to solve the housing problem for the Arabs, by providing space, infrastructure and loans to secure housing for young couples, big families, and families living in insecure, dangerous premises, and also for public buildings. The Christian churches, especially the Greek Orthodox, the Roman Catholic, and the Melkites have enough land all over the country, where good and diversified housing schemes could be developed. One hopes that the churches will rise to this need and challenge.

6 Bank interest in Israel is high, reaching an average of 20 per cent a year. People need loans to pay key money for flats and businesses. People need loans as a down payment to buy or build an apartment or a house. Young people need capital to start a business. A joint churches' or organisations' fund could be a reliable, feasible and possible source for borrowing on reasonable terms.

7 The Christian villagers can gain more from whatever area of land they own, by reclaiming unused rocky land, and by fencing, planting and irrigating it. There is an urgent need to help them, in Jish for example, to have cold storage for their produce, because the villagers are usually exploited by the storage owners, or the vegetable and fruit merchants and dealers.

8 Villagers need to be encouraged, trained and supported to keep and fatten sheep or cattle, or develop the keeping of bees on a market basis.

9 Christian organisations and churches in the West have historic and organic relations with organisations and churches in the Holy Land. The relationships usually are inter-establishments, i.e., churches to churches, church people to church people, organisations to organisations.

Moreover, the national and ethnic dimension plays a major part in establishing the kind and level of the relationship: Franciscan to Franciscan, Greek to Greek, Anglican to Anglican, Lutheran to Lutheran. Such relationships seldom reach the people, the grassroots, the natives, the real, true church, the people, the Christians themselves. There are church people in the country, in all Christian churches, who do not even try to learn to speak the language of the native people. Some have been in Jerusalem, Nazareth, Haifa, Tiberias or Cana of Galilee for twenty or thirty years, and never cared to know the language of their church-goers. It is vital, necessary and important for all concerned to know the people, to meet local people, to encounter the real Christians of the Holy Land. Tourism should include the requirement to meet the people. Meet them in their homes, churches, social centres, etc., learn from them, and get to know them.

10 Youth should be exposed to different cultures and ways of life, in order to know and enjoy and realise that people, regardless of colour, race, creed or country are basically the same. They need food, health, security and respect. Youth-exchange programmes should be encouraged, supported, and facilitated.

I wish to emphasise here that whatever service is good for the Christians is also good for those who are not Christians. Exchange of visits, enjoyment of youth club or community centre should be open to all and enjoyed by all. The theme is ecumenism, and not at all sectarianism. The emphasis is on how much as Christians we can give and share. This is our witness to Christ.

In this respect I like to give as an example, Christian Aid, which has been encouraging groups from Britain to visit Palestinians in their own homes and environment. Such an example is of great value, both to Britons and Palestinians.

4

Christianity in Gaza
Faraj al-Sarraf

In considering the place of Christians in Gaza I shall trace the history of Gaza from ancient times down to the present day.

Ancient History

Gaza, an Arab town, is one of the three most ancient towns in the Middle East, the other two being Jericho and Damascus. Gaza was at the crossroads of the ancient caravans that travelled between the Arabian peninsula, Egypt and Syria. It was also a distinctive military region, since it was close to the Sinai Desert which separated Asia and North Africa. Consequently, Gaza became a passageway for invading military leaders. Any ruler of Syria or Egypt who intended to overrun the Middle East had to take Gaza into account.

The ancient history of Gaza is associated with the Canaanites, the Hittites, and the Ghassanids. Furthermore, the inhabitants of Gaza mingled with the 'Sea Peoples' of the Eastern Mediterranean, including the Philistines who occupied the coast of Palestine between Haifa and Gaza, and who gave Palestine its historical name.

Before discussing the Christian era, the following general points should be mentioned:

1 The majority of the soldiers against whom Alexander the Great fought in Gaza were of the Arab race (Mayer). Both Mayer and the Arab Muslim historian al-Baladhuri confirm the presence of Arab inhabitants

and their oppression by the Byzantines. These inhabitants contributed to the Muslim conquest in 614 AD.

2   The Philistines established several towns in Palestine: Ashqelon, Ashdod, Beit Dajan and Gat. Gaza town was considered as another such town, and occurs in several places in the Old Testament. It is mentioned in detail in 1 Samuel and 2 Samuel, in the stories of Gideon and Samson and Delilah.

3   In the 6th century AD, Gaza became a centre of Hellenistic civilisation and sought to compete with Constantinople, Antioch and Alexandria. Its inhabitants were a mixture of Arabs, Assyrians, Canaanites and other local groups. The majority spoke Aramaic, while Greek was the language of the upper classes.

4   Downey points out that the Jews did not settle in Gaza for long periods of time, and they did not leave behind any historical remains (1963).

The Christian Era

The people of Gaza believe that when the Holy Family returned from Egypt, they passed through Gaza. They rested under a sycamore tree which was later called the 'Salha Sycamore' (the Good Sycamore). The Salha Sycamore remained a holy site until the end of the Ottoman empire. Although the actual Salha Sycamore is no longer there, the place with its sycamores is still visited by the people of Gaza.

The Apostle Philip was the first person to preach Christianity in Gaza (Acts of the Apostles 8.26). Christianity then spread gradually. Mayer states that the first bishop of Gaza was St Philemon, the Philemon to whom St Paul sent a letter. In 290 AD, St Helarion established in Gaza the very first monastery in the world. It was built between Gaza and Meyoma (the port of Gaza at that time). In 331 AD, the inhabitants of Meyoma were converted to Christianity. The site of the monastery is now located near the al-Shati (Beach) Refugee Camp.

In 363 AD, Bishop Iraneon built the Eirene Church (or Church of Peace) at the site where Alexander of Macedonia 'ceased to use the sword on the inhabitants of Gaza.' Between 402 and 407 AD, the St Porphyry Church was built. St Porphyry was able to convince Emperor Arcadius and his wife, Empress Eudokia, to build a church on the site of the Marmenion Temple. The Church is still in use today and holds the grave of St Porphyry who died in 420 AD.

Several bishops from Gaza participated in both the Council of Nicea in 325 AD and the Council of Chalcedon in 451 AD. Moreover, Rustum states that several bishops from Gaza helped in the formulation of the basic seventeen doctrines of the Orthodox church.

The Early Islamic Era

Sayyid Hashim, a forebear of the Honourable Prophet Muhammad, died and is buried in Gaza. Moreover, al-Imam al-Shafi', one of the chief imams in Islam, is also buried in Gaza. The inhabitants of Gaza welcomed the Muslims, and many were converted to Islam. It is recounted that 'Amr ibn al-'As was warned by a Christian Ghassanid about a plot to kill him. The warning saved his life. 'Amr ibn al-'As divided the two churches that existed at that time between the Christians and the Muslims. He gave the large church to the Muslim community, as they were the majority. This site is now known as al-'Umari Mosque. The Christians kept the St Porphyry Church.

Both the Muhammadan and the 'Umari Covenants (Guarantees) established the relationship between the Christians and the Muslims. The Prophet Muhammad granted the first covenant to the monks in the Sinai, while the second was granted by the Caliph 'Umar al-Khattab to the inhabitants of Jerusalem. All Muslims had to respect the covenants. In these covenants, Christians were granted the freedom to practise their religion and their rites. All places of Christian worship, churches, monasteries, etc., were to be respected. Christians were also granted the freedom of work and movement. Religious tolerance was encouraged. Moreover, Arab Christians were exempted from paying taxes and many assumed important public positions.

These measures enhanced the feelings of nationalism and oneness with their Muslim brethren. Christians had fought heroically with other Arab brethren in the well-known battle of Dhu Qar, c. 606, in which the Arabs were victorious over the Persians for the first time. In addition, Arab Ghassanids fought in the battle of Yarmouk against the Byzantines.

The Crusades

Christian Arabs regarded the foreign Crusaders as enemies, and they participated in all battles against them from the start. When the Crusaders occupied Jerusalem, the Orthodox patriarch took refuge in Gaza. He later went to Jordan and did not return until Jerusalem was liberated by Saladin. Saladin restored to the Christians all their properties, their monasteries and their churches, including the Holy Sepulchre. Certain Christian feasts in Gaza became national feasts, such as the 'Bab al-Darum Feast'.

The Ottoman Era

In 1517, at the beginning of the Ottoman era in the Holy Land, Christian Arabs, with the help of Patriarch Atallah obtained from the Ottoman sultan, Selim, a new covenant/convention known as the 'Humayuni Rule'. This convention guaranteed freedom of faith for the local Christians, and allowed foreign Christians to visit the Holy Land. The sultan also repaired the walls of Jerusalem, and in 1530 he gave Patriarch Atallah a document which reaffirmed the Orthodox ownership of the Mar Elias monastery with its surrounding lands.

Some 16th century Ottoman statistics, translated and published by Princeton University, reveal that the percentage of Christian Arabs in Gaza was almost 20 per cent of the total inhabitants, and that Gaza town was the largest town in Palestine. Moreover, the dues and taxes paid to the government were more than double those paid by Jerusalem and three or four times as much as those paid by other towns.

In the 17th century, the Fraternity of the Holy Sepulchre was first established. It was this fraternity that gave the Greeks the power to administer the church of Jerusalem. This created resentment and led to a schism between the patriarchate and the Orthodox laity, a schism which continues to have its effects even today.

At the end of the Ottoman period, Gaza was administratively considered as part of the Jerusalem district. It remained so for a hundred years, until the end of the Ottoman rule. Because of its religious importance, this district was directly connected to the sultan in Constantinople.

The Mamluk and the Napoleonic Era

During the period of the Mamluks, Gaza suffered many disasters. There were pestilence and disease, as well as invasions by the bedouins. Disorder and injustice prevailed. Economically, Gaza was no longer important. The international trading thoroughfares to Gaza were displaced. There was destruction and ruin. The inhabitants of Gaza were reduced to 2,000. Further destruction and displacement were caused by the arrival of Napoleon. His campaign was regarded as another Crusade. It was many years later that the Christians returned to Gaza and re-established their community.

The Mid-19th Century

During the rule of al-Jazzar and Muhammad Pasha Abu Maraq, the oppression inflicted upon Gaza was unique. There had never been any such oppression before. Many families, even the well-to-do, had to sell their children. However, this state of affairs did not last long. In the late 19th and early 20th centuries, things were back to normal.

During that period, Christians traded in grain (wheat, barley, etc.). They used to store them in *ahwash* (courtyards). These *ahwash* stretched from the east of Gaza to the interior of the town, and totalled fifteen. The grain was collected from the farmers in Gaza and Beer Sheba, and was exported to Europe, via the Mediterranean Sea. This trade continued during the British Mandate over Palestine. Christians were also famous for working and trading in gold. A large number of them are still practising this trade. In addition to trading in grain and gold, many Christians worked in municipal councils, and in educational, economic and health institutions.

Most of the Christians at that time lived close to the church in the Zaitun Quarter. They lived there with their Muslim brethren with whom they had all kinds of business transactions, and with whom they were partners. Freedom of faith and tolerance prevailed. In 1856, for example, the Shari'a courts declared that a statement given by a Christian witness was equal to that given by a Muslim. Futhermore, the New Law of Penalties promulgated in 1858 provided for equality among all citizens irrespective of their faith. Towards the end of the Ottoman era, the Christians had two members in the Gaza Administrative Council, as well as an official investigator; two quite high and sensitive positions.

Gaza Christians Today

There are three churches in Gaza today; the St Porphyry Orthodox Church (founded 410), the Latin Catholic Church (1879) and the Christian Mission Church, the CMS (1878). Today many of the Christians have left the Zaitun Quarter (old Gaza), to live in the modern Rimal Quarter. After the 1948 Arab-Israeli War, many Christians left Gaza, and their number was reduced to one third. Today many are also leaving because of the bad economic and political conditions. There are only 2,000 Christians in Gaza. Most are highly educated, with over 150 engineers, and 120 medical doctors.

The Christians in Gaza are involved in the following institutions, which offer their services to all the Palestinians in Gaza.

First, there is the YMCA, which offers educational, technical and sports services, and also operates a kindergarten. Second, there is the Near East Council of Churches (NECC), which operates as a local branch. It offers educational services especially in vocational training. Its medical services include the manufacturing of artificial limbs. Third, there is the Arab al-Ahli hospital, the only non-governmental hospital in the Gaza Strip. This hospital was established by the CMS in 1908, and when the CMS terminated its services in Palestine, the Arab Anglican church in Jerusalem took over. Today the hospital is run by an Arab Board of Directors under the supervision of the Anglican Church. The hospital has 46 beds, and there is also an outpatient clinic. Fourth, there is the Gaza College, a high school college founded in 1943 by the late brothers, Shafiq and Wadi Tarazi. Finally, the Latin Catholics run a modern, well-organised kindergarten, an elementary school, and they are in the process of establishing a preparatory school and a public library. They also render social and medical services free of charge. In addition, both the Orthodox and the Sunday school kindergartens have been operating for some years now.

Conclusion

To conclude, I would like to appeal to all concerned to preserve old Gaza as it is. I would like to see this impressive town with its narrow, ancient lanes and buildings preserved for our future generations. Moreover, I would like to re-affirm that we should all work for the strengthening of our national unity. In Gaza one cannot differentiate between a Christian and a Muslim, either in food, drink, clothing, customs or traditions. Christians have participated with their Muslim brethren in all national activities: in strikes, protests, revolts, etc. We have often prayed together for the rain. We should all work together in preventing the annexation of our land, and in making it completely Jewish. As long as we have right on our side, we should not despair.

We should also discourage our Christian brothers and sisters from emigrating. I would like to point out to them that we Christians are as old as Gaza itself. It is our national duty to stay and build our country. If the Christians in the Holy Land continue to emigrate at the present rate, there will be no Christians left in thirty to forty years' time.

To sum up, I would like to cite the following quotation from Mustafa al-Dabbagh's book: 'The bond which the Arabs have in Palestine, and the historical right which they have therein is everlasting, genuine and indisputable. They are part of it; they have lived in it since the dawn of history before the Jews came to it. They were never separated from it for a single day. Palestine is a gift from heaven; it is deep in the heart of every Muslim and every Christian; those people who make half the total population of the World today. The conflict is not only between Muslims and Jews, it is also between the Muslims and Christians on one side and the Zionists on the other.'

Sources

al-Dabbagh, Mustafa, *The History of Gaza and Palestine* (in Arabic), vols. I-II, Beirut, 1964-66.

Downey, J D, 1963, *Gaza in the Early 6th Century*.

Mayer, Martin, *The History of Gaza*, New York, 1960.

Rustum, Asad, *The Rise of the Greek Orthodox*.

5

Justice and Peace

Jean Zaru

May God's peace, Mercy and Blessings be unto you!

When I received the invitation to participate in this conference I was overjoyed for the opportunity of sharing and learning, of bearing of each other's burdens and joys. There is no greater gift in life than the fellowship of those who share in God, in His truth, justice and peace. Yet I had a sense of unworthiness. A simple lay woman, a victim of so much oppression! What is my message?

I have been confronted with many structures of injustice, political, social, economic and religious. And these structures have been at work in destructive way throughout our community. What has made me take part in all these struggles? Fundamentally there are two reasons:

1 The Gospel has made me sensitive to the suffering which reflects the evil which plagues the whole human race, and opens us to God's redeeming activity.

2 In Judaism, Christianity and Islam, the concept of the divine nature existing in harmonious relationship with human nature and the natural order has been a dominant one. The teachings of these religions which come from my part of the world helped undergird the belief that human beings have rights. Human beings are created in the image of God, and our value comes from this likeness. God's nature is loving, free and just.

God's purpose is to liberate human life from inhuman conditions. These exist because people of free-will have chosen behaviour which disrupts the intended harmony, which would provide justice, peace, and freedom for all. Since I was so directed by my faith, I got involved in the struggle for justice on all fronts, and I could not be selective.

But what is Justice?

> He has showed you, O man, what is good and what does the
> Lord require of you but, to do justice, and to love kindness
> and to walk humbly with your God? (Micah 6.8).

The most crucial issue of the Israel-Palestine conflict is that of justice. Justice means different things to different people. Some people define justice very narrowly, relating it to the establishment of rights based on laws or rules. Others take a broader view of justice, which includes well-being, righteousness, wholeness, and peace.

Under the narrow understanding of justice, the wealthy and powerful are able to have laws interpreted in their favour. They say they are obeying the law, even while they are taking advantage of the poor and powerless. In Occupied Palestine the laws are manipulated by the powerful, making life so difficult and unlivable for all Palestinians, whether living in Israel or in the Occupied Territories. Religious laws, too, are interpreted in favour of the powerful, and this is true also of cultural and economic laws as well. Who benefits from these laws? The Israelis benefit, while Palestinians suffer. Men benefit, but women suffer.

Biblical justice goes beyond law. It includes the concept of wholeness and well-being in all areas of life, social, economic, and political. Grace and forgiveness are also important parts of the biblical understanding of justice. The Holy Spirit continues to motivate us. The Spirit enables us to live in agreement with the justice that God has established, and will help us also to see the fundamental difference between human justice and biblical justice.

Problems of injustice today are not really new. Only the people and situations are new. It is sad that after two thousand years of knowledge of Jesus' life and message, changes for good are only on the surface. Although the following verses from the Bible were written thousands of years ago, they do express the anguish and pain of Palestinians today.

> Listen you rulers of Israel! You are supposed to be concerned
> about justice, yet you hate what is good and you love what
> is evil. You skin my people alive and tear the flesh off their
> bones. You eat my people up. You strip off their skin, break

their bones. The time is coming when you will cry out to the Lord, but he will not answer you. He will not listen to your prayers for you have done evil (Micah 3.1-4).

Woe to you who add house to house and join field to field till no space is left, and you live alone in the land (Isaiah 5.8).

You are doomed! You make unjust laws that oppress my people. That is how you prevent the poor from having their rights and from getting justice. That is how you take the property that belongs to widows and orphans (Isaiah 10.1-2).

I will punish this city because it is full of oppression. As a well keeps its water fresh, so Jerusalem keeps its evil fresh. I hear violence and destruction in the city. Sickness and wounds are all I see. Everyone great and small tries to make money dishonestly; even prophets and priests cheat the people. They act as if my people's wounds were only scratches. All is well, they say, when all is not well. Were they ashamed because they did these disgusting things. No, they were not at all ashamed; and they do not even know how to blush (Jeremiah 6.6-7, 13-15).

Remember, O Lord, what has happened to us.
Look at us and see our disgrace.
Our property is in the hands of strangers;
foreigners are living in our homes.
Our fathers have been killed by the enemy,
And now our mothers are widows.
We must pay for the water we drink,
We must buy the wood we need for fuel.
Driven hard like donkeys or camels,
We are tired but are allowed no rest.
To get food enough to stay alive,
we went begging to Egypt and Assyria.
We are ruled by men who are no better than slaves,
And no one can save us from their power.
Murderers roam through the countryside;
We risk our lives when we look for food.
Hunger has made us burn with fever until our skin is hot as an oven.
In every village our daughters have been forced to submit.
Our leaders have been taken and hanged.

Our old men are shown no respect.
Our young men are forced to grind corn like slaves,
boys go staggering under heavy loads of wood.
The old people no longer sit at the city gate,
and the young people no longer make music.
Happiness has gone out of our lives;
Grief has taken the place of our dances.
Nothing is left of all we were proud of.
We are sick at our hearts, and can hardly see through our
tears.
But you, O Lord, are king forever, and will rule to the end
of time.
Why have you abandoned us so long? Will you ever
remember us again? (Lamentations 5.1-20)

If you visit Palestine today, you will hear every Palestinian's cry, man, woman and child. A cry, a cry coming from the depths, a cry for justice. These words from the prophets can be our words. They are apt descriptions of our situations, and our lives. And in the wilderness of occupation, oppression and exile, we need more than ever the prophets of justice, to proclaim justice, to proclaim the coming of the prince of peace.

Christians have been accused both of failing to promote justice in the world and even more seriously of collaborating with injustice, by encouraging the poor and the oppressed to accept their misery patiently, in the assurance of abundant rewards in a future life. I am very familiar with this conception of faith. All it does is alienate human beings from their proper task in the present life, and induce irresponsibility. For me faith is a source of power. Faith should direct us, and activate us to find human solutions to our situations of injustice. Without a sincere commitment to the healing and reconciliation of a broken world, we could not have either the discernment, or the trust that is proper to the children of God who share already, by grace, in the divine life opened up to us in Christ. To be honest with ourselves, are we not aware of so many Christians who are only seeking salvation through the ecclesiastical spheres of doctrine and worship, without leading an active participation in the quest for a just social order?

According to John, 'Whoever does what is true comes to the light' (3.21). Truth is not only to be thought about, but to be done, and the doing of the truth is a condition of believing it.

In St Luke's account, Jesus started his public ministry in Galilee saying, 'The spirit of the Lord is upon me, because he has anointed me to bring good news to the poor. He has sent me to proclaim liberty to the captives, and recovery of sight to the blind; to set free the oppressed'

(Luke 4.18). According to Matthew, Jesus answered John the Baptist's questions, 'Go back and tell John what you are hearing and seeing. The blind can see, the lame can walk, those who suffer from dreaded skin diseases are made clean, the deaf hear, the dead are brought back to life and the good news is preached to the poor' (11.5).

Jesus did not strive for social or political power. But by very different means he tried to bring justice. first for those who have been denied justice and the good life, the victims of social, economic and political violence. He promoted service rather than exploitation. What a lesson! For today we need to be liberated from people who claim they are serving, teaching, training, healing, but who are exploitative at the same time, exploiting women, exploiting resources, and exploiting nature as well.

We have religious leaders who exploit the Bible in reflecting on the legitimacy, policies and conduct of Israel. They have tried to establish a linkage between biblical Israel and modern Israel. The history of condoning evil in the name of the Bible is a long one. Evils of discrimination, oppression and war are justified by reference to texts in the Bible. David Ben-Gurion called the Bible the 'sacrosanct title-deed to Palestine' for the Jewish people.

An advertisement placed by a large group of churchmen in *The Chicago Tribune* (l July 1946) says, 'because the Jewish people are the people of the prophecy, they are the people of the Land and we knowing him who made the promise, totally support the people and the Land of Israel in her God-given, God-promised, God-ordained right to exist. Any person or group of nations opposed to this right isn't just fighting Israel, but God and time itself.'

How then can we Palestinians claim any right to compassion or justice when, according to many, we are fighting not only Israel, but God Himself?

Christians in Palestine are taking new initiatives to articulate a Palestinian theology of liberation. We begin with the life and teachings of Jesus as the key to reading and interpreting the Bible. Justice and compassion become central themes. God is a God of justice, not a God of war, vengeance and exclusivity.

Religion in my part of the world in both its progressive and reactionary forms has entered and shaped the Arab-Israeli conflict. On the progressive side, there are movements toward a radical alliance with the poor and oppressed. There are activist, reform and peace movements. On the reactionary side, there is narrowness and chauvinism, which easily allies itself with narrow and chauvinistic national and economic interests.

Religion for us is a problem where its structures of dominance have oppressed us, both as Palestinians and as women. And a solution with its vision of liberation and equality has given us hope and generated powerful movements for social change.

The kingdom of peace and justice is not a remote ideal for which we long. It is already at work, transforming the world in which we live. In so far as we have faith, the kingdom takes hold of us and operates in us. This means that through faith we become instruments in the healing and reconciliation of a broken world. We become agents of justice and bearers of the power of the kingdom. Faith, therefore, is more than believing, more than having hope in what God will do without us. It involves active participation in the work that God is doing, in the task of bringing forth justice to the nations.

We have to bring forth true justice to all: to the Palestinians, but not at the expense of Israelis or Jordanians; to women, but not at the expense of men; to humanity, but not at the expense of nature and mother earth. The justice we strive for must be justice for all creatures and for creation itself. Thy kingdom come, Thy will be done.

Isaiah sums up the truth about justice and peace, not only for creatures but for creation as well:

> But once more God will send us his spirit. The waste land will become fertile, and fields will produce rich crops. Everywhere in the land righteousness and justice will be done. Because everyone will do what is right, there will be peace and security for ever. God's people will be free from worries and their homes peaceful and safe (32.15-18).

The Bible begins and ends with promises of peace. In the beginning God created a garden of peace. God gave the best to the man and woman He had created. An abode of peace, order and beauty, with all they needed for a good life. At the end of the Bible another peaceable community appears. There God dwells with people on earth in a city with peace, security and healing (Rev 21.1-4). In between, Isaiah and Micah speak of the peaceful era when swords will be hammered into ploughs, spears into pruning knives (Micah 4.3; Isaiah 2.4).

So the promise of peace is central to the biblical and Christian tradition. Peace on earth, goodwill to humankind is the angel's song at the birth of Jesus. The presence of Christ in our midst is said to bring that peace which passes all understanding (Phil 4.7). Nevertheless, the Christian tradition has held a whole range of views about peace. And we can spend so much time debating these different views, and the split some see between spiritual and historical peace.

I kept asking myself. 'If we say there is something of God in every person, why is it so difficult to see it in others? Why is there so much evil and suffering in the world?' For many years I have struggled with this Christian truth, that we are made in the image and likeness of God, but I was happy to learn that the indwelling divinity seems to be part of all religions.

'The kingdom of God is within you,' says Jesus. 'You are the temple of God,' wrote St Paul. 'He who knows himself knows God,' said the Prophet Muhammad, and this was echoed by many Sufis. This recognition of our shared brotherhood and sisterhood convinced me that it must lead to the disappearance of the injustices of exploitation, oppression and everything that comes from fake beliefs that justify ourselves and degrade others. So acknowledgement of our true selves is revolutionary. It must lead to great changes and to peace. Thus the search for peace and the recognition of reality are identical.

For too long we were told, as Palestinians and as women, to be peaceful (which is to be passive,) to be nice, to allow ourselves to be walked over. They talked to us about the 'peace' that was achieved by pounding the opposition to submission, 'peace' maintained by crushing protest against injustice, 'peace' for the rulers at the expense of the ruled.

We live daily as persons and as communities in the midst of violence. We often find ourselves willingly or unwillingly participating in social organizations that practise and embody violence. We may deliberately act in violent or non violent ways to promote justice. For those who opted for violence against injustice can we say that we would rather see them die than defend themselves. Who will throw the first stone to condemn them? Who is morally superior? When we condemn those who opted for violence, we are demonizing others, so we feel good about ourselves, and we can then relieve ourselves of our responsibility for our sins for treating our brothers and sisters as less than human. As we opt for violence or non violence in our revolution, we know that the liberty to choose is not always there. I believe that the pacifist and non-pacifist who are committed to the struggle for a just future should regard one another on most issues as allies. The problem is not between them, as much as it is between those who support the oppressive structures of the *status quo* and those on the side of liberation. The gospel compels us as Christians not to support the structures which oppress people. This brings us face to face with an impossible alternative today.

There are many contemporary ideas on revolution. Unfortunately, virtually all revolutions have only involved surface changes, such as the transfer of power from one personality to another, or the replacement of one form of tyranny by another. A vital revolution must be concerned with the triumph of human values and human rights.

Christian teachings seem so relevant to ideal revolutions. Although non-violence is at the core of these teachings, it should never be equated with passivity or disengagement in the face of injustice. On the contrary, Christian teachings are very active, highly political, often controversial, and sometimes very dangerous forms of engagement in social and political conflict.

In the last two years, first in Madrid and then in Washington, we all watched anxiously the Middle East peace talks. We should not forget the real issue in these talks is Palestine. The Palestinian people have accepted an extraordinary set of compromises, required of no other participant. We were not represented by the PLO; no one from East Jerusalem was allowed to attend; no one from outside the West Bank and Gaza was allowed to participate, even though Palestinians are one people, more than half of which lives in forced exile outside Palestine. Israel is not committing itself to withdrawal. There is no end to settlements, no negotiation on Jerusalem, no compromise on Palestinian self-determination. The peace which Israel is ready to offer is what we call surrender of our national identity, our political rights, and of the remaining land on which we live. Such a vision is a formula for unending conflict.

No one can suppose that having resisted Israeli rule for decades we are about to give up. The realities on the ground for us are too tragic, too violent. Cosmetic peace is not enough for us. We have no allies, but we do have hope, and we do have a more just picture of the future than Israel has, one which is built on reconciliation and peace. The answer to peace is not exclusivism and unending hostility. It is, rather, reconciliation, sharing and community. There is no military option for Palestinians and Israelis. We should live together and discover how to share the land together.

We have agreed to work for peace. We have cooperated with the conveners. But what worries us is the silence and indifference to our plight, and that mainly in the US. The issues are clear and the dangers are very obvious. Peace is for everybody, not just for the powerful.

But what is peace? Is it only the absence of conflict? Conflict is an inevitable fact of daily life, internal, interpersonal, intergroup and international. Peace consists in dealing creatively with conflict. Peace is the process of working to resolve conflicts in such a way that both sides win, with increased harmony as the outcome of the conflict and its resolution.

We greet one another with peace, we pray for peace. We are called to be peacemakers. We were told the mission of the Saviour is to be a deliverer of peace.

Peace is a state of respect, cooperation and well being.

Peace is the presence of social justice.

Peace is the absence of war, poverty, and hunger.

Peace is freedom from sickness and diseases.

It is employment and health.

Peace is hope for our future, and the future of all God's children and God's world.

Peace is when we have no fear to assemble, to worship, to work, to publish and to say the truth even to the powerful.

Peace is *salam*, well-being for all, with equality, and respect for human rights.

Peace is when everybody feels at home and is accepted, with no barriers of age, class, sex, race, religion or nationality.

Peace is action that is dynamic and positive.

Peace is that fragile harmony that carries with it the experience of the struggle, the endurance of suffering and the strength of love.

Through the ages people have engaged in a universal search for this kind of peace, for ultimate meaning in life, but have turned this struggle into wars to death to gain dominance for a particular ideology, religion, or nation. Our age of unparalleled advancement in education, science and technology has been an age of enormous violence in many corners of the world. Meanwhile the need for imaginative understanding, simple trust and creative cooperation among the peoples was never more urgent. Maybe the time has come when a fresh exploration should be made of the role that our religious experiences and spiritual insights could play in promoting the harmony of humankind and in affirming the presence of a spirit of hope and compassion available to all, by which our lives may be made more whole, more harmonious, as we draw directly upon that power around us, within us and within all life.

We cannot live a day without saying yes or no for peace or for war, for death or for life. But the choice is ours. There is no compromise in the matter. To postpone decision is to decide, to hide the matter is to decide, to compromise is to decide. There is no escape and this is our challenge.

May the Lord bless you and keep you.
May He rest His countenance on you and give you peace.

6

Education in the Holy Land

Jacqueline Sfeir

Introduction

It is important to begin with a comment on the title of this presentation, which one could rephrase as, 'Palestinian Christians: Education'. As it stands the title denies the national identity of the Christians of the Holy Land. The use of the term 'Holy Land', by the international Church has been a convenient escape from having to acknowledge the political dilemma inflicting the area. This practice has been extremely detrimental to Palestinian Christians, and it reflects the historical role of the international Church in reinforcing the alienation of the indigenous Palestinian Christians from their mother culture, by focusing on their religious identity, rather than on their national identity. Religious sectarianism has been a political tool used to divide the national unity of the people since the Roman empire. Religion has been used and abused to produce the existing conditions of religious conflict and reconciliation characteristic of the peoples of Greater Syria, Egypt and Iraq.

In the wake of the Ottoman empire, because of the conditions prevailing in the Arab world, Palestine was easy prey to the political manipulation which favoured the creation of the Zionist state, and now its continued existence. Education is an extension of the existing political situation, and is often used to shape the people to the ambitions and long-term objectives of the governing body. The evolution of education in Palestine carries within it the scars of this reality.

Education: the Palestinian Experience

It is essential to examine education from a perspective that links it with the dynamic process of history, politics and social change. One must go beyond the facts and figures in order to understand the reality of education in a particular country, what affects it, and how it contributes to the shaping of that country's reality, and how it is used to engineer the reality of tomorrow.

Education in Palestine up to the present has been a tool used by those in power at a particular time in the country's history to serve its interests. It has been used to control people and to perpetuate the system of government which, to a great extent, aimed to dominate rather than liberate the Palestinian people.

Education, as a tool, is limited to disseminating information, conveying knowledge, developing skills and, most of all, to shaping attitudes and value systems. However, education, as a process, aims at liberating people, by helping individuals to grasp reality as it is portrayed in their environment, and by seeing their role in view of that reality, and by helping them see how it can contribute in their growth and development.

In Palestine formal education is a tool of control. However, at the informal level, it is a process of liberation. This phenomenon is characteristic of peoples who are persecuted (minorities living in hostile environments, people living under occupation, or under oppressive regimes) and are forced to develop strategies to preserve themselves, and identify what is important to them, and work towards achieving it.

History of Education in Palestine from the Ottoman Turks to the Present

The Ottoman Turks

During the four centuries of Ottoman rule (1516-1918) the policy was to ottomanize the protectorates and to deliberately disadvantage the indigenous populations. This policy led to the disastrous cultural deterioration characterized by an overwhelming state of illiteracy which inflicted the greater majority of the population in Palestine.

It is therefore not strange to find that, in Palestine by the end of the Ottoman era, there were only 95 elementary and 3 secondary government run schools, with a total number of 234 teachers and a student population of 8,248, of which only

1,480 were women.

To compensate for the grave lack in educational services private schools in the form of the 'Kuttab' attached to the mosques were established. There were 379 Kuttab in 1914, with 417 teachers and 8,705 students of which only 131 were women. There also were some foreign schools serving mostly the Christian and Jewish population.[1]

Christian missionaries of various denominations were eager to set up schools in the Holy Land as European influence grew in the second half of the 19th century, and although they were frequently regarded with suspicion as proselytizing institutions, some of their schools became widely respected.

In reaction partly to the burgeoning of the Christian schools and partly to the Turkish bias of state schools, a number of private Muslim schools were established in the later part of the 19th century. The growing demand for education . . . was demonstrated by the increase in the number of private Muslim schools to 379 in 1914, compared with 95 state schools.[2]

The British Mandate

In the spirit of the Balfour Declaration (1917), the government of the British mandate established in 1920 two systems of education, one of which was for the Palestinian Arabs.

> From the 1920s to the 1940s, education took on a new significance as Palestinian society faced a threat to its development and even to its existence (Graham-Brown 1984: 16).
>
> British unwillingness to aid agriculture was paralleled by a comparative neglect of Palestinian education. The Jewish education system, including public schools (with teaching in Hebrew), was only indirectly controlled by the government. It was administered by a Zionist organization, *Vaad Leumi*, and financed by the Jewish Agency and the Jewish community. The Arab public system, by contrast, was

---

[1] Bargouthi, Abdel Latif. 1991. *Education during the British Mandate in Palestine. Forty Years of Misfortune and Twenty One Years of Occupation on the West Bank and Gaza* (in Arabic). Al Taybeh: The Center for Reviving Arab Folklore, p. 222.

[2] Graham-Brown, Sarah. 1984. *Education, Repression and Liberation: Palestinians.* London: World University Service UK, p. 16.

directly controlled by the government and funded mainly from general government revenues, with limited contributions from municipal and local funds. The two education systems were separate but certainly not equal in quality and the Arab system did not keep pace with the growing demand for education (see below) (Graham-Brown 1984: 18).

Table 1
School enrolment ratios of Arabs and Jews, July 1944

Group	Total School-aged Population (5-14)	Number of pupils of all ages	Number of pupils of (5-14)	% of 5-14 age-group enrolled
Arabs and other non-Jewish groups	300,000	104,600	97,400	32.5
Jews	87,000	99,500	84,600	97.0

Source: *Survey of Palestine*, vol. II (Jerusalem, 1946), p. 638.

There were seven elementary, and four secondary grade level schools in the Arab sector. The secondary level consisted of two years of general education, followed by two years of either a literary or scientific emphasis.

Most elementary schools in the rural areas had only four grades. Usually, these schools consisted of only one room, with one teacher for the 40-60 students. In the academic year 1945-46, there were 83 full elementary government run schools, mostly in the cities, with a few in the big villages, or near a group of villages. The total number of schools in that year was 504, with 2,156 teachers and 82,775 students of whom only 20.5 per cent were women (Bargouthi 1991: 227, 232).

For the greater majority of those who went to elementary school, about 40 per cent of the school aged population, only those who ranked in the first three ranks were allowed to continue their secondary education. There were only ten post-elementary educational institutions, each offering a different option. Some gave one or two years of professional training after the matriculation, while others offered one or two years of technical training after the second secondary. These institutions were spread all over Palestine (Bargouthi 1991: 227, 232). In 1942-43 the number of private schools, both Christian and Muslim, receiving minimal subsidies from the government, was 236. There were 322 kindergarten and elementary schools run by the various Christian communities, which did not receive any government funds.

All private schools followed the government curricula in order to qualify for the matriculation exams (Bargouthi 1991: 236, 237).

The total number of students enrolled in the government schools in 1946 was 21,468. For the same year the number of students enrolled in rural schools was 6,382 and 15,086 in urban areas (Bargouthi 1991: 75). The total number of Arab students enrolled in schools in 1946, then, was 65,353.

According to the Government of Palestine, Department of Education, Annual Report of 1945-1946, the Arab non-governmental schools, some of which were foreign schools (Italian, French, German and English) serving Arab students, were divided as follows:[3]

Type of Schools	Number	Number of students
Muslim Higher Council	11	2,023
Catholic	113	18,593
Protestant	30	5,023
Orthodox	30	4,184
Other Christian	9	1,436
Other (unofficial)	120	12,623
Total	313	43,885

1949-1967 Gaza and the West Bank

In 1948, and after the establishment of the state of Israel on 80 per cent of mandatory Palestine (when the Palestinian Arab population constituted two thirds of the population of Palestine),[4] the West Bank became part of Jordan and the Gaza Strip was administered by Egypt.

According to Janet Abu-Lughod ('The Demographic Characteristics of the Palestinian Population . . . ') in 1952 the number of Palestinians on the West Bank was estimated to be 742,000 (of which 364,000 were refugees), while that in Gaza was 179,000 (of which 101,000 were refugees). By 1961, the Palestinian population was 806,000 in the West Bank, and 369,000 in the Gaza Strip.

In her study, 'Palestine Open University Feasibility Study' (published in 1980) she estimates the numbers of Palestinians to be 604,000 in the West Bank, and 330,000 in the Gaza Strip. In this period (1948-1967), education for the Palestinian population reflected the diversity of political conditions under which they lived.

In the West Bank the Jordanian system of education was

[3] al-Dabbagh, Mustafa. 'Education in Palestine During the British Mandate in Palestine.' In *The Palestinian Encyclopedia* (in Arabic), vol. 3, part 2, p. 47.

[4] 'Israël et La Palestine: Points de repères historiques.' In *En Terre Sainte Aujourd'hui, La Vie Hors Série Notre Histoire*, no. 26, Octobre 1989, p. 20.

implemented, while in Gaza it was the Egyptian. Palestinians in the diaspora, of course, were subject to the system of education of the host countries in which they found themselves, whether in Jordan, Syria or Lebanon.

In the West Bank and Gaza there are three types of school administrations:

1 The government schools
2 The United Nations Relief and Works Agency for Palestinian Refugees (UNRWA) schools
3 The private schools which are mainly Christian. According to UNRWA statistics, in 1969-70, 5.9 per cent of the school population of the West Bank were enrolled in the private schools (approximately 2,658 pupils), with none in the Gaza Strip. In 1984-85, 1.8 per cent of the school population of the West Bank were enrolled in the private schools (approximately 1,165 pupils).[5]

It is not an easy task to account for the break-down of numbers, for there are drastic differences in numbers given by different official sources. For example, in Table 24 in *The Palestinian Encyclopaedia* discussing education in Palestine, we find the following information:[6]

Statistics of the Jordanian Ministry of Education
(only the West Bank figures are reported here)

Type	Pre-Schools & Elementary	Preparatory & Secondary	Total	%
Year 1956-57				
Gov.	74,300	21,000	95,300	66.4
UNRWA	27,300	3,600	30,900	21.5
Private	14,400	2,900	17,300	12.1
Year 1963-64				
Gov.	88,900	31,300	120,200	66.8
UNRWA	33,300	5,300	38,600	21.4
Private	13,900	7,300	21,200	11.8

[5] UNRWA/UNESCO Statistical Yearbook 1948-85 in al-Dabagh, Mustafa. 'Education in Palestine During the British Mandate in Palestine.' In *The Palestinian Encyclopedia* (in Arabic), vol. 3, part 2, p. 47.
[6] Bashour, Munir. 'Education Under Occupation in the West Bank and the Gaza Strip.' In *The Palestinian Encyclopedia* (in Arabic), vol. 3, part 2, p. 721.

While the UNRWA statistics for the same years are as follows:

Type	Elementary	Preparatory & Secondary	Total	%
Year 1956–57				
Gov.	21,200	8,000	29,200	33.8
UNRWA	43,800	4,800	48,600	56.3
Private	7,300	1,300	8,600	9.9
Year 1963–64				
Gov.	15,600	11,700	27,300	29.0
UNRWA	51,900	9,200	61,100	64.8
Private	3,500	2,400	5,900	6.2

1967 to date: the Occupied Territories

After the Six Day War of June 1967, the West Bank and Gaza Strip fell under the Israeli military occupation, referred to as the Occupied Territories. The civil administration of the Israeli military occupation took over the sector of education. The role of the civil administration is mostly that of censorship and control over the existing Jordanian and Egyptian systems of education.

According to The Council for Higher Education,[7] there are 1,419 schools in the Occupied Territories, 643 being private schools, and 487 kindergartens. The number of school-aged pupils (excluding pre-schools) in the private sector is 44,394, and constitutes 7.85 per cent of the school population in the Occupied Territories.

The most drastic reality of Palestinian education under Israeli Occupation in recent years is the series of measures taken against the popular uprising, the *Intifada*. A major disturbance to the education of Palestinian children has been the closure of schools throughout the period. The UNICEF report, 'The Situation of Palestinian Children in the West Bank and Gaza Strip' (published July 1992), describes these school closures. The extent of the disturbance can be gauged by considering the extent of the closures. The estimates of average percentages of school losses are as follows:

	1987–88	1988–1989	1989–90	1990–91
Gaza	35%	46%	35%	43%
West Bank	75%	50%	50%	35%

[7] In 1977, a group of Palestinian educators, associations of professionals, and representatives of charitable organizations, formally established the Council. Today, the Council is recognized internationally as the body most responsible for the development of Palestinian education at all levels.

Education in Palestine:
Goals, Objectives and Curriculum

'The Ottoman system of education . . . was limited to the training of administrative and military personnel or to religious instruction' (Graham-Brown 1984: 16).

'The British Mandate government was acutely aware of the ideological significance of education, particularly in a situation where national consciousness was growing. The British attempted to discourage and suppress nationalist ideas. The curricula displayed, as Totah indicated, a blandness of approach to political and cultural issues which amounted to a form of disinformation. This, however, did not halt the spread of nationalist influence in the schools, particularly in secondary schools, as the period of British rule was punctuated by political turmoil in Palestine and in the surrounding Arab countries.'

. . . One of the effects of the new nationalist ideas was to lessen religious and sectarian divisions. 'The study of Arab language and literature and the history of Muslim civilization . . . and the momentum of the nationalist movement outside the school, combined almost to obliterate the difference between an Arab Muslim and Arab Christian completing the secondary school course.' Thus developed a tradition which is still alive in the Israeli-occupied West Bank and Gaza Strip today, that students and teachers are in the vanguard of political action and debate, carrying considerable weight among the politically active sections of the community. This pattern was reinforced by the existence in the towns of numbers of informal youth organizations, clubs, scouting organizations, and so on, which also served as centres for political debate.

Teachers in the state schools found themselves in a difficult situation. 'As civil servants they were expected to execute their orders, even though orders came from a foreign government whose policy they disliked at heart. But as patriots they were under a more compelling obligation to uphold the national ideal to conform to the wishes of their community.'

Teachers were not allowed to form a union or to join clubs and associations which might promote political discussion. They were also forbidden to publish any material other than textbooks, without the approval of the Department of Education. As a result no coherent expression of their views reached the government.

' . . . Most importantly, with a growing nationalist consciousness among the Palestinians, the idea became implanted of education as a universal solution, a means of individual advancement and cultural modernization' (Graham-Brown 1984: 20-21).

Up to 1967 the policy of unification between the East and West Banks of the Jordan was so strong that it led to shifting all the political, administrative and economic decisions to Amman, thus reducing the significance of the West Bank cities. For all practical purposes the system of education was one for both the Jordanians and Palestinians (Bashour, pp. 131-231).

The evaluation report on educational policy, submitted to the Second Regional Conference of the International Council for Curriculum and Education by the Ministry of Education in Jordan (February 1990) showed that the curriculum in Jordan was designed under circumstances which had been changing drastically in the present period. The Report showed up the weaknesses of the Jordanian curriculum, which were due in the main to the extent of change in the curriculum. The main weaknesses include that, the objectives are not specifically defined; the curriculum does not reflect the changing needs of the society; and the curriculum is based on segregated subjects and lacks integration. There is no continuity between grade levels, and the curriculum does not provide adequate options for technical training.

In addition to the limitations pointed out in this report, the Jordanian curriculum is, of course, 'Jordanian', which in the view of Palestinians, lacks a vital component, the national one. In view of the policy of unification, the Palestinian question was not focused upon, but was addressed as the 'Arab Question', with a deliberate minimization of the Palestinian perspective, whether historical or political.

During the Israeli occupation of the West Bank and Gaza, the system of education has 'fossilized', after it had been ripped of the 'Arab' component which characterized both the Egyptian and Jordanian curricula. The situation was aggravated by the systematic policies used by the Israeli military authorities which aimed at undermining the existing system of education. The measures used by the Israeli occupation are very similar to those used during the British Mandate, compounded by the repeated closure of schools and a significant drop in teacher training, whether pre-service or in-service. This was in addition to the overt abuses of human rights directed at the schools, such as turning a number of schools into prisons during the *Intifada*. The July 1992 UNICEF report describes the effects of the closure as follows:

> The impact of the closure on the schools of the West Bank and Gaza Strip has been dramatic. Virtually no school has been able to complete a year's syllabus since December 1987. The constant interruptions of the educational process has had severe effects on achievement. Most immediately affected are lower elementary students in the process of basic skill acquisition . . .
> In 1990, the Tamer Institute for Community Education

83

administered an achievement test to 2,000 fourth and sixth grade students in the West Bank from UNRWA, government and private schools. Results showed that children who were in the primary grades were having great difficulty acquiring the basic skills in Arabic and Mathematics. For example:

– only 245 of the fourth graders could measure accurately (with a ruler) a given line segment

– only 2.3 per cent of the primary four sample, and 22.8 per cent of the primary six sample were able to produce the required number of sentences in a composition. The sentences produced lacked correct structures, relevant ideas, and appropriate vocabulary.

The implications of this reality gives a further dimension to Israeli diplomacy, as described by Nahum Goldman in a British Parliamentary session: 'Sometimes diplomacy in the Middle East is the art of delaying the inevitable.' In view of the educational scene depicted above, one can reword the statement to imply that the Israeli strategy in the Middle East is to prolong the process (in this case the peace process) as long as possible, to allow for disintegration to set in, so that the opportunities for maintaining a viable infrastructure in the Palestinian community are reduced to an absolute minimum. In all probability, the Israeli strategy would aim at eliminating such possibilities altogether. This strategy has been planned and implemented throughout the various stages of the Israeli take-over of Palestinian land, beginning with the establishment of the Zionist state, and carried through throughout the course of the occupation. It is only those who refuse to see what is happening who are unaware of such intentions.

Towards a Palestinian National System of Education

The overwhelming political and economic conditions, which the Palestinian people are undergoing in the Occupied Territories, has not at all submerged the continuously increasing sense of urgency that they feel concerning the need to develop a system of education that is relevant to them. During the extended school closures of 1987-1990, the Palestinians of the Occupied Territories developed various forms of alternative education to compensate for the school closures. Although the attempts were not very successful in meeting the needs incurred by the closures, and in spite of all the restrictions and measures taken by the occupation forces to obstruct the development of these alternatives, a very rich dialogue was initiated, as to what we are looking for in a national system of education. Although the dialogue is on-going, and has become a topic of discussions at the formal and informal levels of the educational scene in Palestine, the overwhelming and increasingly repressive measures taken by the Israelis to disable the Palestinian population, are rendering almost impossible the task of going through a systematic process of development. The latest measure taken by the Occupation authorities has been the closure of the Occupied Territories. This closure does not only segregate the Palestinians from the Israeli territories, but it has divided the Occupied Territories into pockets. One cannot commute from one area to the other without military permits, which are extremely difficult to obtain.

The developments described above have not been happening in a Palestinian vacuum. Education has been on the Palestinian agenda, together with the other critical issues of health, economy and social services. The problem is not confined to Palestinians in the Occupied Territories, but is general among all the Palestinian people wherever they are. Bassem Srhan, in an article published in *Shu'un Falastinyya*, the PLO's journal of studies, argued the need to go beyond conveying a sense of national identity to Palestinian children. He stressed the need to emphasize the thinking process, instead of learning by rote; to replace selfishness by an ethic of work for the benefit of the community; and, finally, to emphasize the possibility of changing undesirable social traditions (Graham-Brown 1984: 140-141).

> [Rosemary Sayigh] says, there was an awareness of elitism and academism of the Arab education systems and their lack of relevance to the Palestinian situation, 'but so far no resistance group, from the most revolutionary to the most conservative, has sufficiently raised itself above the day-to-day crises to consider this vital problem.' She adds, on the whole the masses in the camps only want more schools, not a different system.

Educational development and the changing of an educational system is a challenge anywhere. One has only to look at developed countries to realise how much it takes to produce minimal changes in a system of education even when all the support systems exist. In Palestine this change has already been started, and it involves more than the formal educational institutions. However, we will be able to embark on the development of a national system of education only after independence has been achieved.

The International Church of the Holy Land: A Double Edged Sword

In the introduction I objected to the use of the term, 'The Christians in the Holy Land' to describe the Christians *of* the Holy Land. The Christians of the land are the Palestinian Christians. 'Palestinian Christians' is the appropriate label of the Christians of the Holy Land. 'Palestinian' gives them their national, cultural and historical identity. 'Christians' gives them both their religious and universal identity. Unfortunately, it has not been the wish of the Western world to acknowledge the richness of the Palestinian Christian identity, and it has chosen to submerge it in the Christian component, in the hope, perhaps, that the Palestinian component would vanish!

The history of Christians in the Holy Land has been continuously laced with imperialism and colonization. The local Christian community has been overshadowed by the international Church. It has been divided into all the denominations to ensure that this or that church has a representation in the Holy Land. In a subtle way the churches have been a tool of colonization, if not political, then cultural. The persistent sense of the negation by the mainstream Christian West of an Arab Christian presence is a reminder of the fact that, more often than not, the international Church has not recognized the local church, and has been insensitive to the indigenous culture of the native Christians. This reality has been the source of the resentment towards the international body of the Church, felt both by Palestinian Christians, as well as by Palestinians in general.

The Role of Christians in the Development of Education in Palestine

It is true that the missionary schools played an important role in educating the Christian Arabs at a time when education was scarce. However, their inability to recognize and respect the indigenous church, instead of consolidating the local Christians in Palestine led to the exact opposite. The Christian schools not only brought in their respective language and culture, but were a means, whether intentional or not, of dividing the already fragile Palestinian Christian community, and alienating it from its mother culture. Because the emphasis was on religious, rather than national identity, the school, instead of retaining the educated local Christian, provided him with a direct link to the

West, and became a catalyst to the evacuation of the Palestinian Christian community.[8]

Christian Arabs have been sensitive to the threat that cultural colonization would involve their up-rooting from their heritage. They have tried to affirm their national identity, and have been at the root of the Arab national movement. However, they have not been able to resist the challenge that was presented, both by the colonizing church, and by the political ambitions of the West concerning the Middle East in general, and Palestine in particular. In Palestine this awareness was translated in the 30s and 40s into the development of a new type of private school which was neither Christian nor Muslim. It was national, and had the slogan, 'Religion is for God and the homeland is for all.' Such was the case of Bir Zeit School which has now developed into a University, the Nahda College in Jerusalem and Gaza College in Gaza.[9]

As has been demonstrated in my historical preview of education in Palestine, the importance of the private school sector, which is predominantly Christian, is receding, in view of the growing availability of public education. Because the Christian school has managed to maintain a relatively acceptable standard, and because the Christian school still holds a certain prestige, we find that its presence now is more a function of class than it is of need. This aspect, however, is definitely not conducive to playing a cementing role for the Christian community in Palestine. It is becoming more evident that the survival of the Christian school is based on the collection of school fees. For that reason, the Christian school is beginning to disadvantage poorer Christians, except, of course, in the case of parish schools, or schools that are strongly subsidized by the international Church. This perpetuates the cycle of social discrimination, which in this case is based on socio-economic factors, rather than on purely religious ones, but, more often than not, on both.

The National Church:
Confirmation of the Palestinian Christian Identity

The dichotomy arises again when we consider Christian schools. They can play an important role in helping to bring about a process of educational change, rather than insisting on retaining a sectarian nature.

[8] UNRWA/UNESCO Statistical Yearbook 1948-85 in al-Dabbagh, Mustafa. 'Education in Palestine During the British Mandate in Palestine.' In *The Palestinian Encyclopedia* (in Arabic), vol. 3, part 2, pp. 237-240.
[9] *Ibid.*

Neither the government nor the UNRWA schools have the leeway to foster the internal reorganization necessary for the promotion of such change.

The local church can act as a national body by making itself available through the schools to do what has been done before through the same means, but now with a new consciousness of the importance of acting within the national and cultural context of the Palestinian church. The Lutheran School system, with five schools in the central region of the West Bank, and the American Friends (Quakers) School in Ramallah, have already started to play that role.

7

A Study of Muslim and Christian Students' Attitudes Towards Each Other at Bethlehem University

Jeanne Kattan

This paper presents the results of an empirical study measuring Muslim and Christian Students' attitude towards each other. The survey sample consisted of 300 students studying at Bethlehem University. A questionnaire was designed to elicit the respondents' amount of agreement with a series of assertions. Each statement was answered on a 5-point Likert scale. The results indicate that the respondents have highly positive attitudes towards each other. The personal factors of age, place of residence, and religion do not have a very significant effect.

Introduction

Since its foundation in 1973, Bethlehem University has been serving the local Palestinian community. The main purpose of the university is to provide higher education for the Palestinian youth; an education geared towards community needs in order to provide employment opportunities for its graduates.

In the Bethlehem University Catalogue of 1990-1992, it is stated: 'Bethlehem University, a coeducational institution open to students of *all faiths*, is sponsored by the Vatican to serve the higher educational needs of the Palestinians of the West Bank and Gaza.' It is also stated that ' . . . the University seeks the development in the students of the highest ethical, moral, and spiritual values. The University proposes to enhance the individual student's religious beliefs.'

Since its foundation, Muslim students have naturally been the majority (approximately 97 per cent of the population of the West Bank and Gaza are Muslims). However, as Bethlehem University is situated in the Central West Bank (the Bethlehem, Jerusalem and Ramallah areas), and since the majority of the Christians live in those areas, approximately 35 per cent of the student population is Christian.

It would therefore be interesting to study the Muslim and Christian students' attitude towards each other in an institution 'open to all faiths' and an institution committed to 'enhancing the individual student's religious beliefs.'

Purpose of Study

This study is conducted as an effort to answer the following questions:

1 What are the Muslim and Christian students' attitude towards each other?

2 Are these attitudes effected by personal variables such as age, place of residence (city, village, camp), and religion?

Methods and Procedures

Subjects

The sample was randomly selected from the five major schools at Bethlehem University: Arts, Business, Education, Science and Nursing (including Physiotherapy). The sample included both females and males; first, second, third and fourth year students; as well as students from cities, villages and camps. The 300 students who responded to the questionnaire represent 26 per cent of the population of the Schools involved in the study (1,152 students), and 18 per cent of the entire Bethlehem University student population (1687) students. The respondents were 178 Muslim students and 115 Christian students.

Measure and Data Collection Procedure

A questionnaire was designed to elicit the Muslim and Christian students' attitude towards each other. The questionnaire elicited the respondents' amount of agreement with a series of 18 assertions. A five-point scale, varying from strongly agree to strongly disagree, was used, and the respondents were required to circle the letter coinciding with their reaction to each of the 18 statements.

To avoid a 'halo effect', (i.e. indiscriminately supplying positive ratings for every item), negatively stated items for which the direction is reversed were included. Thus 9 statements were positively stated while the other 9 were negatively stated. When scoring, the negative item scales were inverted so that their scores were additive with those of the other items of the questionnaire.

Moreover, to disguise the purpose of the questionnaire in order to ensure that item responses were valid (awareness may colour responses), filler items were included. 17 other items were randomly dispersed among the actual items to prevent respondents from inferring the purpose of the study. These dealt with their attitudes towards students from the other sex, students from other regions, and students from other social classes. In scoring, these 17 items were disregarded.

The questionnaire was in Arabic to ensure full comprehension of the statements. The questionnaires were distributed by the various lecturers in class, and the responses were collected on the spot to ensure some degree of spontaneity.

Description and Analysis of Data

Description

The questionnaire included 9 positively and 9 negatively stated statements. For the positively stated items, the Strongly Agree scale was assigned 5 points; 4 points were assigned for Agree, 3 for Undecided; 2 for Disagree and 1 for Strongly Disagree. For the 9 negatively stated items the direction was reversed; i.e., Strongly Disagree was assigned 5 points, Disagree 4, etc. Thus the highest score any respondent would get was 90 (18 items × 5 points = 90).

Data Analysis

Table 1
Means and standard deviations total, by religion,
by region and by year of study

	Means X	SD
Total	69.064	9.106
Muslim	69.994	8.715
Christian	67.739	9.717
Village	70.561.	7.360
Camp	71.810	12.260
City	68.640	9.068
Year 1	70.111	8.588
Year 2	68.450	9.389
Year 3	68.286	8.985
Year 4	69.163	9.756

Table 1 indicates that the mean of the attitude in general is 69.064/90. This indicates a highly positive attitude.

To check whether the respondent's place of residence (city, village and camp), his/her age, and his/her religion would affect the results, means were calculated for these personal factors.

As Table 1 indicates, the differences between the means are not high. They range from 67.73-71.81 (the difference is 4.5 per cent). It seems that although these factors have some influence they are not very significant.

It is interesting to note that the mean for Christian students was the lowest, 67.739, and that the mean for the students from the camps was the highest, 71.810. It could be that Christian students feel more threatened as a minority. As for the students from the camps, it could be that this group is usually more politicised and that religion doesn't play as important a role or it could be a sampling issue; there were 16 respondents from the camps in the sample, (which is, however, representative of their number at the university).

To conclude, the means indicate that the students are quite favourably disposed towards each other, and that the personal factors are not very significant.

The analysis above only indicates a general attitude; it does not provide in-depth information. Therefore a deeper analysis of the students' responses was carried out. This closer look revealed some interesting data.

First, the 18 statements were broken into four divisions, and the statements in each division were grouped in such a way as to provide an answer to a question.

Division 1

Here questions 1, 2, 9, 10, 12, 15, 17, 18 are included (see Appendix). All these questions indicate how the respondents perceive each other, or how they feel about each other.

Table 2
Percentages of the respondents' strong agreement
or strong disagreement and the percentages
of the respondents' agreement or disagreement
on statements 1, 2, 9, 10, 12, 15, 17, 18

	SA/SD	A/D	Total
Statement 1	42.50%	48.5%	91.0‰
Statement 2	38.50%	54.2%	92.7%
Statement 9	57.20%	34.4%	91.6‰
Statement 10	51.85%	39.8%	91.6%
Statement 12	13.00%	10.7%	23.7%
Statement 15	51.50%	28.1%	79.6%
Statement 17	45.20%	27.4%	72.6%
Statement 18	45.80%	34.8%	80.6%

As Table 2 indicates, 91 per cent of the respondents expressed their respect for the students of the other religion (Stat. 1); 91.6 per cent agreed that they have a lot in common with the students from the other religion (Stat. 9); 79.6 per cent feel close to each other (Stat. 15); and 80.64 per cent disagreed with the statement that they have deep problems with students from the other religion (Stat. 18). Moreover, 91.6 per cent stated that it was possible to make friends with students from the other religion (Stat. 10). (Stat. 2) is the reverse; here it is stated that friendship between them is impossible; 92.7 per cent disagreed quite strongly with this statement while 72.65 per cent disagreed with the statement that religion is a key factor in their selection of friends (Stat. 17). However, despite these positive feelings towards each other, i.e., the respect, the closeness, and the friendship, only 23.7 per cent agreed with the idea of intermarriage (Stat. 12). This is to be expected as this is, more or less, a social taboo.

Division 2

Here statements 7 and 16 are considered. These two statements indicate how the respondents perceive their religion *vis-à-vis* their national identity.

Table 3
*Percentages of the respondents' strong agreement or disagreement
and the percentages of the respondents' agreement
or disagreement on statements 7 and 16*

	SA/SD	A/D	Total
Statement 7	33.8%	55.2%	89.0%
Statement 16	48.8%	36.5%	85.3%

Table 3 indicates that 89 per cent of the respondents agreed with the statement that they are Palestinians and that their belonging to two different religions is not really important (Stat. 7); while 85.3 per cent agreed with the statement that they are Arabs and that their belonging to two different religions is not really important (Stat. 16). This is to be expected in our context as nationalism is paramount in a society under occupation.

Division 3

Here statements 4 and 8 are considered. These two statements indicate how the respondents perceive the value of dialogue.

Table 4
*Percentages of the respondents' strong agreement or strong
disagreement and the percentages of the respondents' agreement
or disagreement on statements 4 and 8*

	SA/SD	A/D	Total
Statement 4	63.2%	27.1%	90.3%
Statement 8	50.8%	35.8%	86.6%

Table 4 indicates that 90.3 per cent of the respondents agreed that they have many chances at Bethlehem University to exchange ideas with their colleagues from the other religion; this has made them sensitive to the way the others think (Stat. 4). Moreover, 86.6 per cent disagreed with the statement that there is no value in such a dialogue (Stat. 8).

Division 4

Here statements 6, 11, 13 and 14 are considered. These four statements indicate how the respondents feel about Bethlehem University and the Bethlehem University staff *vis-à-vis* religion.

Table 5
Percentages of the respondents' strong agreement or strong
disagreement and the percentages of the respondents' agreement
or disagreement on statements 6, 11, 13 and 14

	SA/SD	A/D	Total
Statement 6	39.1%	26.1%	65.2%
Statement 11	50.2%	19.7%	69.9%
Statement 13	31.1%	20.0%	51.1%
Statement 14	37.8%	10.0%	47.8%

Table 5 indicates that 69.9 per cent of the respondents agree that they can express freely their religious beliefs at Bethlehem University (Stat. 11); and 65.3 per cent agree that Bethlehem University provides them with a place on campus to practise their religious rites (Stat. 6). There is a chapel and a Muslim prayer room on campus. It could be that many new students are not aware of this fact, or that the prayer room is not considered 'proper'. The lowest mean 3.29 for Stat. 6 was recorded for Muslim students while the highest mean 4.13 was recorded for Christian students.

On the statements regarding the staff, only 47.8 per cent of the students agree that the staff don't differentiate between them because of religion (Stat. 14). Here there is not much difference between the Muslim and Christian students; the means recorded are 3.19 and 3.18 respectively. On the other hand, 51.1 per cent agree with the statement that they prefer the staff member to be from their religion (Stat. 13). These results are quite revealing. They probably indicate that students have more positive attitudes towards each other than the staff, and that there is more tolerance among the younger generation.

Conclusion

This study has investigated the Muslim and Christian students' attitude towards each other. The mean of the attitude in general was quite high, 69.064/90. This indicates that students have very favourable attitudes towards each other. The factors of age, place of residence, and religion do not seem to effect the general outcome significantly.

In addition, an in-depth analysis has demonstrated that as part of the Bethlehem University community, students have the chance to express and practise their beliefs freely. They are also able and willing to engage in dialogue with their colleagues. Moreover, the analysis has revealed that students at Bethlehem University not only perceive each other favourably but they feel that they have a lot in common, and that they are bound together by strong ties of friendship. They strongly refute the claim that there are problems between them. Their identity as Palestinians and Arabs seems to override their identity as Muslim or Christian.

These results are expected. Muslims and Christians share the same history, the same language, the same culture and the same destiny. Moreover, under occupation, both are facing the same political, economic and social pressures. They are working together for the achievement of a better future.

The findings of this study are quite encouraging. Although the sample does not represent the entire society, and although it represents 'the educated class', they are the future generation. It is to be remembered that the sample represents both females and males, it represents young people from cities, villages and camps (it is worth mentioning here that over 60 per cent of the Palestinians in the West Bank and Gaza are below 18). If we have succeeded in imbuing tolerance and openness in our youth, then the future definitely looks brighter.

Note The author of this paper does not claim that the findings of this study can be generalised for all the West Bank and Gaza. It is hoped that other bodies and institutions would replicate this study for comparative purposes.

Appendix

Following are the 18 Statements in the questionnaire that are related to the Muslim and Christian students' attitudes towards each other.

1 We respect each other despite the differences in our religious beliefs.

2 Friendship with students from the other religion is not possible.

3 I do not object to visiting the holy places of the other religion.

4 The dialogues I engage in with students from the other religion have introduced me to their way of thinking.

5 I have never visited the holy places of the other religion.

6 I am not provided with a place to practise my religion on campus.

7 We are all Palestinians; our belonging to two different religions is not really important.

8 I do not see any value in engaging in a dialogue with students from the other religion.

9 We have a lot in common despite the differences in our religious beliefs.

10 I can make friends with students from the other religion.

11 I can freely express my religious beliefs at Bethlehem University.

12 It is not acceptable to marry a colleague from the other religion.

13 I prefer to have a teacher who has the same religion as myself.

14 I do not feel that teachers from the other religion differentiate between us.

15 I do not feel close to the students from the other religion.

16 We are all Arab students; our belonging to two different religions is not really important.

17 Religion is a key factor that determines my relations with the other students.

18 I have very deep problems with students from the other religion.

8
The Significance of Jerusalem to Christians
Albert Aghazarian

1 The Centrality of Jerusalem in Christianity

Jerusalem is a city which has a multitude of histories. Each specific history differs in its meanings, significance, and details. The history of Jerusalem for Jews centres around the first and second temples and the modern state of Israel. For Muslims, Jerusalem embodies, concretely, the experience of pluralism and tolerance in Islam. It is the place where Islam accepts and embraces previous revelations. Jerusalem acts as the launching ground, the earthly connection, for spirituality. My focus will be the aspects of the city that are meaningful for Christians.

For many, Jerusalem is a great symbolic centre. For others, it is the epitome of weird cults: a city run like a necrocracy where the dead have more influence than the living. Jerusalem's place in Christianity is illustrated accurately by medieval maps which show Jerusalem as the core, the centre, the middle where the three known continents were thought to be joined together. Jerusalem is most importantly the place where all of Jesus' life converges. In his Gospel Luke wrote, 'When the days drew near for him to be taken up, he set his face to go to Jerusalem' (9.51) . . . in order to fulfil 'everything that is written about the Son of man' (18.31) . . : 'because it is impossible for a prophet to be killed outside of Jerusalem.' (13.33).[1] The highlights of his life are all

---

[1] All Scripture quotations are taken from the New Revised Standard Version of the Bible. Nashville, Tennessee: Thomas Nelson, 1990.

associated with Jerusalem: from preaching in the temple, to the Agony in the Garden of Gethsemane, along the Via Dolorosa to the crucifixion, and finally the resurrection and ascension into heaven. Opposite the Holy Sepulchre is the Anastasis or Catholicon, where a circle of white marble symbolizes the 'centre of the universe.' This symbolism is especially apt for Christians because of their focus on the Paschal mystery of Christ, i.e., his death and resurrection. It is appropriate that the 'centre of the universe' should be next to the site of this mystery. While among Western Christians the celebration of Christmas assumes the greatest importance, among eastern Christians it is the resurrection which is the most essential event to celebrate. The mystery of resurrection holds a message of hope, of the ability of the oppressed to triumph. This image has more meaning for people under occupation than the act of birth. The altar of every church in the world is a symbol of the resurrection, the tomb of Jesus. Some may say that the altar symbolizes the sacrifice of Abraham, but the fundamental significance is the same since the historical place of both events is Jerusalem.

Virtually from the beginning of the early church Jerusalem has been considered to be the 'Mother of all churches.' In the Gospel of Matthew, this image is evoked in the lament, 'Jerusalem, Jerusalem, the city that kills the prophets and stones those who are sent to it! How often have I desired to gather your children together as a hen gathers her brood under her wings, and you were not willing!' (Matt 23.37). With this in mind, the struggle of so many denominations over every inch of the Holy City should be seen not as un-Christian but simply as children yearning to be closer to their mother. Jerusalem is truly a mother figure for Christians, both through her role in Jesus' life and because she gave birth to the early Apostolic churches which then were able to spread throughout the world. It was in this city that the first Christian community was formed. In St Luke's second work, the Acts of the Apostles, Jerusalem is said to be the place of the first community, 'faithful to the teaching of the Apostles, to the brotherhood, to the breaking of bread, and to the prayers.' (Acts 2.42; 4.32).

2 The Historical Background

Throughout the first three centuries of the Christian era Jerusalem was the launching pad for the apostles after Pentecost. The Roman destruction of the city in 70 AD transformed the mother of all churches into the pagan city, Aelia Capitolina, which pushed Christian activity underground. However, recent archaeological evidence in the Holy Sepulchre and elsewhere indicates that despite these obstacles, Christian pilgrims were already secretly making their way to Jerusalem in the 1st century AD.

By 313 AD Constantine had converted to Christianity, and pilgrimage to Jerusalem became an established trend, no longer a clandestine phenomenon. Constantine's mother, St Helena, aided the physical reconstruction of Jerusalem as a centre for Christians by building the Holy Sepulchre. The trend of establishing structures to mark Jesus' footsteps through Jerusalem was set into motion. It was in and around these sanctuaries that a very strong liturgical life first developed. St Cyril of Jerusalem (313-387), who is famous for his catechetical teachings, described the sanctuaries as witnesses to the mystery of Jesus. His ardent teachings added strength to the growing religious life of Jerusalem Christians.

The fourth to the seventh centuries witnessed the arrival of the 'desert fathers' to Jerusalem and its surroundings. These are the fathers of Christianity, the monks who came from Asia Minor, Armenia, Greece, Georgia, Egypt, and Syria. Monasteries such as Mar Saba, St James, St George, and St Theodosius were founded and then sustained the monks in their ascetic and hermitical lives. Thousands of monks vied with each other to endure greater and greater levels of physical hardship. The monasteries still exist today and are maintained as spiritual oases in the desert. Around the same time there was also a tremendous proliferation of churches within Jerusalem. The Council of Chalcedon in 451 AD created a significant schism in the Christian Church over Christological issues such as the nature of Jesus. This turning point in the history of Christianity has created a lasting split which affected the course of subsequent history.

One may argue that the struggle for Jerusalem was an element in the exhaustion of both the Byzantine and Persian empires. In the year 614 AD, the Persian empire wrested Jerusalem from the hands of the Byzantines. The Persians demolished churches, including the Holy Sepulchre, and took what was then believed to be the 'true' cross. The Byzantine empire had been dealt a severe blow and in order to strike back every possible resource had to be used for the mobilization of forces. In 628 the Byzantines recovered Jerusalem as well as the cross, but only at a heavy cost. Both kingdoms were exhausted, leaving a convenient gap which eight years later was filled by the brisk march of Islam.

The Muslim period of Jerusalem began with the peaceful take-over by Caliph 'Umar in 636 AD. Patriarch Sophronius, the patriarch of Jerusalem, handed over to 'Umar the earthly keys of the city. However, in Orthodox tradition surrender of the earthly city does not undermine the celestial aspects which are eternal. 'Umar issued an edict which gave Christians access to their holy sites and the freedom to worship. It is noteworthy that the Christians pleaded with 'Umar to exclude the Jews from a similar agreement, but he would not agree, and extended the same concession to both. His edict to the Christians assured them of 'the safety of their persons, their goods, their churches, their crosses – whether they be in good or bad shape – and their worship in general. Their churches will neither be touched nor destroyed; they and their dependants will not undergo any damage and it will be the same for their crosses and their possessions.'[2] In the spirit of maintaining Christian worship in the city, St Sophronius declared:

> Here, it is Jerusalem we proclaim,
> where God has lived bringing about miracles.
> Here we announce Golgotha,
> where God took the cross upon himself.
> Here we sing of the resurrection,
> where God rose from the tomb.
> Here we preach Sion . . .
> where Christ appeared risen from the dead.
> Here we glorify the Mount of Olives
> from where God ascended to the heavens . . .[3]

Despite the political changes in Jerusalem, pilgrims continued to flock to the city, and local Christians continued their religious lives in the churches and sanctuaries. Throughout the Muslim period the pilgrims and Christian residents witnessed periods of greater or lesser tolerance and protection. When the bishop of Gaul, Arculf, visited the region in 670 he encountered no resistance to his activities. However, the English pilgrim Willibald, did not enjoy such ease of travel when he visited in 724. At one point the Church of the Holy Sepulchre was destroyed by order of the unbalanced Caliph Hakim and later rebuilt by the same regime. These tumultuous vacillations were due to either the whim of the caliphs, the relationship between Byzantium and Dar al-Islam, or internal political pressures. At a later period, the good relationship between Charlemagne and Harun al-Rashid helped mitigate some of the many difficulties inherent in undertaking a pilgrimage.

The Crusades came crashing violently into Jerusalem in 1099 AD. After a blood-bath, the crusaders held the city for two centuries, expelled Orthodox groups (whom they considered heretical) and massacred Muslims. They ruled without mercy as conquerors, putting substantial energy into creating new realities on the ground. They attempted to repopulate Palestine with Christians without success. But

---

[2] A Issa, *Les minorités chrétiennes de Palestine à travers les siècles*, Rome 1975, p. 111.
[3] Quoted by C von Schonborn, *Sophrone de Jérusalem*, Paris 1972, p. 120.

they did forbid Jews and Muslims access to Jerusalem in certain periods, built and restored churches throughout the city, and converted some mosques into churches. Everything they did was with the aim of creating a new religious geography and demography in the Holy Land. Whatever way the Crusades are judged, they undeniably left behind much bitterness and wide gaps between Christians and Muslims, and between Christians and Jews, as well as important monuments.

Forty-two years after the Crusades ended with the fall of Acre, the Franciscans became the next western Christian element to arrive in Jerusalem. They were inspired by a peaceful meeting between Francis of Assisi and Sultan al-Kamil. The Franciscans legally established themselves as the guardians of Catholic holy places, thereby assuring a Catholic presence in the city. By the early 19th century, local Catholics had joined together with the Franciscans and formed the diocese known as the Latin patriarchate of Jerusalem.

Although the *millet* system of allowing different religious entities authority to govern themselves is thought to have been established in Ottoman times, the spirit of the idea can be traced back through the millennium. The region of the Holy Land has always been a group of groups, never a single entity. During the Mamluk and early Ottoman period the situation of Christians stabilized, partially due to this *millet* system. Every denomination was granted internal autonomy under a patriarchal leader who had juridical authority on matters of personal status. The leader of each community was answerable to the central authorities and was responsible for assuring that the group contributed the required taxes and did not rebel.

As the Ottoman empire began to weaken, after two hundred years of well organized and prosperous rule, the emerging European powers began seeking greater roles in the region. The different religious denominations were to be mobilized in such colonial manipulations. There has long been a scholarly discussion of when exactly the decline of the Ottoman empire began, but undoubtedly the concrete symptoms of disintegration became evident with the challenge posed by Muhammad 'Ali and his son Ibrahim Pasha. They embarked on an effort to carve out the historic Mamluk kingdom comprising Egypt, Syria, and the Arabian peninsula (1831-39).

Britain's key role in aiding the Ottoman repulsion of the Egyptians under Muhammad 'Ali and his son had ramifications of enormous importance. The competing powers embodied in the developing European states sought to manipulate religion towards their own national interests. The Russians sought protection for the Orthodox in Jerusalem and the Ottoman empire as a whole. France and Austria adopted the Catholics. The British extended protection to the Druze in Lebanon as well as to the Jews in Jerusalem whom they tried to convert to Protestantism through Christ Church's London Mission for Jews. As of 1858 Britain declared that any Jew going to Jerusalem or into Ottoman lands could apply for the status of a protégé of the British empire after six months residence, with all the rights and privileges involved. This kind of policy marks the beginning of far reaching demographic changes in the whole region.

These alliances between states and religious groups, and also specific issues of the Holy Land – how it should be governed, and by whom – played a role in the outbreak of the Crimean War. A very important result of the war was the establishment of principles of Status Quo to govern holy places and to protect the diverse character of Jerusalem. These principles were decided upon in the Congress of Paris in 1856 and every international congress since has confirmed the Status Quo (e.g., Berlin 1878, Versailles 1919). The fact that Jerusalem is legally a *corpus separatum*, as defined by UN Resolution 191, and the lack of its proper judicial status up to the present is an indication that any solution to the current conflict must also resolve the unique status of the city.

3 Contemporary History Since 1948

In the Rhodes agreement of 1949 which set the armistice borders between Jordan and Israel, Palestinians were deprived of the right to return to homes which were in what then became Israel. The same agreement deprived Jews of the ability to travel to East Jerusalem. After the June 1967 war, Levi Eshkol, prime minister of Israel, in the presence of Teddy Kollek, the mayor of West Jerusalem, pledged not to interfere with the delicate balance in the city. Despite this promise, in the same month the Moroccan Quarter of the Old City was completely razed. The justification given was to provide proper access and space around the Western Wall.

In April 1968, Pinhas Sapir, Minister of Finance, signed an order confiscating one hundred and twenty-nine *dunams* of land which had been known as the Jewish Quarter before 1948. According to all reliable sources Jews did not own any more than twenty percent of this quarter. The justification given for the confiscation was public utility. The legal follow-up procedures by Palestinians to prevent confiscation of their land yielded no results. The Israeli explanation was that the Jordanians had deprived the city of its pluralistic nature and had not allowed Jews to live around and worship at the wall between 1948 and 1967. No reciprocal gesture was made to the Palestinians who had been prevented from returning to their homes inside Israel after 1948. At the present time, not only are Christians and Muslims from the area surrounding

Jerusalem being prevented by Israel from worshipping in the city, but they are also being severely deprived of educational, medical, economic, and social interaction with Jerusalem.

Israel's efforts to secure religious rights for Jews does not extend to either Christians or Muslims. The Israeli occupation of East Jerusalem in 1967 was the first total disruption of the pilgrimage of Christians from the East. The stream of thousands of Christian pilgrims from Arab and Islamic countries to Jerusalem every Easter has dried up significantly since 1967. One lamentable and serious consequence has been the reduction of intercommunal contact to the level of the élite. Before 1967, local Jerusalem families would squeeze themselves into as few rooms as possible for the duration of Easter in order to rent out space to the pilgrims. Pilgrims would often stay with the same family year after year, bringing small gifts as tokens of appreciation to their hosts. This yearly event established strong bonds between the Christian communities all over the Middle East and those in Jerusalem.

Israel's serious interference with the principles of the Status Quo governing holy places began with the abrasive intervention between 1968 and 1970 in the dispute over Deir al-Sultan, which is the rooftop of the Church of St Helena. Israel intervened blatantly in order to give the Abyssinians the advantage over the Copts. This then led to Israeli state involvement with Ethiopia to the detriment of Egypt.

Following in the same trend as the take-over of the Jewish Quarter in 1968, a systematic drive began in 1980 to settle the Muslim Quarter with Jewish families. Thus far, fifty-three houses have been acquired and one hundred and twenty are still in litigation due to claims of absentee ownership. Jewish settlement of the Old City reached new heights in April 1990 with the take-over of St John's Hospice from the Greek Orthodox patriarchate. At the present time purchases are being attempted, and plans are being laid for Jewish settlement in the Christian and Armenian Quarters.

Israeli and Jewish sources in international forums seek to minimize the importance of such settler groups as Ateret Cohanim, but the residents of the Old City experience their provocative presence daily. It is important to note that these groups have access to public funds in Israel and international support from powerful sources in the West. These groups are threatening the delicate balance of pluralism within Jerusalem by attempting to Judaize Muslim and Christian areas.

In conclusion, it should be noted that there has been no legislation in Israel concerning the rights and privileges of Christians in the Holy Land. Experience on the ground indicates that oral pledges are insufficient to guarantee such rights. For example, the issue of taxation keeps recurring and causing friction between church authorities and the state. The ever dwindling number of Christians has been a cause of alarm for church leaders concerned with the future of their communities. The new conditions have contributed concretely to the emergence of the concept of the local church, replacing the previous denominational structures. Intermarriage among Christians of various denominations has become more common than ever. Since the *Intifada*, one may clearly discern the churches' involvement in Palestinian issues. This might explain the issuing of thirteen public joint statements by the local church. The emergence of 'Palestinian Liberation Theology' is also an element indicating such an orientation. Increasingly it is becoming evident that the local church is definitely a potential factor in contributing to the complicated task of resolving the Jerusalem issue.

THE CHURCHES IN THE HOLY LAND

9

The Spiritual Meaning and Experience of the Roman Catholic Church in Jerusalem

Maroun Lahham

Jerusalem is the Holy City for all the sons and daughters of Abraham, Jews, Muslims and Christians. It is the cradle of Christianity. Jerusalem has been the witness to the mystery of Jesus, the Word of God made flesh for the Salvation of humanity.

This is why Jerusalem is the spiritual home for all Christians. And this is why, in Jerusalem, there is no possibility of monopoly. This is true for all the monotheistic religions who hold Jerusalem holy. It is true for all the Christians and for all Christian Churches who remain witnesses for Jesus and His message of Salvation in the land from the beginning up to the present time.

It is in this universal context that the Catholic Church in Jerusalem is situated. This is the case also for the churches of other denominations, whose presence is due to historical circumstances, generated from ancient liturgical or ethnic developments that occurred in the beginning, or that have developed early on in Jerusalem.

Historical Preamble

The first question to answer is: 'Who are the Christians of the Holy

Land?' The Holy Land for all the churches of Jerusalem consists of the following territories: Israel, Palestine (or the Occupied Territories, the West Bank and the Gaza Strip) and Jordan. These three parts are also distinct political realities.

All, or almost all the Christians in this area are Arabs, whether Jordanians or Palestinians. They constitute the first component of the local church in all its variations. Together with this Arab component of the local church, there has always been the universal Christian presence. These Christians come to the Holy Land, either as pilgrims, residents, scholars, monks or religious. To these components a third is added in the Hebrew speaking Christians, Roman Catholics and Russian Orthodox, who are Christians of Jewish origin, and who live in the Hebrew-speaking communities.

The figures depicting the Christian presence in the Holy Land are as follows: in the area of Israel, Palestine and Jordan, the total population ranges from 10 to 11 million inhabitants. Six million and a half are Arab, Palestinians and Jordanians, and four million are Israeli Jews.

The total Christian population is approximately 300,000, half of which lives in Israel and Palestine. The break-down of these figures between the various Christians denominations is debatable. Each denomination has its own version. Permit me to speak of the Catholic presence for the sake of precision. Catholics of all rites (Roman Catholics, Melkites, Maronites, Syrians, Armenians) constitute slightly less than half of the 300,000 Christian population. Christians of Hebrew expression number only a few hundred. There are also some 20,000 Messianic Jews, but they appear to wish to remain Jews who believe in the message of Christ, without seeing themselves as part of the Church.

The following question needs to be addressed to the Palestinian and Jordanian Christian: 'Who are you? What do you represent?' The response is both an answer and an aspiration: I am Christian, I want to be only that, free of all of these denominations. We, Arab Christians, are the successors of the first Christian community of Jerusalem. It is futile to get involved in the controversy of ethnic purity and church affiliation in order to define who holds the prestige of being in direct lineage to the first Christian community. The honour goes to him who works within the actual mosaic of the church towards unity of heart and the growth of Christian love, which constitutes the unique and distinctive trait of all of Christ's disciples.

The very first community of Jerusalem was that of Jesus and his disciples, followed by the church formed by Mary and the disciples after Pentecost. This was the first Judaeo-Christian community. Along with it was the church of the Gentiles of Jaffa and Antioch. This first Judaeo-Christian community eventually fused with the church of the Gentiles which was made up of the cosmopolitan population living at the time

(Romans, Greeks, Syrians and Arabs).

The first liturgy of St James gave birth to the Syriac liturgy of Jerusalem. It was not long before the Syriac language was replaced by the Greek, due to political and cultural factors. This was followed by the changing of the liturgy. I am aware that this is a controversial domain into which I would not like to delve. Nevertheless scientific research and objective studies of the formation of the Jerusalem liturgies can only profit the Church of Jerusalem as well as the Universal Church.

The most important thing is that the Palestinian and Jordanian Christians of today, no matter what church they belong to, identify with the first Christian community of Jerusalem, in spite of the centuries of political changes and continuous moulding of the peoples, languages and races.

The Roman Catholic presence in Jerusalem has been consolidated by the communion which existed between Jerusalem and Rome until the schism occurred between Constantinople and Rome. Even after that date, and for a number of years, Jerusalem remained united to both Constantinople and Rome. Political and military isolation, rather than the dogmatic differences between them, was responsible for the total separation between the Churches.

Due to the communion which existed between Rome and Jerusalem, the Catholic presence was consolidated through the exchanges relating to the theological disputes which shook the church of the orient. This is how, for example, we find Sophronius travelling between Jerusalem, Alexandria and Rome fighting monothelism. The communion was also manifested by the pilgrims' diaries as they travelled through the Holy Land. Such is the case of the anonymous pilgrim of Bordeaux (333), and of Etheria who left us with a unique witness of the Holy Week liturgy of Jerusalem, when St Cyril was bishop of the Holy City. Other pilgrims preferred to settle in the Holy Land, and made it their country by adoption. This was the case of St Jerome, who considered himself a native of Bethlehem. His continuous quarrels with more than one Palestinian bishop are a proof of his determination to be considered a native of the Holy Land. Many followed his example, such as Rufin and the two Melanias who established a monastery on the Mount of Olives. Later on, the Benedictine monks took over; and that is where Charlemagne found them in 808 in Jerusalem.

In the Middle Ages, the pilgrimage movement grew in spite of the dangerous roads of Palestine. With the onset of the 11th century, we meet the Crusaders, a much discussed historical phenomenon, especially from the religious perspective. With them, the link between the eastern and western churches was re-established. This however did not improve the relations between the two churches. The dogmatic differences had already been established, and new political motives due to the French military presence acted to widen the gap between them. With these new wars, this land knew another form of melting of peoples, races and religions.

It is in this epoch that the patriarchate of Jerusalem, that is the Succession of St James, was doubled. Since then, we witness the simultaneous presence of both the Roman Catholic and the Greek Orthodox patriarchates.

The Holy Land owes to this epoch an increase in churches of which the main monument has been and still is the Basilica of the Holy Sepulchre which, in spite of the abuse of time and man, remains the first sanctuary of the world; and the cathedral of the three patriarchs of Jerusalem, Greek Orthodox, Roman Catholic and Armenian Orthodox.

After the Crusader era ended, the Franciscan presence, which began at the beginning of the 14th century, continued the Roman Catholic presence in the church of Jerusalem. It is with the true Franciscan spirit of simplicity and openness that Christians know that it is their universality and openness which marks the wholesome personality of the Christian church in the Holy Land. This is why the individual Catholic of the Holy Land is encouraged by the hierarchy to understand and appreciate his brethren in the other churches, each of which has its own liturgy and patrimony. The variety among the churches, then, is a great enrichment: Roman Catholic, Greek Orthodox, Coptic, Syrian Armenian, etc.

In this perspective, then, the Catholic presence in Jerusalem has an ecclesial, cultural and ecumenical dimension.

Ecclesial

The church is universal by definition. No culture is alien to the faith. And the liturgy which is the very celebration of the Mystery of Salvation here and now has to express itself in all cultures and languages. The Arab expression of the Roman Catholic liturgy has in fact enriched the presence of all who believe in Christ. The celebration of the faith in the Roman Catholic rite, together with the Arab genius, has made it possible for the Arab faithful to belong to the local and Universal Church. Its existence, like that of all the other churches in the Holy Land has a double dimension: that of nourishing the faith of its faithful, and that of welcoming the Universal Church which celebrates the mystery of faith according to the same liturgy.

On the other hand, the sense of belonging to the local culture is so strong that is overcomes all barriers of ritual, and enables the Roman Catholic faithful to identify with the two thousand years' history of the faith in the Holy Land. The long list of saints and hermits is part of her glory, as is the impressive Arab religious heritage that began in the Holy Land, and produced the golden age of Arab Christian literature, from the 8th to the 14th century. The Catholic church, as well as all other eastern rites, feels comfortable in the midst of these realities, knowing all the while that all the churches of Palestine share the same sentiments and sense of belonging, without any claiming exclusive appropriation of their common history.

Cultural

Even though the Roman Catholic shares this dimension with his Christian brethren, his faith is characterised by a certain particularity. While he is deeply rooted in his language and culture, the Arab Roman Catholic is open to another culture and other ways of thinking and perceiving, evaluating and acting. In considering the service he wishes to render his country and church he strives to find an appropriate balance between two equally important tendencies, one looking back to the origins of the church, and the second looking to the future. He attempts to ensure an innovative element in the continuous process of inculturation. Inculturation is a vital process for the Christian communities of the Holy Land, who are a minority, and who need to face the world with confidence and trust.

Ecumenical

It is true that the ecumenical movement at the international level is going through a crisis which we think is healthy. It is also true that ecumenism does not have a long history in the Holy Land. Nevertheless circumstances have completely changed, and the credibility and the future of all the churches of the Holy Land depend on their sincere collaboration. In major questions of justice, peace and human rights, there cannot be a specific Catholic, Orthodox, or Protestant answer. These issues deal with the internal problems of the churches, but do not address the existential problems of a people or a church in crisis. The answer needs to be a Christian one, and should reflect the consciousness of all the church of Jerusalem, which must be entirely at the service of the same people facing the same problems.

The Catholic Church of the Holy Land decidedly wants to be ecumenical, open to all ecclesial communities, and to participate in the diverse services with all the means available to her: its own ecclesial experience, its openness to, and knowledge of the Western world, its international contacts, and its various services and institutions (social, medical, pastoral, catechetical, scholastic and academic).

Conclusion

In Jerusalem, every Christian has his place. Jerusalem is his spiritual homeland. The different churches of Jerusalem, in continuity with the mother church, share the same mission of service and hospitality to the churches of the world. They are equally responsible for their faithful in the local church. They strive to help their members in their various trials as they search for justice and peace. They help them to have an accurate picture of the mission of their church, and to identify their own role in it. They encourage them to realise that their own individual existence, like that of the local church, depends on the conception they form of their relationship with the universal church which is dispersed all over the world.

Those who know the ecclesial reality of Jerusalem speak favourably of a mosaic where each church has its place and where the whole forms a beautiful image of Jesus Christ Lord and Saviour. The Roman Catholic church has its place in that mosaic. It prays and makes her own the big movement of hope that runs through the Christian world of today, that all will be one in Christ.

10

The Armenians of Jerusalem and the Armenian Quarter

Harry Hagopian

1 The Armenian Quarter of Jerusalem

On 14 September 1993, the Armenian Patriarch of Jerusalem, His Beatitude Torkom Manoogian, re-inaugurated the historical building 'Bardizatagh'. Like the many other residential quarters that have flourished in the compound of the St James Monastery over the last one hundred and fifty years, Bardizatah also bears witness to an uninterrupted Armenian presence in the Holy Land.

In his speech, the patriarch recalled that Jerusalem has been a spiritual fount for Armenians for more than fifteen centuries. Whether walking along its hallowed alleyways or kneeling in prayer in its churches, Armenians have been constantly reinvigorated and strengthened by the faith of their ancestors. They have stamped their indelible presence in Jerusalem: their rugged individuality, when combined with their fighting spirit and nascent optimism, has contributed to the character of a city that cradles three monotheistic religions, and to a land that witnessed the first church of Pentecost.

It is perhaps fitting to clothe the patriarch's words with the sense of realism that permeates the lives of all Armenians in the Holy Land today by tracing the modest beginnings of such a presence from 301 AD, when Armenia declared Christianity its state religion, and monks as well as pilgrims started the long trek from the distant land of Mount Ararat to the sepulchre of Christ. So, who are the Armenians in the land of Christ, and what is their heritage in a nation of diverse communities?

The Armenian Quarter occupies the south west section of the city, lying within the walls of Jerusalem. Its area is one sixth of the Holy City within the walls, and its character and architecture have been carefully preserved throughout the centuries.

The history and development of the Armenian community in this land is intimately intertwined with pilgrimage. As early as the 5th century, the Greek hagiographer Cyril of Scythopolis wrote about four hundred Armenian pilgrims *en route* to the River Jordan. Burckhardt, the famous 19th century peregrinator who 'discovered' Petra, also refers to eight hundred Armenians who had been to St Catherine's in Sinai.

The Armenian Church of Jerusalem was mobilized to provide for the physical and spiritual needs of such a constant flow of pilgrims. At first, the hospices were in the form of single rooms or halls. Later, as their numbers steadily increased, they were organized around courtyards with separate entrances. Today, within the monastery, there are twenty such courtyards – each bearing the name of a town – Tokat, Adana, Smyrna, Crimea – or simply that of the builder.

The Armenian monastery of St James was considered the largest hospice in the city. Other than accommodation, it housed three huge stables for mules and camels, granaries, mills, storerooms for olive oil, wine, copper plates and bakeries. The pilgrims travelled overland to Jerusalem in big caravans. Special rest houses called *houketouns* (houses of the soul) were provided on the way. There was a large one, for example, in Aleppo, and others were dotted along the way in Damascus, Gaza as well as in Jaffa and Ramla. Upon arrival in Jerusalem, the pilgrims were lodged in the dormitory-like hall of the *houketoun* until they were assigned individual rooms. On the night they arrived, they confessed their sins and, after offering prayers at the tomb of St James, they were led to the Holy Sepulchre where they would touch and kiss the doors of the sanctuary.

Most pilgrims came before the Lenten period and spent the forty days of Lent as well as Holy Week in the city, leaving after the Feast of the Ascension. As such, the pilgrimage season usually lasted three months and was the major source of income for the monastery. However, there were also special monk emissaries called *nviraks* who were sent to the diaspora to encourage pilgrimages to Jerusalem and raise funds for the church.

Pilgrimage could, of course, be a risky business with pilgrims forced to navigate wars and epidemics, as well as the often hazardous routes leading to the Holy Land. Until the 17th century, pirates threatened those who came by sea – as did violent sea storms – and many pilgrims' ships sank on the way. One commemorative slab reads:

> The pilgrims coming from Constantinople were swallowed by the sea – clergy and lay people, men and women alike. In commemoration, the patriarch erected a cross for the salvation of their souls and engraved this inscription, so that whoever reads this inscription would say: May God have mercy on their souls.

Pilgrims also had to prepare themselves spiritually for the journey. An 18th century Armenian pilgrimage annual, written by Bishop Hanna, narrates how pilgrims had to renounce bad habits and become humble and modest. Before setting out, they had to confess their sins, receive Holy Communion and write their testament. Those who died while visiting the Holy Land were considered privileged and believed to be blessed on the Day of Judgement, as they were buried in physical proximity to the tomb of the Lord.

The improvement in land transport, paralleled with cheaper shipping fares from Odessa and the development of the railroad, led to a wave of popular pilgrimages with numbers reaching record heights of eight to ten thousand a year. However, both the Armenian genocide of 1915 and the Bolshevik revolution of 1917, dampened considerably this traditional type of popular pilgrimage. After the 1920s, pilgrimage by land persisted, mainly from neighbouring Arab lands. That, however, only lasted until the Six Day War of 1967.

For its part, the Armenian patriarchate felt morally obligated to provide facilities for the pilgrims, some of whom would spend as long as six months in Jerusalem. The annual growth in the number of pilgrims led to the expansion of the Armenian Quarter within the city. With the additional income, the patriarchate invested in property – a move which proved wise and which continues to yield a substantial income today.

In fact, property and pilgrimage have always been closely interconnected. In the 19th century, during the Crimean War of 1854-1856, no pilgrims could reach the Holy Land from Turkey or the Caucasus. As a result, the Armenian brotherhood sank deep into financial crisis. Patriarch John (1850-1860) decided that the patriarchate could not continue to be at the mercy of epidemics or wars and decided to invest in real estate. In the following years, double the original number of pilgrims came and, with this additional income, the patriarch bought precious land outside the Jaffa Gate. Even though the brotherhood considered any investment outside the city walls unsafe, the patriarch persevered and became the pioneer of such ventures.

The residential neighbourhood in the Armenian Quarter was centred around the Sanctuary of St James, established in 430 AD. Around that holy site sprang up a monastery, hospices and hospitals. St James is the patron saint of Armenians in Jerusalem, with the monastery and the brotherhood named after him. St James is also considered one of the five main holy places in Jerusalem, after the Holy Sepulchre and several early sanctuaries.

The northern section (the martyrium of St James), St Menas and St Sergius, with their barrel-vaulted ceiling and bi-apsidal chapel, are still intact today with the exception of the tile decoration of the early 18th century. The central design of the church follows the requirements of Armenian liturgy and ritual, while the capitals and some architectural details date from the Crusader period. The central dome with its cross-ribbed design is a copy of the dome of the Armenian church of Haghpat. It could be said that the Cathedral of St James stands as a happy marriage of Byzantine, Crusader and Armenian influence. Structurally, no changes have occurred in the cathedral since 1161. Decorative elements were added in the 16th, 17th and early 18th centuries – for example, one of the most striking features of the cathedral is that the church walls were originally completely covered by late 15th century frescos.

St James monastery, along with St Catherine's and Mar Saba, is one of the oldest functioning monasteries in the Holy Land. For the last fifteen hundred years, not a single day has passed without two or three daily services being held at St James.

The first lectionary of Palestine (St Thoros' Collection, Codex 121) was translated from Greek into Armenian in Jerusalem and was used both in Jerusalem as well as in Armenia. This 5th century document, covering the period from 5 January to 29 December, charts all the feasts of the Jerusalem church – as well as where they were celebrated. In short, it is the liturgical calendar of the Jerusalem church and is the oldest known document in the world to include the corpus of feasts, sites and dates in the Holy Land. The Greek original has been lost and survives only in the Armenian translation. Father Charles Renoux, discoverer of Codex 121 and a renowned authority on the early development of Jerusalem liturgy, believes the lectionary was compiled during the period 417–439.

As the foundation of St James Cathedral was contemporaneous with the desert fathers in Palestine, the church possesses a great number of relics and reliquaries of saints of the early church in Palestine and of some of the Apostles. Within the church, there is a chapel called St Macarius, the first bishop of Jerusalem, under Constantine and Helena. According to the oral history of Jerusalem, as well as some literary sources, his remains are interred in this chapel.

The present decorative splendour of St James Cathedral is partly due to the efforts of Patriarch Gregory the Chain-Bearer (1712-1749), considered one of the greatest of the patriarchs of the Holy See. On his ascension to the throne, he found the patriarchate in dire financial straits and wandered on foot in Armenia with a chain round his neck. He spent seven years going from church to church collecting funds, and refused to remove the heavy chain until all debts were repaid. His name, along with that of Gregory of Baronter, is mentioned during the Holy Liturgy in the Armenian churches of Jerusalem.

Coming out of St James Cathedral, one can see on the left the *symandra* (wooden bells or clappers) which were in use up to the 1830s when Ibrahim Pasha of Egypt allowed Christians to sound bells. Today, the sounding of the *symandra* marks the beginning of church services.

In the forecourt of St James, there are many funerary inscriptions – one, for example, of Patriarch Abraham, 'who died in the reign of Salaheddin, 1192', and another tombstone of 'Bishop Vartan of Kars, 1238'. To the left, a flight of stairs leads to the patriarch's residence, built in a palace-like fashion by Balian, the architect of the Ottoman Court. Hung on the walls are portraits of monarchs who have visited the Armenian patriarchate, including Franz Josef and Eliza of Austria, Kaiser Wilhelm and his wife Augusta Victoria, as well as King George and Queen Mary of England. Although Queen Victoria did not visit Jerusalem, she sent her autographed picture in 1869 in recognition of the services rendered by the Armenian Patriarch Yessayi in releasing a British ambassador who had been taken hostage in Ethiopia.

A staircase to the right of the churchyard leads to the former cloister and refectory which has stone and marble tables and ceramic walls. It was founded in 1391 by Patriarch Gregory the Egyptian, destroyed in the earthquake of 1547, and then rebuilt by Patriarch Philip in the same year. The ceramic walls were plastered by the monk Elia of Caesarea, in the period of Gregory the Chain-Bearer.

A climb to the roof reveals the 5th century chapel of the Holy Apostles, with its gabled roof and 5th century lintel. Within the Cathedral of St James and on the rooftop, there are forty altars where Holy Mass is said according to the church calendar. In the north west of the monastery is the medieval chapel of St Thoros, founded in the Cilician era and expanded during the period of Gregory the Chain-Bearer.

It is now assumed that there was an active scriptorium in the monastery by the year 450 AD. The value of these manuscripts lies in their textual contents. Armenian monks, who were very much part of the desert community from the 5th century, translated the Greek and Syriac texts into Armenian. These translations travelled from Jerusalem to Armenia where they were copied. Some are the only surviving copies of important works of the church Fathers, as many of the originals have been destroyed.

Three monasteries had prolific scribal activity: they were St James, the Holy Archangel's and St Saviour – in addition to the Armenian monastery at Ain Karem. The first printing press in Jerusalem was an Armenian one, set up in 1833, with printing facilities in many languages. It is still used today, despite the existence of a more modern one, to print the annual liturgical calendar which is sent to all Armenians in the diaspora. During the last century, there also existed a large photography workshop founded by the monk Essayi in 1855 and active until 1885.

Strolling through the Armenian monastery, one comes across hundreds of inscriptions on the lintels of rooms from the 1600s to the 1800s mentioning the pilgrims who made donations for the upkeep of those buildings.

Simeon of Poland, an Armenian traveller visiting Jerusalem in 1615, noted the varied functions of the monastery when he wrote that it housed 'millers, scribes, candle-makers, bead-makers, stone masons, tailors and a goldsmith . . . '

On the southern side of the big courtyard, a small iron gate leads to a new series of courtyards. In this vicinity can be found the library, the museum, the high school and the Holy Archangel's convent.

The Gulbenkian library, once known as the Tourian library, was founded in 1929 by the Armenian philanthropist Calouste Gulbenkian in memory of his parents. It houses around one hundred and twenty thousand volumes in many languages, as well as an important Armenological collection with almost eight thousand titles on Armenian themes in foreign languages. There is also a separate section of about four thousand titles of old Armenian printed books. The library also features many periodicals and magazines, including the first newspaper *Aztarar*, which was started in Madras in 1795. It is interesting to note that the first Armenian book was printed in Venice in 1512, and the first Armenian Bible in Amsterdam in 1666.

The Holy Archangel's convent (also known as the Olive-Tree Convent, due to its association with the High Priest Ananias and Christ's trial) is a 12th century church with a typical Armenian porch entrance. Following the restoration work done in 1988, hundreds of writings and anonymous crosses incised by pilgrims, in addition to other inscriptions, were revealed.

When the Franciscan friars were expelled from the Cenaculum on Mount Zion in 1551 by the order of Suleiman the Magnificent, the Armenian monks housed them for seven years in the convent and put two altars and private quarters at their disposal. After the 15th century, however, the convent was converted into a nunnery.

Outside Zion Gate is situated St Saviour's convent – the site of the traditional House of Caiaphas where Peter denied Jesus three times and the cock crowed. Within the last century, Byzantine mosaics found to the north and south corroborate the oral tradition of the House of Caiaphas. In the courtyard of the church lie the patriarchs of Jerusalem from the 16th century. The earlier patriarchs were buried in the parvis of St James. Alongside them are also buried the emissaries (*nviraks*) who went to remote lands to raise funds for the church of Jerusalem.

Recent excavations have unearthed rare Herodian frescoes as well as pavements with flagstones, a sophisticated drainage system, a Byzantine mosaic floor, and the remnants of a wall from a Crusader church.

To the west of the monastery is the Armenian cemetery where monks, pilgrims and members of the Armenian community in the Holy Land have been buried for centuries. In the upper end of the cemetery lies a monument in memory of the twenty-three Armenian soldiers who fell in the battle of Arara when a contingent of around five hundred Armenians fought alongside the allies during the First World War.

Outside the Holy City of Jerusalem, there are three monasteries. The oldest one is in Bethlehem, near the Church of the Nativity. It has many Justinian remains (6th century) and an old chapel known as the University of St Jerome. Dating from pre-Crusader times, it underwent extensive renovations under the reign of Patriarch Gregory of Baronter who converted it into a hermitage. An ascetic figure himself who would usually retire to pray in a cell located in an orchard in Bethlehem, the patriarch attracted other ascetic groups to Jerusalem and started an anchoritic settlement either in the Judean desert or in Sceta.

For the last five hundred years, the Armenian Convent of Jaffa has been an epicentre of organized monastic life. Jaffa, being a port city, was the window to the outside world, and was considered second only to Jerusalem in the whole of Palestine. The Armenian Convent of St Nicholas, situated on the sea front, was the first shore haven for many pilgrims travelling to the Holy Land by sea. Gregory the Chain-Bearer expanded its facilities to receive and host the increasing number of pilgrims. The archives contain most of the correspondence between the convent and the Jerusalem patriarchate, highlighting the role of the former as the pilgrims' link between the Holy Land and the outside world. In fact, its importance can also be underlined by the fact that Patriarch Petros of Tokat was buried there.

At its zenith and until 1948, the Armenian community of Jaffa numbered six thousand – with schools and cultural centres. Today, the shifting political sands and an emigrant trend have reduced their numbers to a mere four hundred.

Another important station for pilgrims coming to Jerusalem was the Convent of St George in Ramla – a venerated sanctuary holding the relics of St George. As a major site of pilgrimage, worshippers flocked to the convent for three days on the eve of the Feast of St George, made vows and offered communal meals (*mataghs*). This communal offering of *matagh* is an ancient practice in the Armenian church tradition which underlines the inherent belief that all peoples are equal before the Almighty.

The Armenian genocide, perpetrated in vicious waves by the Ottoman Turks and peaking in 1915 with a blood-soaked legacy of over one million hapless Armenian victims, resulted in momentous changes in the life and witness of the patriarchate. Communities in countries as diverse as Syria, Lebanon, Egypt and Cyprus, which until then had come under the jurisdiction of the Jerusalem patriarchate, were transferred to that of the Catholicossate of Cilicia at Antelias. Today, the Jerusalem patriarchate has jurisdiction over the ten-thousand strong Armenian communities of Israel, the West Bank and Jordan.

In 1921, Archbishop Yeghishe Tourian was elected as patriarch. His reign led to a period of religious rejuvenation and cultural renovation in the life of the local Armenian community. Patriarch Tourian re-organised the seminary (shut during the Ottoman period), founded the library and resumed publication of *Sion*, the official organ of the patriarchate which had first been printed in 1866 by Patriarch Essayi. Since then, five patriarchs have succeeded him, and the present incumbent, Archbishop Torkom Manoogian, is a dedicated churchman and an international ecumenical figure.

The last seventy years have been active years for the patriarchate as it has attempted to strengthen the Armenian community of the Holy Land. Its seminary is training many young students, and it is jointly helping restore the Church of the Holy Sepulchre – with the Greek Orthodox and Latin-rite Catholic churches. In addition, ecumenical co-operation between the Armenian patriarchate and its sister churches in Jerusalem is equally strong. This spirit of collaboration, which fosters unity in diversity, is being focused on all issues affecting Christians in the Holy Land – inevitably including current political issues, not least the status of Jerusalem itself.

The Armenian patriarchate of Jerusalem has also contributed throughout the years to the safeguarding of the Holy Places. During the Persian invasion of 614, Armenians relied on their historic ties with Persia and used their good offices to help restore the Holy Sepulchre – with the Greek Patriarch Modestus expressing his thanks to Catholicos Komitas. Likewise, the Armenians were helpful in promoting Christian interests during the Fatimid rule in the 11th century, since many Armenians – such as Badr al-Jamali who was the Grand Vizier of Egypt for twenty years between 1074 and 1094 – were of Armenian parentage and held key posts in the country.

Equally, the Armenian role should not be overlooked in protecting the interests of the other eastern churches (Syrians, Copts and Ethiopians) during the Ottoman and Crusader times, when some communities were expelled from Jerusalem for short periods because of their political affiliations. This resulted from frictions caused by ancient theological discrepancies between the Latin church (as the religion of the ruling class) and the Greek and other eastern churches.

In their relations with Christian communities abroad, Armenians have received a favourable verdict from foreign travellers. Louis de Rochechouart, for instance, noted in 1463 that, ' . . . Armenians are, of all, the most friendly to the Latins', and Father Eugene Roget also described Armenians in 1632 as, 'most zealous, civilized and affable'. For a small minority community, such words are encouragement indeed in the struggle to remain loyal to an Armenian witness in Jerusalem that has continued uninterrupted for well over fifteen centuries.

2 The Armenian Community

The Armenian community of Jerusalem is perhaps the oldest one outside Armenia. As early as the 5th century, when caravans of Armenian pilgrims began to arrive in the Holy Land, some of those pilgrims decided not to return home. Thus, Armenian communities started in different parts of Palestine and Jordan – as far away as Karak – and many families still carry names indicating their origin from different towns in Palestine. Recently, near the kibbutz of Nir David in the Jordan Depression, a jarful of Armenian coins was found dating back to the 13th century.

3 The Origins

After Etchmiadzin, Jerusalem has been the main focus of Armenian Christian attention. Though Armenian connections with Palestine go back to Roman times when King Tigranes of Armenia (95-55 BC) invaded Syria and Northern Palestine, other Armenians were to be found in the Roman Legions.

The main turning point in the attachment to the Holy Land began, however, with the adoption of Christianity as the state religion of Armenia in 301 AD. St Jerome, in his letters of 386 AD, mentions Armenians among other pilgrims of different lands visiting the Holy Land. Monks from all parts of the East, Asia Minor, Cappadocia, Armenia and the Caucasus met in the Judaean desert and gave impetus to the early period in the formation and development of the church from the 4th to the 7th centuries.

The Universal Church was therefore shaped in the semi-arid wastes between Jerusalem and Jericho, in the wilderness of the valleys beyond Bethlehem and the River Jordan. Thousands of monks flocked to this Judaean wilderness, staying in caves and newly-established *lavras* (monasteries). Hundreds of Armenian ascetics were part of this movement. Euthymius, an Armenian bishop of Melitene, for example, is considered to be the organizer of Palestinian desert monasticism. He came to Palestine to live in a cell in 405 AD. Later, he established his *lavra* on the way to Jericho. It was consecrated by Juvenal of Jerusalem in 428 AD.

St Euthymius was a great monastic reformer, and he drew up regulations and a comprehensive code of life for all aspects of monastic life. Many of the towering figures of desert monasticism – such as St Sabas – were initiated by him. Cyril of Scythopolis, himself a monk at the St Euthymius monastery, was a contemporary biographer of the major figures of desert monasticism. Through Cyril's texts, we learn about other central Armenian personalities in the monastic life – those like Sophronius, or the Armenian from Sebastia, who was the successor of St Theodosius, and who enlarged the monastery fourfold.

Another bishop with a tremendous impact on the desert monks was St John Hesychast, who belonged to a noble Armenian family of Roman colonia. Armenian anchorites were so numerous in some of these monastic settlements that they had their separate chapels in Mar Sabas and St Theodosius. There was also a sizeable community in St George of Choziba.

In the same period, there were also other Armenian monasteries active in and around Jerusalem. In the second half of the 19th century, in 1869 and 1894, the remains of a number of Armenian monasteries were found, with mosaic floors and Armenian inscriptions. A cluster of them was found on the Mount of Olives, pointing to an important monastic concentration on the summit of the Mount of Olives around what is today the Russian convent with the tower.

In 1894, north of Damascus Gate, a seven by four metre mosaic was unearthed, commemorating Armenian soldiers in the Roman army who were killed for their Christian faith. This chapel, known as St Polyeucte, is constructed over a cave full of bones. Considered to be one of the earlier known examples of a cenotaph, the inscription reads: 'To the memory and salvation of all Armenians whose name only the Lord knows.'

Precise statistics about the numbers of Armenians in the 17th and 18th centuries are not available; however, a census in 1902 puts their number at twelve hundred. In the 19th century, many Armenians were craftsmen, mainly watchmakers, photographers and goldsmiths. Some were also involved in carpentry, especially furniture work, whilst others were blacksmiths and master masons – hence a family name such as Benneyan, which means builder. Some held public office: directorates or consular posts in foreign regions, like the United States and Prussia, as well as in both Jerusalem and Jaffa.

This period is also remembered as a time of war, epidemics and starvation. Many Armenians, including seminarians, went to the army never to return. A rare diary, kept by Patriarch Mesrop Nishanian (then a priest), recounts those horrors. A month before the arrival of the British in Jerusalem, all the patriarchs and bishops of Jerusalem were exiled to Damascus. They were forced to stay there for a year. After the British capture of Jerusalem, there was an influx of Armenian refugees, survivors of the genocide. In 1920, their numbers in Palestine reached twenty thousand.

With the monastery in Jerusalem full to overflowing, community centres, clubs and schools were started. They prospered and became active in the social, economic and cultural lives of the country.

The 1948 Arab-Israeli war resulted in serious demographic dislocation and in waves of emigration. The Armenian community in Jerusalem has presently shrunk to around three thousand. Yet, they have the advantage of inheriting an infrastructure of organized communal life.

Armenians play a significant role in the social, cultural and economic life of the region today. They have become pioneers in industry, photography, ceramics and jewellery, as well as being musicians, medical doctors and dental surgeons, lecturers and teachers in universities and institutions of higher education.

The survival and the vitality of this small community is further proof of their firm attachment to their faith and culture, and to an unyielding sense of destiny and preservation as living testimony of their own identity and their wider ethos.

11

The Spiritual Significance and Experience of the Churches: The Lutheran Perspective

Mitri Raheb

Background

The history of the Evangelical Lutheran Church in the Holy Land started in the year 1841, when an Anglo-Prussian bishopric was founded in Jerusalem. Through the works of Bishop Samuel Gobat, Johann Ludwig Schneller, Kaiserwerther Deaconices as well as the Jerusalem Foundation, various Lutheran Congregations came into existence, especially in Jerusalem and in the south of Palestine.

In 1959 a synod, comprising representatives of these different congregations came together proclaiming the birth of the Evangelical Lutheran Church in Jordan, which was also then officially recognised by the king of Jordan.

In 1979 the synod elected the first Arab bishop as the head of the church to succeed the German Propst, who had been considered until that time as the spiritual head of the church.

The Lutheran Experience in the Holy Land

The work of the Lutheran Church in the Holy Land was a distinguished one, since it was not connected with, nor interested in, the traditional Holy sites of Palestine.

Rather, the Lutheran church has invested in five main areas.

School Work

It is very interesting to note that the first task of the Protestant missionaries who came to Palestine was not to build churches, but to establish schools. School work preceded church work, and church work was an outgrowth of educational work, and not the other way around. Education and spreading knowledge have been top priorities of the Lutheran church from the beginning.

This fact is related to the Lutheran heritage, which underlines the importance of the Holy Scripture, enhances its knowledge, encourages its reading and embraces its practice in daily life. Today the Evangelical Lutheran Church operates five schools with 2,700 pupils in five cities in the occupied territories. Christian education in Palestine is very much needed today; one look at the political landscape of the Middle East will be sufficient to show that it lacks any sign of logic. The policy of Israel, as well as that of most of the Arab states, often appears to be irrational, incalculable, and incomprehensible. Religion too often appears to be naive and fundamentalistic.

That is why knowledge, training and education are important for the future of Palestinian society in general, as well as for the Christian community in particular. Education is essential for the democratization of the Middle East, for the development of the region, and for building up a wealthy and sane society. At a time when religious fundamentalism is gaining weight, a responsible and open-minded faith is very much needed.

Social Work

From the beginning Protestant work in Palestine has focused on social work with orphans, the socially marginalized, poor, and sick people. It was as if the church was feeling that her mission is nothing else, but an echo of the mission of her Lord, who was sent to bring good news to the poor, to proclaim release to the 'captives and recovery of sight to the blind, and to let the oppressed go free' (Luke 4.18). Due to this humanitarian dimension, the Lutheran Church as well as other churches in Palestine has founded hospitals, rehabilitation centres, orphanages, and other social institutions.

Welfare services, however, are not enough. Committed Christians realise today that poverty and oppression are not accidental, but are rather the result of repressive policies to increase wealth and power selfishly at the expense of others. Therefore it is very important for the church today to work for social justice, and to engage herself in building up a healthy and a well developed infra-structure in Palestine.

Contextualized Theology

No one denies, as a matter of fact, that the Lutheran experience has focused on the right understanding of the Holy Scripture. For this reason preaching, biblical study and exegesis have been crucial elements in the Lutheran experience.

Up to the present time churches in the Middle East have been engaged in either recalling the patristic theology or importing Western theology. The church was (and this is part of the Palestinian reality) a consuming church. It is time to develop a Palestinian Christian theology, which reflects our situation and deals with the problems of the Christian communities today. In fact Christianity is not an eternal law, but rather a gospel of God, who was incarnated in Christ in a certain space and a certain time. Such an incarnated contextualized theology must be ecumenical to face the problems in the region which challenge all the churches without exception.

The Relationship with the World-wide Christian Community

Developing a contextualized Palestinian Christian theology is a great necessity not only for the local church, but also for the Universal Church. It is not a secret that many western Christians, especially Protestants, are mis-using the Bible to fit into their ideology.

The uncritical and a-historical equating of today's state of Israel with biblical Israel, the theologian's shock and guilt over the holocaust, and Israel's victories over the Arab states, have led many Western theologians to mythologize the state of Israel. The other side of this mythologization was the denomization of the Palestinian people. The local Palestinian church has a mission to the Universal Church, in underlining the justice of God as the hermeneutical key in reading and interpreting the Bible, thus becoming the voice of the voiceless.

Dialogue with the Two Other Monotheistic Religions

Christians in Palestine are living in a multi-cultural and multi-religious context. They are living as a minority among two majorities (Islam and Judaism). The Christian Church must redefine theology to give it a new content, since the role of religion is often either ignored and underestimated, or politicized. Religion, correctly understood, is a positive relationship between God and human beings, simultaneously forming the basis for all relationships between one human being and another, as well as with the environment.

In this regard, the position of human beings in religion has to be clarified. A theology of creation can be very important for us in Palestine, where three religions and two nations have to exist. Such a theology holds that every human being, no matter what his religion or nationality is, is created in the image of God. To protect a human being's rights is therefore a divine law. To be religious, therefore, means simply to be a true human being. Dialogue among all people of goodwill is essential in creating conditions of maximum justice, tolerance, and development in the region.

These are some of the experiences, concerns and hopes of the Evangelical Lutheran Church in the Holy Land.

12

The Birth and Experience of the Christian Church: The Protestant/Anglican Perspective. Anglican Identity in the Middle East

Riah Abu El-Assal

The History of the Diocese

The Protestant (Anglican) bishopric in Jerusalem was established in 1841 in co-operation with the King of Prussia, who had a vision of a world-wide Protestant union, with Jerusalem as its centre. In keeping with the aim of the church to bring Christianity to the Jews of Palestine the first bishop, Bishop Michael Solomon Alexander, was a former Jewish rabbi converted to Christianity.

The second bishop, Bishop Samuel Gobat, was a Swiss Protestant who turned his attention towards the local Christians and ordained the first three Arab Protestant (Anglican) priests. Together with the Church Missionary Society (CMS), Bishop Gobat was responsible for the establishment of many schools in the Holy Land. His efforts were not wholly appreciated by the churches already established in the region, who feared that his intention was to proselytize among their members.

In 1882, due to dissatisfaction among the Germans, the Anglo-Prussian agreement was annulled and the bishopric reconstituted as an Anglican bishopric in 1887.

In 1905 a great step towards the indigenization of the church was taken with the formation of the Palestine Native Church Council. In the Council local clergy and laity united together under the guidance of the CMS to establish a self-governing, self-supporting system. The CMS hoped that local Christians would be more successful than foreigners in winning Muslims to Christ.

In the following years the diocese saw many historic changes; the break up of the Ottoman empire, the establishment of the Kingdom of Jordan and the Republics of Lebanon and Syria, and in 1948 the establishment of the State of Israel, which brought about the division of the diocese, the isolation of the Anglican community in Israel and the massive task of coping with the refugees and persons displaced by the war of 1948.

In this period of general disarray, the church provided much-needed leadership and humanitarian help, not only to its own members but to all those affected by the upheaval – Christians and Muslims. Bishop Henry Stewart organized the building of houses to shelter needy families. The Nasser family, Anglicans from Bir Zeit in the West Bank, founded the now famous Bir Zeit University in their own home. There are many more examples of Anglican presence, including, of course, perhaps the best-known spokesperson for the Palestinians in the Western world, Dr Hanan Ashrawi, who was born to an Anglican family.

Some of the leadership in the early years after the division of the diocese was not so positive. In the south of Israel, Nichola Saba, at the instigation of the District Commissioner, tried to persuade the local Anglicans to sell the possessions of their church and emigrate to Brazil! However, this move was strongly opposed by the Council. The property passed into the hands of the Israeli Custodian for Absentee Property who administered the property of Palestinians not considered residents of the country by the government.

In 1954 and 1956 another two priests left Israel, leaving only Rafiq Farah to care for the flock, until the diocese in Jordan, Lebanon and Syria sent the late Revd Khalil Duaibis to help him in 1958.

In the West Bank, in Jordan, in Lebanon and Syria the Anglican refugee communities also faced great difficulties. The people had lost their homes, their possessions and their jobs.

The so-called Six Day War of 1967 made communication between the Anglicans of Israel and the bishop in Jerusalem easier, but made it more difficult for the bishop to reach other parts of the diocese.

Recently the Anglican churches and institutions in Amman worked hard to care for the influx of refugees from Iraq and Kuwait.

In Israel, there is a significant number of Christians among the immigrants from Russia, some of whom have already found their way to our churches.

In West Beirut the congregation worshipped for many years in the building of the Near East School of Theology, since their lovely waterfront church of All Saints had to be abandoned at the outbreak of the civil war, and was very badly damaged. It occupies a symbolic position on the line between the Muslim and Christian sectors of Beirut. We are happy that now that the city has been reunited, it can once again be used for worship.

The newest congregation in the diocese was established in 1990, in Aleppo, Syria.

The Constitution of the Diocese

The diocese of Jerusalem is one of the four dioceses which make up the Province of Jerusalem and the Middle East.

From 1974–76, under the supervision of the Vicar General, Robert Stopford, the diocese was completely restructured. The two bishoprics – of Jerusalem and Jordan, Lebanon and Syria – were reunited to form the diocese of Jerusalem, comprising the Holy City, Israel, Jordan, Lebanon, and the Occupied Territories of Palestine and Syria. In place of the Archbishop it had had since 1957, Jerusalem now again had a bishop. Provision was made for an assistant bishop based in Amman to maintain relations with Lebanon, Syria and Jordan. 1976 saw the first Palestinian Anglican bishop, Faik Haddad, installed in Jerusalem.

Our present bishop, Bishop Samir Kafity, is presiding bishop of the Central Synod of the Province. The bishop is the representative of the Anglican Communion, and the successor of the bishops of the Church of England in Jerusalem. He participates in the Lambeth Conferences.

The diocese is run according to the Anglican tradition, with the bishop as its head, and a House of Clergy and a House of Laity representing the different congregations. Regulations control the number of representatives sent by each congregation to the Houses, which together with the bishop form the Church Council. This last meets annually to decide on matters relating to the spiritual and other needs of the church and its institutions.

The constitution of the diocese provides that at least one representative from each of the regions (Israel, Jordan, Lebanon and Syria, and Palestine) sits on each of the various decision-making committees, including the finance committee, authorized to run diocesan business between meetings of the Church Council. The bishop has the power of veto in matters relating to the clergy.

Some twenty-eight congregations make up the diocese, of which six are primarily English speaking. Some of these share the building in which they worship with Arabic speaking congregations, as in St George's Cathedral in Jerusalem. St George's also hosts a number of small guest congregations.

Through the ministry of its thirty-two institutions, particularly in the fields of education, special education for the handicapped and medical care, the Anglican church serves all members of the community, Muslim and Christian alike. The diocese is responsible for two major hospitals, in Gaza and Nablus, for a number of specialist vocational schools in Beirut and Jordan, for some excellent primary and secondary schools, and for homes for the elderly and the orphaned.

In Jerusalem and the West Bank, Anglican schools face closures and great hardship due to strikes and curfews in the wake of the *Intifada*. In Israel they face discrimination through the refusal of the government to grant them the funding due to them.

At present several candidates from the diocese are in training for ordination in different places in the world, including the USA, Europe, Australia, Beirut and Cairo. The number of candidates for ordination has increased in recent years.

The Diocese and the Political Structures within which it functions

The Anglican church in Jerusalem and the Middle East is recognized as a religious community in all the areas in which it serves. (In Syria its members are all expatriates.) The decisions of its ecclesiastical courts are also recognized, although there are serious problems with some governments, for example in Israel where there is a conflict with the government over some of the above-mentioned absentee property.

The Israeli government also refuses to grant the Anglican Church tax exemption, which is granted to the Roman Catholic Church. Tax exemption would mean that medical and educational materials and equipment, badly needed by the hospitals and schools run by the church, could be imported much cheaper (as could cars for the clergy!).

Anglicanism within the Islamic and Judaic Context of the Middle East

The rise of religious fundamentalism has contributed tremendously to making the national identity and affiliation of individuals a secondary matter in our region, not only for Arab Christians, but even for Arab Muslims. In some Arab countries fundamentalist groups are opposing anything which is not Muslim, at all levels and in all spheres. This has forced some Arab Christian minorities to live a life of alienation in the homelands of their fathers and grandfathers, or caused them to experience periods of intense worry and psychological and physical instability with respect to their fate and the future of their children and properties. So much so that some have felt compelled to abandon their homeland, identity and roots. However, they escape from one reality of alienation to another of exile in the West.

It is important to point out that this situation is not new. It is not the result of an historical accident, nor is it the result of the experiences of the Arab nation over the last forty or even one hundred years. In Israel for the first time since the year 70 AD a Christian minority is living within a Jewish majority. Relations between the two communities are burdened by the history of anti-semitism in the Western churches and by discrimination against the Jews in Europe, and complicated by the modern movement of Christian Zionism. But the confrontation between Judaism and Christianity in Israel is shrouded behind the tensions between the Jews and the larger Arab community to which the Christians belong.

Arab Christians were and continue to be an inseparable part of the Arab Nation which extends from the Arabian Gulf to the Atlantic Ocean. Let it suffice to point out that we were present, perhaps among the Arab converts to Judaism, in Jerusalem on the day of Pentecost, as recorded in the Acts of the Apostles (2.11). Just as the Christian faith spread in Asia Minor and other areas of the Roman empire until it reached Rome through the early apostles, so it spread throughout the Arabian peninsula through the Apostle Thomas, who found his way in AD 50 to the Indian sub-continent by way of the Arabian peninsula.

From the 4th to the 7th centuries AD the first Arab Christian kingdom was established with its capital at Edessa, now Urfa in Turkey. This was the golden age of Arab Christianity when there were thirty-six bishops in Hauran in Syria and as many as sixty-three in Palestine.

We are part of the Arab nation, bound by a single language that we speak with its many dialects. We have no civilization, no history, no culture nor heritage other than the Arab civilization, culture, history and heritage. Despite all external influences, we do not live the culture, civilization or traditions and customs of the English, or, more lately, the Americans. Yet this evident historical reality does not mean that there is no problem of disharmony between who we feel ourselves to be, where we come from, and our present reality. During the First World War the Revds Elias Marmura and Butros Nasser were exiled by the Turks of the Ottoman empire because they were looked on as English.

We could speak at length about the experience of Christian minorities in Syria, Lebanon, Iraq and Egypt. A bitter reality is experienced by Arab Christians in the land of the 'Black Gold', Saudi Arabia, where it has been impossible for most, if not all, to establish any harmony between their Arab and their Christian identities. Some have felt compelled to abandon outwardly their faith, simply in order to protect their financial interests. As soon as they have achieved this they escape to the West, seeking to compensate for what they have lost with remarkable spiritual and doctrinal zeal.

To understand this disharmony better, let us go back again in time. In the first era after the appearance of the Arab prophet Muhammad and the rise of Islam as the dominant and decisive force in the Arab East and North Africa, a new uniform reality was created which in many cases led to a confusion between the two religious understandings, to the point where it resulted in a large percentage of Arab Christians being torn away from their Christian faith. This happened for two important reasons:

> 1 The theological question pertaining to the doctrine of the Holy Trinity:
> What reached the Arabian peninsula of this doctrine was not the trinity of Father, Son and Holy Ghost, but a belief in the triad of father, mother and son, as we see it reflected in the text of the Qur'an (Sura 5, v. 116; Sura 5, v. 77; Sura 4, v. 169). By way of contrast, Islam preached a clear monotheism.

> 2 The political question, or the matter of spiritual and ecclesiastical imperialism:
> Local Christians, most of them Arabs, had protested against the imperialism of the Byzantines and others. Therefore, it was no wonder that the Arab Christians supported the Islamic conquests which were, in essence, Arab conquests.

I believe that the relations of the 'outside' to the 'inside' in the Middle East have always been characterized by some form of 'Christian over Christian' caste behaviour. In this connection it is important to study the Catholic and Protestant missionary societies which, in my view, deepened the gap between the Arab Christian and his true identity, roots, and loyalties.

The Arabic language and Arab culture has enriched even those not originally Arab. Aramaic thinking, Hellenistic thinking and Roman thinking, as well as the Jewish religion, necessarily influenced those Arabs who had been converted to Christianity. It was natural for the Arab Christian to drink from the springs of those who were sitting on the thrones of the church. This influence came through reading the Scriptures and repeating the liturgies, and led to Arab Christians giving their sons and daughters Christian names which were originally Hellenic and later westernized, and following Christian customs and habits.

I may point out here that colonialism does not occupy land only, but also infiltrates the spirit and the mind. I think this has had the greater effect, deliberately or otherwise, in shaking the confidence of Arab Christians in their own Arab identity. The division of the church into different denominations as the result of various heresies, each with its own spiritual, if not temporal, army, and each with its own customs, most of them far removed from the Arab heritage, have had a similar effect.

What occurred in the 6th and 7th centuries, the spread of heresies, was repeated during and after the Crusades, and again with the coming of the missionary movements, so that the Catholics among us became more Catholic than the Pope, the Orthodox more Greek than Alexander the Great, the Anglican more English than the Archbishop of Canterbury, the Lutheran more German than Luther, and the Southern Baptists more American than George Washington.

Anglicans among us, despite the suffering we underwent at the hands of the British during the Mandate, continued meticulously to maintain the Anglican form in our churches: the prayer books, life style, and even the cathedral talk, which was always in the King's English. With some of us, it reached the point where Anglicans insisted on taking high tea at four o'clock Greenwich Mean Time. Some continue to this day to believe that an Englishman, and after him an American, is *naturally* more competent than an Arab! This is a phenomenon found not only in the Anglican church. The Greek churches continue to believe that their hierarchy should be Greek, the American Baptists have their 'home boards' in which Americans supervise the work of local churches and the Roman Catholic holy sites are tended by expatriate Franciscan friars.

In Israel again, Jewish fears over recent developments in Europe are being linked to the spectre of anti-semitism as a basic tenet of Christianity, and currently we are witnessing very negative articles in the Israeli press on the role of the Anglican church in Israel and Palestine, which has been also accused of being a tool of the PLO.

For their part, Muslims in the region reacted very sensitively to statements by the Anglican hierarchy in the West concerning relations with Arab countries, such as the Archbishop of Canterbury's declaration that the 1991 Gulf War was a just war. In Israel we have attempts to sow discord between the Christian and Muslim communities, for example by referring to church support for local Christians as 'Crusades'. The Anglican community, often perceived as a westernized community, is particularly affected by such charges.

In the Holy Land we are particularly aware of the lack of understanding of local Christians shown by pilgrims from the West, many of whom visit the Christian Holy Places, with Jewish Israeli guides, and are warned not to leave the group because of the dangerous Arabs around. Most of them are not aware that these 'dangerous' Arabs they see are their brothers and sisters in Christ.

The pressure on Middle East Christians in general, and in particular on those identified with Western churches, is responsible in large part for the serious exodus of Anglicans from the region.

Anglicans and Other Middle East Christians

The diocese in Jerusalem is active in both regional and world-wide ecumenism. It was one of the founder-members of the Near East Council of Churches, formed in this century. It has also served with sister churches in developing the work of the Council into a full regional ecumenical Council, comprising all Orthodox, Oriental Orthodox, Anglican and other Protestant churches, and Catholic churches in the Middle East, into what is now the Middle East Council of Churches. Through the Central Synod the diocese is represented on the World Council of Churches and continues to support its ecumenical activities.

The diocese is resuming its special relationship with the Lutheran Church of Jordan, and it is in partnership with the Finnish Lutheran Mission in Lod, the Association of Churches and Missions, South Western Germany (EMS), the Church of Scotland in the Holy Land, the Presbyterian Church of the USA, the United Methodist Church, USA, World Vision International, the Association of Evangelical Churches in the Middle East, the Uniting Church of Australia, and others.

The recent decision of the Anglican community in Britain to permit the ordination of women to the priesthood was registered with great disapproval by our Orthodox and Catholic friends in the region, who are also very perturbed about the discussion on homosexuality in the Anglican community. I would like to urge a discussion of these issues among the Anglicans of the region, to work out our own position regarding them.

Personal Significance of Being an Anglican in the Middle East

As an Arab Palestinian Christian living in a Jewish state in a predominantly Muslim region, I have experienced all the problems of identity described above. In general I may say that nothing of the culture of this region – which is my culture – confirms my identity as an Anglican, i.e., as a member of a church which has its roots in English culture. I feel it is self-evident that such a situation must lead to severe inner tensions which negatively affect our ability as pastors to give the required guidance to our people.

I would also like to mention my increasing difficulty with our official name, the 'Evangelical Episcopal Church'. Originally the term Evangelical was intended to emphasize our attachment to the Gospels and the right of Anglicans to seek spiritual sustenance in the Gospels, a right denied by the eastern churches to their lay members. However, since Christian fundamentalists have taken the term 'evangelical' to describe their mission I fear that the term can give rise to misunderstandings.

Future of the Dioceses and the Province

The future development of the diocese of Jerusalem, and indeed of the province, depends largely on the outcome of the peace process, in turn influenced by the United States' conception of its role as sole remaining superpower, as it will be defined by President Clinton.

In a region of open borders and prosperity resulting from stability and new trade markets, Christians, especially Anglicans with their traditional links with the United States and Europe, would be predestined to play a central role. Peace and stability in the region would make it possible to resolve the inner conflict in Middle Eastern Anglican Christians.

If, however, the region continues to be racked by instability, and Muslim and Jewish fundamentalists increase their influence in their respective communities, I fear that we will see further emigration of the Christians of the region until there are none left at all! Our efforts must be focused on preventing this exodus. I would like to see more effort on the part of Anglicans, together with fellow-Christians, to bring our situation home to those outside the region, so that we may gain world-wide support in our struggle to keep the community alive.

13

The Spiritual Significance and Experience of the Churches: The Orthodox Perspective

Gabriel Baramki

The Orthodox Church is the indigenous church of the land where Christianity itself originated. How are we to feel as Christians in the land, as the people who have lived there from time immemorial? We can relate to the first Christians as simple people: simple folk who followed the exemplary life of Christ. Although of different backgrounds and different races in the land where Christ lived and taught, they simply followed His teachings. They lived, and related to the land in which they lived.

This is how I look at Orthodox Christians who have been living in the Holy Land for generations. At times, we were the majority, at others, we were simply part of the larger society. With the advent of Islam, we continued to live there as Christians, relating to one another and living in harmony with the community and with our surroundings. I look at this in the way that I look at a Palestinian house that has been lived in by successive generations, across the centuries. It is built with the material of the land as endowed by God – built with plenty of stones and rocks! It is massive, but is in harmony with its surroundings. It stands solid and is built for successive generations, not just for one or two centuries, but for the whole span of our history. We look now at how people lived all their lives and developed these houses; adjusting them to keep in harmony within the structure of our society. In retrospect, we recognise how this Palestinian house was built and how suitable its construction was, and is at a time when we are concerned about the political and social environment. We wish to ensure that this house remains cool in summer and warm in winter – to balance the outside elements. Thereby it will remain serene and in harmony with its physical surroundings.

This is also how I look at the Christians of the land, living in harmony with their brethren and neighbours, who have been oppressed just as they and their brethren are now oppressed, occupied, and fighting for liberation. They fight for their humanitarian rights side by side with the other indigenous people who have other faiths. So the Christians of the Holy Land not only fought the Ottomans and rose up against them, but in earlier times fought foreign Latin Christians during the Crusader period, and the Romans before them. But at all times they were Palestinians, and felt as one would expect an indigenous people of a land to feel anywhere else in the world.

The land is central to the life of our people and especially now. We say that while Christianity is spiritual, in practical terms, we must keep our feet on the ground – our ground. We have to live in our land in order to experience both the spiritual part of our Christianity and to have physical experience of life in the place where Christ himself lived and taught. To us, these things are not only symbolic, but factual. They are there. You cannot separate the physical presence of the Church of the Holy Sepulchre in Jerusalem from the immense concept of the Resurrection. When you are there, you feel it all around and within you.

So 'being' is important. Bishop Cragg said that we have a feeling that goes back to 'the being', and that you cannot separate the geography from either the whole panorama of history nor the spiritual experience of belonging. This is how I see these things as an Orthodox Christian, who has lived there all his life: as did our ancestors before us.

I often wonder how it is that I am a Christian, and how my ancestors at the time of Christ, became Christians. Now there are those who demand that I leave my land. I am expected to lose the right to be in the land of Christ, simply because my ancestors became Christian. I am not asking this question of this audience here but of all Christians everywhere who are supposed to be fighting for Christianity in this Holy Land. This is, I think, the crux of the issue when we talk about the Christians of the Holy Land, be they Orthodox or of other denominations. Are we Palestinian Christians, because of our Christianity, to lose our physical rights of tenure and become as homeless wanderers cast adrift in a new diaspora?

14

Relations between Religions in Historic Palestine and the Future Prospects: Christians and Jews

Salim J Munayer

As I am speaking about the relationship between Christians and Jews, my perspective comes from being a Palestinian Christian and a citizen of the State of Israel. As a Christian from a Greek Orthodox background, born in the city of Lydda, no doubt my view has been shaped by the reality of the State of Israel and the relationship between Palestinians and Israeli Jews, especially in view of the situation in the occupied West Bank and Gaza.

I am a teacher at Bethlehem Bible College responsible for academics. Almost every day as we study the Bible, we are confronted by the reality of the relationship between Palestinians and Israeli Jews. Add to that the fact that I am the Head of Musalaha, a ministry with the aim of bringing about reconciliation between Palestinian Arabs and Israeli Jews on the basis of the Scriptures. In other words, my view of the relationship between Palestinians and Israeli Jews is shaped by who I am, with what I am involved, and what I experience every day.

Most of the current discussions and articles related to the relationship between Christians and Jews come from the perspective of western Christians and Jewish people. In those discussions there are several main issues.[1] To quote Naim Ateek, 'As a Palestinian Christian, it is very interesting to note that such dialogue groups have never been too successful in attracting the participation of indigenous Christian Arabs . . . The basis of dialogue between Jews and western Christians since the creation of the State has been three-fold: anti-semitism, the Holocaust and the existence of the State of Israel.'[2] Though these may be important issues they do not have much relevance for the indigenous Palestinian Christian. For this reason, I must make a distinction between the western Christian community and the local Palestinian Christian community.

From my own experience of participating in the dialogue groups, most of the western Christians who reside in Israel are preoccupied with being allowed to remain in the land, and with their religious freedom. This issue has been highlighted as a result of the anti-missionary law.[3] Another phenomenon on those dialogues is that often Christians are asked to compromise on their belief in the uniqueness of Jesus, and on their commitment to communicate their faith in Jesus as the Messiah to the Jewish people. One of the greatest weaknesses of dialogue between Christians and Jews is that it involves a very small cross section of the population and does not touch the mainstream of Israeli society.

I would now like to address the Christian Jewish relationships which I consider most important: the relationship between Israeli Jews and the local Palestinian Christians, as opposed to the relationship between the Jewish people and the corporate Christian world.

Under the Ottoman empire. Christians and Jews in the Holy Land functioned under the *millet* system, a system which allowed local minorities a degree of autonomy. Each of those communities struggled to survive as non-Muslim communities. As minorities they did not share the same relationship as Jews and Christians in Europe, where there was a Jewish minority and a Christian majority.

The major factor in the 20th century that changed the relationship between Christians and Jews in the Holy Land was, and continues to be, the struggle between the Palestinian national movement and the Zionist movement which set out to establish a homeland for the Jewish people. There is a dichotomy here. The Zionist movement succeeded in establishing a state and the Palestinians are still struggling.

In this struggle Palestinian Christians took a leading role in the

---

[1] 'The Tantur Dialogue on the Holy Land', by Thomas F Stransky, CSP, *The Catholic World*, Jan-Feb. 1991, pp. 44-46.

[2] 'An Arab-Israeli's Theological Reflections on the State of Israel after Forty Years', *People, Land and the State of Israel*, p. 106.

[3] 'Christians in Israel: Situations and Expectations', by the Revd Fr. Frans Bouwen; *Freedom of Religion and Conscience in Israel*, by the Liaison Committee of the United Christian Council In Israel, November 1976.

nationalistic struggle, and the role of religion became secondary. I must say that in this struggle some racist and anti-Jewish statements have been expressed, but this has to be looked on in the context of the nationalist struggle. Because the Palestinian people see themselves as semitic people, the anti-semitism of Europe to a large degree is foreign to them.

As the nationalist struggle intensified before and after the Second World War, many Jewish refugees were coming from Europe to Palestine. The Palestinian Christians, of course, did not see themselves responsible for the Holocaust. As a matter of fact, I myself came to the horrifying realization of the Holocaust only in my adult life as I was studying in school, and during my visit to Germany. The discussion of the Holocaust between Jews and Christians is foreign to the Palestinian.

The major factor that has influenced the relationship between Palestinian Christians and Jews was the formation of the State of Israel. As a result of the war in 1948, many Palestinians, including Christians, found themselves refugees. Those who were able to remain in the State of Israel came to a new reality; the reality of being a minority not only in a Muslim society, but a minority in a Jewish state. Those years were very difficult as the Palestinian people in the State of Israel were under military law. They had to learn how to relate to their new reality. As a result of the formation of the state, much land and property owned by Palestinians was lost, not to mention the human cost of that era. As I talk with my parents and people of their generation, they tell me that those were very painful and difficult years. They were struggling to survive economically, and to re-establish the religious and economic institutions to meet their needs. It was not until martial law was abolished in the mid-60s that their civil rights were restored to a greater degree.

For western Christians the establishment of the State of Israel raised several theological issues, about the role of the Jewish people, and the relationship between the Church and the Jewish people. Western Christians sought a new perspective on the role of the Jewish people which accorded with the Bible. Some saw in the establishment of the state a solution for the persecuted Jews in Europe, and a sign of the end times. But for the Palestinian Christian, the creation of the State of Israel was a painful experience, a feeling that an unjust act had been committed against them. And from that suffering the Palestinian Christians asked themselves whether the establishment of the Jewish state was God's will, and, if so, why were they suffering?

The main objective of the Christians in the Holy Land who were made citizens of the State of Israel is to ensure that their nationalistic, ethnic, and religious identity be equal to that of the Jewish people in the state. Often this group of Christians feels that their destiny has been shaped and determined by a Jewish majority. There is a tension in the way Israel defines itself. Israel describes itself as a democratic state, on the one hand, but on the other, as a Jewish state. In many respects, the two definitions, democratic and Jewish, contradict each other.

The Jewish people, by themselves, struggle to define the questions, Who is a Jew?, or, Which strand of Judaism is the official one? At present, the Orthodox strand seems to be in the forefront. However, this does not represent truly the sentiments of the majority of the Jews in Israel, a fact which creates tension among the Jewish people themselves. Another related question is, Which law will eventually shape the State of Israel? Is Israel going to go according to the Western model of a democratic state, and have a constitution that she does not have now? Or will the Jewish law, the *Halakah*, take more and more precedence. Often it depends on the political games between the different religious parties when it comes to forming the coalition government. The vagueness of the situation reflects also on the Christian community.

Over the years there has been an increase in the extreme Jewish religious nationalist movement, emphasizing the desire that the State of Israel be exclusively Jewish. Its members have strong negative feelings toward Christians. They want to make into a law certain Jewish interpretations of *Halakah*, which say that Christians are pagan worshippers, and that they defile Jerusalem. They would propose that a non-Jew who wishes to live in a Jewish state would have to accept three conditions: according to Rambam, these conditions are: 1) acceptance of the seven commandments of the sons of Noah, from the book of Genesis, 2) tax regulations, and, 3) a condition of slavery.[4]

Even the former Sephardic Chief Rabbi of Israel, Ovadia Josef, seems to believe that Christians are pagan worshippers. Amnon Rubenstein quotes the Chief Sephardic Rabbi as saying that there is a need for a commandment to burn the New Testament, and separate the Old Testament from it (*HaEretz*, 23 Oct. 1979). It was reported in the newspaper *MaAriv* (14 June 1985) that the New Testament had been found in the library of army bases and burned by the rabbi of the base. Moreover, Rav Zvi Yehuda Kook, the rabbi most respected by the Jewish nationalist movement, defines Christians as pagan. Obviously defining Christians as people who worship a pagan God has implications for the Palestinian Christian today. Today in many of Israeli's religious Jewish schools it is forbidden to teach the New Testament.

In addition, in June 1985, extremist groups related to Meir Kahane

---

[4] See Y Harkabi, 'Fateful Decisions', 1986, chapter 4, section 7, *The State of the Stranger in the Jewish State*, who wrote the book out of concern about the danger of the militant religious right wing.

circulated leaflets advocating that Christians be kicked out of the country, especially from Jerusalem. There are anti-Christian and 'anti-crossism' sentiments in some sectors of Jewish society. It is a new phenomenon that was not expressed by Jewish people in the West.

The following pointers characterize Palestinian Christians who are citizens of the State of Israel:

1 Palestinian Christians call for equal rights in all spheres of life. They want to highlight the fact that they are Palestinians, that they have the right to express their Palestinian identity and culture in the framework of the State of Israel, and that this identity will not be suppressed.

2 As the majority of Palestinians are law abiding, they have the right to receive the same economic opportunities, as their fellow Jewish citizens. It is an important factor in stabilizing their communities, and in fighting against the emigration of the Christians, which is due to housing and economic conditions.

3 The Palestinian Christians in the State of Israel are calling for freedom of religion for all religious groups, not only freedom of worship, but the freedom to be able to express their faith to others without restrictions.

4 Christians are called to be peacemakers. Palestinian Christians call for peace between Israeli Jews and Palestinians. Palestinian Christians want to see an end to the occupation in the West Bank and Gaza, so that their people will be able to form their destiny and to shape their future. Most Christian Palestinians in Israel want to see a Palestinian State alongside Israel, with both states co-existing in peace.

These factors are a condition for a fruitful and healthy dialogue between Jews and Christians in Israel. Many people, especially Westerners, approach the subject of the relationship between Jews and Christians from a theological perspective. But the reality of the life of Palestinian Christians affects seriously their ability to dialogue with Jews.

Another significant issue that is colouring the relationship between Christians and Jews in the Holy Land is the terrible situation of the occupation in the West Bank. We cannot avoid the subject. It is one of the fundamental issues that is affecting the relationship. The daily misery, the killings, and the economic conditions sometimes make it impossible to see a positive light in the relationship between Jews and

Palestinian Christians in the occupied territories. For the majority of the Palestinian Christians in the occupied territories, their experiences with the Jews differ to a large degree from the Palestinian Christians living in the State of Israel. In the occupied territories the Jew is the policeman. the soldier, or the employer. In almost all of these encounters the Palestinian experience is negative. The inability to have control over the basic elements of one's livelihood, land, water, identity is a frustrating experience. Seeing how more and more land is being confiscated, more civil and human rights have been taken away, perceiving that maybe there is no future for oneself and one's children can lead many to hate the Jewish people. In this encounter, many Palestinians in the occupied territories experience aggressiveness, humiliation, and the violation of human dignity which leave deep scars. Those scars cause people to be angry, bitter and, in some cases, to have a blind hatred for the Jewish people.

It is such a pity that both Jews and Palestinians who have suffered so much are now inflicting suffering upon one another.

One other important issue that influences the relationship between Christians and Jews in the Holy Land is the question of Jerusalem. The status of Jerusalem will affect, and already is affecting the relationship between Jews and Christians.[5] Some western Christians will accept the fact that they have access to the Holy Places, and can study in the Holy Land, while Palestinian Christians for their part are concerned about the process of elevating the Jewish Quarter of Jerusalem above the others. Taking over houses in the Old City, like St John's Hospice, alerted many to ask how the Jews see the future of Jerusalem, not only in relationship to the Christians, but also to the Muslims, and to the whole issue of the Mosque or the Temple Mount. Palestinian Christians see Jerusalem as their spiritual, cultural and national capital. And to a large degree, it is already their capital. The question of Jerusalem is the most difficult one. It is a great concern that all communities that live in Jerusalem, Jewish, Christian and Muslim, would be able to prosper, without this being at the expense of the other.

What are the future prospects?

As long as one community has the upper hand over the other, it will be very difficult to have healthy relationships between the communities. It is important to realize that the struggle between Israeli Jews and the Palestinian people will not come to a solution until the issue of the occupied territories is resolved. Resolution of this issue will open a new horizon for the encounter between Palestinians Christians and Israeli Jews.

---

[5] *Jerusalem, Past and Present in the Purposes of God*, ed. Peter Walker, Cambridge, 1992.

Palestinian Christians and Jews, as a result of their experiences as minorities, should have a greater sense of understanding and compassion for one another. Both communities must have the courage to return to the Scriptures that both share – the Bible. We need to emphasize the biblical truth that we are all created in God's image and His likeness, and as such that we have a responsibility towards each other to fight against the mutual dehumanization and demonization of the Palestinians and the Jews.

We need to go back to the biblical message that election is related to the blessing. For when God chose Abraham, He chose him to be a blessing to all nations. Of Abraham's election, God says (Gen 18.19), 'For I have chosen him so that he will direct his children and his household after them, that he will keep the way of the Lord by doing what is right and just, so that the Lord will bring about for Abraham what he has promised him.'

As Arabs and Jews, calling ourselves children of Abraham, we are called to behave like Abraham's children. Our father, Abraham, desired that his children would be reconciled to each other.

The major issue of land and peoplehood is that if we are created in God's image, and if God is the Lord of nations, of history and of all the earth, then there are two people on this piece of land. Perhaps it is God's election or destiny that Palestinians and Jews learn to live and to share God's creation together.

It is a difficult task to rise above the pain, the anguish and the hatred, and to ask for God's mercy to acknowledge that we are human beings, and that God is the only absolute. We need to seek Him and his grace and mercy so that He can help us to find ways in which we can accept each other, respect each other, and bless each other with our heritage.

The lesson of history, especially for minorities in the Middle East, causes them to look for assurance for their survival, not only from the ruling community. There is a need to find a way in which human rights, religious freedom and expression can be guaranteed to all and protected in the Holy Land.

Palestinian Christians and Israeli Jews need to recognize that much pain has been inflicted on each other. We need to move from blaming each other to reconciliation and restoration.

As a Palestinian Christian, even though I have personally suffered many acts of injustice, I am asking God to give me the power to forgive and to reconcile. If I am called a Christian Palestinian, I have a commitment and obligation toward my Palestinian people and their future and welfare. At the same time I have an obligation to my Lord to love my enemies, to break the circle of hatred and enmity and violence, to be a peacemaker, and to look for practical ways for peace between Jews and Arabs. We as Palestinian Christians can play an important role, and be an avenue of peace.

I ask the Jewish people to go back to the Scriptures, to their history, and to see what they have already achieved, and to open their hearts to the desire of their fellow Palestinian brothers and sisters, to rise above hatred, paranoia and insecurity, and to find a way of mutual respect and common prosperity. As Palestinian Christians, we need to assure the Jewish people of our sincere desire for peace.

These are the foundations for the future. I conclude with a verse from the First Letter of John, 'If anyone says, I love God, yet hates his brother, he is a liar. For anyone who does not love his brother, whom he has seen, cannot love God, whom he has not seen. And he has given us this command: Whoever loves God must also love his brother' (4.20f.).

VIEWS FROM OUTSIDE

15

Beginning at Jerusalem
The Church's Story –
Then and Now
Kenneth Cragg

I

Great literature needs and finds great beginnings. Consider Melville's *Moby Dick*, opening with, 'Call me Ishmael . . . ' and at once the reader is enigmatically summoned into the sea-drama of the Ishmael who is both theme and narrator, and whom we will know at the end as the sole survivor of the whale-boat, *Pequod's*, fate. Or Hamlet, with the harassed sentry on guard challenged – in an odd reversal of how it should be – by the soldier coming to relieve him. There is the un-answered question of the whole play: 'Who goes there?' 'What a piece of work is man.'

Where does Christianity begin and how? Who were 'the first Christians?' The Letter to the Ephesians (1.12) addresses them as 'those who first trusted in Christ.' But they were only the first generation in Ephesus. What of their predecessors before the faith reached that city? You will all have your ideas.

I want to make my candidate for 'the first Christian' the man alongside Jesus on one of those Good Friday crosses. The reason why will permeate all that follows. I mean the brigand of whom Luke tells us, who said: 'Lord, remember me when you come into your kingdom' (Luke 23.42). We must perceive him reading the crown of thorns, if not also the titulus overhead about 'the king of the Jews.' In the dust and agony of that hour, he sensed a 'kingdom' and wanted to be part of it. He was, surely, the very first recruit to what became the core and heart of Christianity. However dimly, he had glimpsed the clue to Messiah in one who, not being overcome by evil, was overcoming evil with good by a love that prayed forgiveness on the perpetrators. In the event that would later be described by the faith that knew it as 'the sin of the world,' there was a sovereignty waiting to be read as kingly in the meaning of 'the kingdom of God.'

This nameless man – shall we call him Bar-Emunah, 'the son of faith'?- had realised where God was, namely there in this mysterious sufferer. He was assured by Jesus of inclusion in 'the kingdom.' What there transpired became the central theme of the first apostles. It passed steadily through them into credal faith. They, to be sure, had priority over this late recruit, yet he – Bar Emunah – had preceded them, fugitives as they were, in what would become the very heart of their Gospel. As intimates of the Galilean ministry only they could integrate its story into the final text of faith. But that text came finally to the full only from the Passion. Jesus suffered as he did because he taught as he did, and, suffering, he continued to teach. The whole was a seamless robe like the one over which the soldiers diced. It was beyond the Cross and the Resurrection that those disciples of the teacher became apostles of the Lord. The final crisis, which had shattered them into despair and dispersion, reinstated them in courage and discerning faith. In their transformation the Church was born, but only thanks to the meanings the climax had transacted.

There were three of these meanings. The first was the realised Messiahship of Jesus, now defined, identified and achieved in the terms Bar-Emunah had agonisingly recognised. The second was the opening out of 'peoplehood to God' to all and sundry on the sole basis of faith, irrespective of birth, sex, race, or culture, with none 'already there' through special privilege denied to others, and with 'all believers' equally welcome. That 'church-event' – as we must call it – followed hard on the 'Christ-event' and as its necessary sequel. The third was the emerging theology which came to read both these events as being what they were thanks to the very nature of God – 'God in Christ reconciling the world.' (2 Corinthians 5.18). Christian faith came to God 'in Christ' only because 'in Christ' God was fully understood. Only as these were seen and known to be inseparable could there be faith in either. 'The Christ of God' (Christology) was the disclosure of 'God in Christ,' theology's sufficient referent.

This threefold thing is what 'began in Jerusalem', deciding, developing, defining, what created the first Christians. We can see them fleetingly anticipated by the yearning of one who did not survive the throes of his dawning faith. But the reason for starting with him will now be clear. We can best explore our three dimensions by his light, acknowledging that all faith needs to say was implicit in the loyalty and love of those first apostles.

II

Everything both before and after the climax of the Passion had to do with what could be described as 'the verification of Messiah.' The who? and how? and when? and where? of that concept had long preoccupied the Jewish mind. It was a central focus of Jesus' ministry. The question turned on what was the Messianic task. That hinged on reading the situation the task had to address. Was it the power of Rome as something to be thrown off? Was it Jewish liberation by a renewal of Davidic-style kingship or Aaronic priesthood, or some dual action of both? Was it the whole nation somehow saving itself by a pure Sabbath? If so, should this be sought by a 'remnant' – in despair of 'the whole' – withdrawing to the wilderness? There were other theories also and a wild diversity of zealots for them.

It is important for us to recognise that this Messianic hope owed itself to the biblical doctrine of creation and human creaturehood. That concept meant that history had a purpose of good, under God, but entrusted to man. The Jewish faith included this basic humanism but saw 'the human' as somehow distinctively committed to Jewry, to their story, their territory, their peoplehood (though these denominators of history, land and ancestry characterised all peoples alike). Via Abraham, Jacob/Israel and so David, Jewry understood a unique covenant through which their history, their destiny, would express and realise the divine ends for which all history – thanks to creation – was designed. It was never clear how other than Judaic humanity, the 'Gentiles', would participate in divine-human destiny, except somehow via the 'chosenness' of Jewry.

Messianic identity was all the more puzzling when it was perceived, in bitter experience, that it was precisely Judaic history that had gone awry and failed to deliver the true human-ness under God. Despite 'the Law and the Prophets', wrong, sin, evil, and exile supervened. This was the situation the Messianic hope had to address. It was bound up with the vindication of God Himself. For if there was to be genuine faith in the purpose of creation, there would have to be hope through and beyond what creaturehood in history had done to it. Broadly, through numerous conflicts of mind, and jostle of ideas, this was the place for 'the answer' which Messiah would supposedly be.

We must keep that inclusive understanding in mind in the light of Christian origins. But, first, we must note how Jesus' own ministry was spent in this ambiguous scene. The Gospels make this very clear. His teaching and healing not only challenged the establishment but were perceived by many as portents of the benedictions they awaited. In the mystery of his personality Jesus seemed well cast to fill the role of the awaited one. Certainly, if he had chosen to go the zealot way, Pilate would have had more to do than wash his hands. Christian faith believes there was another logic. Jesus perceived that his message, lived and preached, encountered hostility, that his pathway was descending into sharp engagement with evil forces, pride, expediency, callousness and wrong. His was a darkening path. This is partly the clue to the contrast between Galilee and Jerusalem, and to the necessity he felt to bring his meaning to the central shrine of Jewish sanctity and tradition. The Gospels make very clear this sense of things impending, of suffering ahead, of enmities his Gospel evoked which would later be characterised as 'the sin of the world.'

The precedent of 'the suffering servant' was in his mind, as of one, or ones, who had borne calumny and shame as the price of fidelity to truth, and whose travail availed to liberate and redeem those who understood its meaning. It would seem to have been the 'genius' (or as Scripture would say 'the Sonship') of Jesus to trace in this tradition the very clue to 'Messiah.' At least, after Easter, the first Christians came to see it so, and it seems incredible that they could have done so without him, or in contradiction to his mind. He was made perfect as 'the author of salvation,' by 'the things that he suffered' (Hebrews 5.8: *emathen . . . epathen* – a Greek play on words – 'learning . . . suffering'). 'Learn of me,' he had said, and the Cross was where the lesson was most inclusive. What it taught was that the love that suffers is the power that redeems, that only when evil is forgivingly borne is it borne away so that 'forgiven-ness' may be ours. This is what Bar-Emunah had first identified and received. The Christian faith and the Christian Church began at the same place. In the event where we could inclusively register, qualitatively, 'the sin of the world' we could know 'the Lamb of God' who bore it away (John 1.29).

III

Messiahship, realised in these terms, could not fail to be inclusive, incorporating all humanity in its embrace. For it was not concerned politically with Rome, nor exclusively with Jewry, nor unilaterally with 'chosen people.' Whoever would could come. Any and all – 'believing on this Name,' i.e., realising this love, – were freely admissible to grace within an open peoplehood to God. The age-old problem of what to think about 'the Gentiles' would be resolved by their inclusion, and thus the Judaic would truly become the index to the human in universal terms, all nations bringing their glory and honour into this kingdom.

This is what 'began at Jerusalem,' what transpired in the New Testament – not abrogation or supersession, but fulfilment. This Messiah-Jesus belonged with the primal inclusiveness of biblical creation, but also fulfilled the destiny of Abraham and 'his seed.' This is why Jerusalem is birthplace to Christianity, but only as 'the base-camp' of a new worldwideness, a 'diaspora' of grace which (as we know from Paul's Gentile offertory) always looked back fraternally to the city and people of its origins.

It is, therefore, strange to read in *Pilgrims to the Holy Land* by Teddy Kollek and Moshe Perlman:[1]

> Christianity, . . . sprang up and developed far from the scene of Jesus' last ministry, notably in Antioch and other parts of the Middle East and the eastern Mediterranean, where his disciples recounted his teachings, his parables, the stories of his miracles in his lifetime and his resurrection and ascension. Jerusalem itself . . . remained comparatively untouched by the views expounded by the latest victim of Rome.

Hardly so. One only has to ask why his disciples should have been so far from 'base,' in the first place? Had Jerusalem been untouched there would have been no thrust to take them into ventures beyond it. Nor must we allow the implication here that the new faith was some Hellenist entity. All its first apostles were Jews. The Gospel and the Church were Jerusalem-born, precisely in not being Jerusalem-confined. It was from Jewish factors that they had their genesis.

It is true – as New Testament scholarship readily allows – that there were tensions between Jerusalem and the dispersion, between strong traditionalists and new communities. For the strains and pains of the new openness were sharp and costly. Perhaps, also, we may read in the structure of the Gospels themselves strenuous issues between ardent custodians of the words of Jesus and those who centred his significance squarely in the Passion.[2] However, it is fair to see in the New Testament itself, as a document, the evidence of an achieved inclusiveness. For

---

[1] New York, 1970, pp. 28-29.
[2] I.e., the people who cherished what have come to be known as 'the Q sayings,' (from *Quelle* – 'a source') if they were a clear cut community among the early Christians. But they could in no way have been unaware of what had happened to their teacher in the final climax of the Cross.

without this its problems, indeed its very pages, would not exist. Men do not send epistles to a dispersion that is not in being, nor would they want to do so if it were not understood to be one fellowship. 'Gospels' are not necessary where there is no retrospect to fill them, no clientele to want them through widening lands and lapsing years. The Christ-event and the church-event explain and fulfil each other.

IV

What 'began in Jerusalem' in these terms – our third point – must be understood as having 'begun in God'. So much John's prologue insists: 'In the beginning was the Word . . . ' – that 'Word' of creation originating the world to which, in due time, after history had disclosed its waywardness, Messiah would have to relate. 'And the Word was made flesh and dwelt among us . . . All was from God and in God.' It cannot otherwise be rightly understood for what it was. Such is the import of the Incarnation. If we may employ a metaphor from drama, we have 'the mind which gives it being' in the stage-enactment which gives it expression. Authorship is both. This was the faith the Church came to express in the terms, during early centuries, which its culture afforded, concerning 'being' and 'substance' and 'person.' Within them there was always the Hebraic conviction that God is 'Self-given' in events, in history where experience spells knowledge. That instinct enabled the theology of the first, and subsequent, Christians to take the event of Christ's Passion as the index to the very nature of God. They were only warranted in doing so if, conversely, they could think that it was ultimately in such love as they saw in Christ that divine power and sovereignty were defined.

Ongoing Christian story in the lands of its initiation I must leave to others. Through all vicissitudes and chances, tragic and heroic, splendid and mundane, 'God in Christ,' 'the Christ in God,' has been its theme, its mandate and its confidence. These its creeds have enshrined and its sacraments transacted. These are its witness still – the sum of its being and the heart of its vocation. For these the mysterious gift of tongues: for these the promise of the unfailing Spirit. Here, in this 'temple of his body,' is the risen-ness of Christ – the Christ according to Jesus, 'pioneer and consummator of our faith.' (Hebrews 12.2).

This founding Christian theology, inter-relating the Christhood of Jesus crucified and the nature of God, became in the New Testament the ground of Christian ethics, the criterion and motive of Christian behaviour. To 'believe in the forgiveness of sins' was not only to receive it through Christ but to practise it 'in Christ.' The 'mind' he had, they were to share. As 1 Peter said, they were to 'follow his steps' (2.21). This is the meaning of 'his Easter in us.' It has been said that Jesus, through Holy Week towards Gethsemane, was 'riding into the setting sun.' If so, then it was also into the new day of 'knowledge and love of God,' the dawn of community in open grace.

Let me leave it there. It only remains to remember how the authorial Luke in his second treatise for Theophilus, the Greek 'lover of God,' captures the entire meaning in the record of Pentecost. Peter in his sermon is enthusing in 'the Christ-event' – 'this Jesus, crucified, made Lord and Christ,' but his context is 'the Church-event.' Jerusalem the locale; Jews and devout men of every nation (however circumscribed Peter's geography): 'wind and fire' the symbols of the whence and whither, and 'mere Galileans' vocal to the ends of the earth in all human audition: and all in the energy of the Holy Spirit, the power and the wisdom of 'God told in Christ,' and Christ 'the telling of God.'

I have reflected how everything began 'at Jerusalem' with its Galilean antecedents. Let us not think that this is all remote from our present fears and hopes, our own deep preoccupations. For if we are rightly to discern our contemporary vocation and to fulfil it aright, we must know from where our very being derives.

16

Christians in the Holy Land

Michael Nazir Ali

I speak as someone who has some little experience of the world-wide church, principally, of course, the churches of the Anglican Communion and United Churches, but also Christians of many other denominations, because the Anglican desire has been in many cases, in India and in the Middle East and in Ethiopia, not to proselytise but to assist. It is true that Anglican churches have come into being from time to time in these places, but where ancient churches exist our policy has been to strengthen them and to work for renewal in their corporate life.

As I meet Christians from different traditions, I find that the Holy Land is important for Christians all over the world. I understand language about every place 'being hallowed ground'. Nevertheless, I find that Christians in different parts of the world hold a special place for the Holy Land in their hearts, and not only the Holy Land but also for Christians from the Holy Land. I remember, as a very young man, finding myself sitting next to a Christian from Bethlehem on Christmas Eve in a church. That totally and quite radically altered my perception of Christmas, for that year at any rate, and I still think of that encounter; it was very special. Christians should want to be in solidarity with all those who seek justice and peace anyway, but particularly with those who seek justice, and with justice, peace, in the land of our Lord.

So that is the perspective from which I come, and as I go around the world and meet Christians from different parts of the world, I am very conscious of a change in Christian demography. This is often overlooked. The reality now is that the majority of Christians are not to be found any more in the so-called Christian West, but in Africa, in Asia, and in Latin America. One result of this may be that the church is less powerful, and that Christians may be more powerless in world terms, but it also affords opportunities for solidarity among the poor and the oppressed which have not been taken into account as much as they might have been. The change in Christian demography affords a new opportunity for Christians from the Holy Land to relate to the poor and the oppressed in other parts of the world.[1]

I confine my reflections to five areas, the significance of the place, the significance of the people, the church's contribution to progress, participation in politics by Christians and a programme for peace. Christians from the Holy Land have strong views on all of these matters, but these are reflections 'from the outside' on how things look to Christians who are very deeply interested in fellow believers from the Holy Land, and who have love and concern for them.

The Christian faith is not only historical, but it is also geographical, in that God's revelation was made at a time and in a place, or rather, in different places. The significance then of 'the Bible lands', is there for Christians and, of course, these 'Bible lands' are not limited to the Holy Land, they can be made to stretch from Ethiopia to north west India, perhaps, what is now Pakistan! But the Holy Land, nevertheless, has a very special place among the Bible lands and a place that we cannot ignore as the locus of God's revelation of himself, of his covenant with his people and of his universal purposes. All these things have to be held together in a kind of tension. But because it is a locus of God's revelation, it is also a place for *reverence*. Many of the parts of the world where the Christian faith and Christian churches are growing very rapidly, have what we may call sacramental cultures; people have a strong and a high view of the value of the visible and of the capacity of the visible and the material to mediate the spiritual. The material then can mediate the spirit and the land, naturally, is important in that respect. But opportunities for pilgrimage to the Holy Land, for people from many different parts of the world, have, paradoxically, become more circumscribed in a world of greater mobility, and it may be that Christians from the West are perhaps taking more than their fair share in this respect. I was very pleasantly surprised by encountering some Nigerian Christians in Jerusalem about two years ago. They said that they had persuaded their government to provide facilities for them to visit Jerusalem, just as it provided facilities for Muslims to perform the *Hajj*. That kind of thing will happen more often.

The whole question, then, of reverence for the land, for what has happened there, for the people who have lived there, has to be taken

---

[1] See further Barnett, D B.1982. *World Christian Encyclopaedia*. Oxford.

seriously. But along with reverence there also must be *reflection*, and once again I find that the West, or western churches, have taken many of the opportunities for such reflection for themselves and have not usually easily afforded such opportunities for others on the same scale.

Where reflection is concerned, of course, the history of Christian reflection about the Land goes back, as has been said, to St Jerome and perhaps even before that. The realisation by Christians that to be in the Holy Land is itself an opportunity to reflect on the biblical witness, on the tradition of the church and on its history has to be noted in this context. Perhaps we could note here the contribution of archaeology, and its emergence particularly among those who were concerned to locate the origins of biblical witness in what are material remains in the Bible Lands. The development of archaeology has been closely allied to the development of biblical studies. But there are other kinds of biblical work immediately related to the Land – the allied work that is going on on the Dead Sea Scrolls and the patient establishing of the text, translation, commentary and theological discussion of the significance of some of these texts.

One matter that I wish to note here has particularly to do with Palestinian culture, and this tradition goes back to Abraham Rihbany's book, *The Syrian Christ*. It may go back even earlier, but is carried on today by people like Professor Kenneth Bailey of the Tantur Ecumenical Institute and others. In the 19th century it became very fashionable for people to imagine that it was possible to recover a sense of the biblical witness by observing the customs and the culture of the people of the Bible lands, and especially of Palestine. This was done in an amateur way for a long time, but Kenneth Bailey has made this kind of approach to the study of the Bible more widely accepted. His approach, which is two-pronged, looks at the Bible from the point of view of contemporary Palestinian culture, and tries to illuminate the text from that point of view. That is the beginning of contextual theology. The other great service that he has performed is to highlight the work of the classical Arab commentators throughout the ages, especially from the 8th to the 14th centuries. In fact, Bailey has claimed that next to Latin and Greek there is more Christian literature only in Arabic than in all the other languages! If that is so there is a great deal of research work to be done.[2]

Significance of the place and *significance of the people*. Already, at the time of the Exodus, we read that when the Israelites left Egypt they were joined by a great crowd of oppressed people who experienced the Exodus also as their liberation. And then we find that some Old

[2] Rihbany, A M. 1916. *The Syrian Christ*. Boston: Houghton Mifflin, and Bailey, K E. 1983. *Poet and Peasant Through Peasant Eyes*. Grand Rapids: Eerdmans.

Testament scholars, like Norman Gottwald and Walter Brueggemann, are saying that the arrival and the settlement of the Israelites in Canaan can also be understood in the context of a proletarian revolt against the hierarchical priest–king axis of the Canaanite states. Thus it can be seen as a popular movement in Palestine itself and not just as the arrival of people from outside.[3] And then, of course, there is the function of the Melchisedek accounts in the Hebrew scriptures. We find that the father of the faithful, Abraham the patriarch, makes a tithe offering to Melchisedek who offers him bread and wine (Gen 14.17-20). What is the significance of Melchisedek, already King of Jerusalem, in that context? So we find that from the very beginning there is a kind of mixed population, even according to the accounts in the Hebrew scriptures. But I think we have to say that the people of Israel do have a special place, as it were, in the economy of God. And what is this special place? That is the question they must ask of themselves and that we have to ask about them. And one finds, in reading the Hebrew scriptures, that a particular hermeneutical key is, indeed, the whole question of justice. In the covenant itself we have an encounter with a just God who demands justice from his people, and the prophets are full of this demand for justice, 'Let justice roll down like waters and righteousness like an ever living stream.' (Amos 5.24), and also in Micah the reference to doing justice, to loving kindness and to walking humbly with your God. (Mic 6.8)

Justice is a hermeneutical key to the Hebrew scriptures in many ways. Naim Ateek, in his manifesto for Palestinian liberation theology, has used this in choosing the title *Justice and Only Justice* for his book. He refers to Deuteronomy 16.20 where the word for justice that is used in the Hebrew is *sedeq*. He points out that the rabbinic exegesis of this is that the first justice in this verse refers to justice within Israel, and justice for the people of Israel. But the second justice is justice for the stranger, justice for the neighbour, and justice for those outside the household of Israel. The implication is that justice for one group, even if that group is Israel, cannot be at the expense of justice for others. Justice within Israel and for Israel has to go hand in hand with justice for the stranger.[4]

The Vatican II document *Nostra Aetate* states that there is a continuing covenant which God has with the Jewish people. I affirm this, but also believe that this covenant is a covenant for fulfilment in Christ just as any other kind of preparation for other cultures and for other people. It

---

[3] Gottwald, N K. 1979. *The Tribes of Yahweh: A Sociology of the Religion of Liberated Israel*. New York: Orbis; Brueggemann, W. 1977. *The Land. Place as Gift, Promise, and Challenge in Biblical Faith*. (Overtures to Biblical Theology) Philadelphia: Fortress.

[4] Naim Stifan Ateek. 1989. *Justice and Only Justice. A Palestinian Theology of Liberation*. New York, Maryknoll: Orbis, p. 177.

is not simply that the Jewish people have been replaced by the Christian Church. God has a continuing purpose for them, but that purpose can only be illuminated and fulfilled in Christ. The particularity of the Hebrew scriptures already shows within itself a kind of yearning for universality. The prophets are aware already that if Yahweh is really the God of the whole world, of the whole universe, then he must have a purpose for all the other peoples of the world. This is sometimes seen in a centripetal way, and sometimes even in a centrifugal way, where it is understood that Israel cannot for ever be the centre of the universe, that God's purposes must be fulfilled in many different ways (e.g. the Book of Jonah; Isa 19.25; Amos 9.7).

Of course, it is in the Church as the Israel of God that this universality begins to be realised, but the Church is not yet all tribes and all nations and all peoples worshipping God and praising his work in Jesus Christ. From the very beginning, however, there has been a universal aspect to the Church, a universality which begins to realise what is potential already in the Hebrew scriptures. In this continuing work of being the Israel of God, the Church is not excused this demand for justice, as justice is a hermeneutical key to the Hebrew scriptures, so it must remain for the whole Bible as the Church receives it.

In addressing the significance of the people, reference needs to be made to the continuous Christian presence in the Holy Land. This itself is a kind of miracle. There were many parts of the world where the Church was strong and stronger, perhaps, than in the Holy Land and where it was completely wiped out by the force of historical circumstances; North Africa, for example. This continuous presence encompasses different Christian traditions, and I find that Jerusalem in particular and the Holy Land in general, is a microcosm of the world church. There exist, of course, many tensions within the Christian communities in the Holy Land, but it is very encouraging for a visitor to the Holy Land to see the universality of the church reflected in the place of its origin, that the church has not lapsed into tribalism. This presence has continued through the dispersion of the Jews and the destruction of Jerusalem, the setting up of a pagan city there, and predates Islam. It is a living testimony to faith in the land where it arose. The world and the world church are greatly concerned about the survival of Christian communities in the Holy Land – even in preference to the survival of historical sites and monuments, valuable as they are.

Islam is also an Abrahamic faith. Jerusalem was the first *qibla* to which the Muslims turned in prayer, and perhaps one of the reasons for this was that Mecca was still in the hands of the pagans and the Ka'ba was still full of idols. There was no other option for the Prophet but to direct his followers to turn to Jerusalem for prayer until Mecca had been liberated. The Qu'ran repeatedly claims continuity with the Hebrew and the

Christian tradition – 'We believe in God and the revelation given to us, and to Abraham, Ismail, Isaac, Jacob, and the Tribes, and that given to Moses and Jesus, and that given to all the prophets from their Lord: We make no difference between one and another of them' (Qur'an 2:136). This is an explicit claim to continuity. I find it disturbing when people refer to 'Judaeo-Christian' values or ethics as necessary for particular areas of life such as business, thus seeming to exclude the contribution other faiths could make. Of course, some Jews deny that there is such a thing for their own reasons, but I am disturbed by this because it specifically seems to exclude Islam, and yet in different ways the Christian Church and Islam have inherited common as well as differing aspects of the Hebrew heritage. If there is to be an ethic, whether in business or anywhere else that is to be developed, care should be taken that it is something that can be affirmed by Jews, Christians and Muslims together, and must be so affirmed in a world that is becoming increasingly multi-faith and multi-cultural.

We need to recognise not only the survival of Christian communities in the Holy Land, but also to recognise their contribution. The identification of the holy sites and their preservation has been the task of the Christian communities of the land. To preserve these sites from thieves, from the weather and from war, over the centuries, were not easy tasks for Christian communities in the Holy Land, and as we go around these sites we need to salute these people who have so courageously preserved them. The problems did not have only to do with thieves, weather and war. The *dhimmi* status was conferred on Christians by the Ottoman empire. But to be a *dhimmi*, to be a member of a recognised minority, goes much further back in Islam than the Ottoman dispensation, particularly with respect to the preservation of buildings or Christian churches. The fact of the *dhimmi* status of the communities had an impact on the preservation of these sites.

A picture of the Church of the Holy Sepulchre before the Ottoman empire began to open up in the middle of the 19th century, reveals it to be in a terrible state of repair. The manifesto that 'Umar gave when he accepted the capitulation of Jerusalem nowhere mentions the repair of churches. There is not one mention of repair, and in the Dar al-Islam this has been a problem throughout the centuries in many different parts of the world. People have been able to keep their churches, but very often not to repair them. So the survival of these monuments and sites in the face of these difficulties needs to be saluted. Although being a *dhimmi* actually did limit Christian participation in many different ways, Christians and Jews both made a very significant contribution to what has come to be known as Islamic civilisation.

The transmission of Hellenistic learning, for instance, to the Muslims, which they greatly developed and then in their own turn communicated to people in Western Europe is a case in point. This would not have been possible without the contribution of Oriental Christians such as 'Abd al-Masih al-Himsi who was a translator, and Ibn Masawaih who was an Assyrian Christian and a physician in the court of the 'Abbasid caliphs. Alongside this contribution to mainstream civilisation wherever they lived, there were also Arab commentators and scholars in Christian theology. Professor Kenneth Bailey points out that there is a great deal of material available in the Arabic language on Christian thought and biblical commentaries, for example in the writings of Ibn al-Salibi and Hibbat Allah ibn al-Assal.

Participation in Politics

The marginalization that *dhimmi* status meant for Christian communities must have been one reason why Christians were such enthusiastic contributors to the *nahda* (or Arab renaissance) when it happened. It was for them a chance of re-entering the main stream of political and socio-economic life in their country. The contribution of Christians to the *nahda* is out of all proportion to their numbers. But there is a question that needs to be asked about this contribution. Kenneth Cragg has pointed out that the Christian Arab nationalists accepted the dominant factor of Islam in Arab political and social life, and they acknowledged the cultural and historical influence of Islam.[5] This is right because Islam has actually shaped Arab culture in a way that is formative. But the point remains, having accepted that, as to what is the distinctiveness of the Arab Christian contribution to Arab nationalism, and to the particular circumstances of each country. This question could be stated in terms of values, of rights of people, and also in terms of renewal in communities. I have always appreciated greatly the Palestinian aspiration for a non-confessional state. This aspiration has come mainly from the frustration and tragedy that has been produced by having to deal with extreme forms of Zionism. This aspiration is also crucial today in responding to other kinds of fundamentalism.

A Programme for Peace

Central to this must be the freedom of access to the holy places for Jews,

[5] Cragg, K. 1992. *The Arab Christian. A History of the Middle East*. London: Mowbray.

Christians and Muslims, and for all kinds of Jews, Christians and Muslims. Christian communities have to be rid of the parochialism that sometimes one finds in the Holy Land. A non confessional homeland for all Palestinians, and a recognition of the right of Israel to secure borders – these will not return Israel to a monolithic state (if that ever existed) because there are other kinds of people who will still remain within those 'secure' borders. The aspiration for a non-confessional homeland needs once again to be underlined. A Palestinian *Aliyah* has been referred to by Riah Abu El-Assal to complement the Jewish one The world church should ask itself what role it has to play in promoting such an *Aliyah*. Relief, development and mission agencies of the world-wide church need to ask how they can assist in this. The necessity for a comprehensive peace settlement in the Middle East is central to this. What happens to Palestine has to be understood in the context of the whole of the region. Such a settlement must guarantee the basic freedoms of association, of belief and of speech for all of the people in the region. This is not something that we can take for granted in every country in that region. And a final question remains for Christians of the Holy Land: what do you feel is your vocation, your calling, for ministry in the worldwide church? Perhaps Palestinian Christians have a ministry to offer the world church which is based on their perception of justice. Has this been worked out fully? The world church needs this ministry. It should be a ministry that unites and does not divide. It should be a ministry to the poor and to the oppressed. There are many Christians in many different parts of the world and, indeed, other people who are waiting to listen to this testimony of Christians of the Holy Land.

17

Pilgrimage to the Holy Land, Yesterday and Today

Michael Prior

> Why all this voyaging? What do
> we hope to find beyond those icons
> in darkened bedrooms, beyond the broken
> statues, fallen columns, the rubble
> of stones, the babble of tongues?
> What are we looking for
> and what shall we do
> if ever we find it?

This question, posed by a modern poet is *apropos* of journeying in general.[1] However, there is likely to be a significant difference between a journey and a pilgrimage: 'A visitor passes through a place; the place passes through the pilgrim.'[2] The notion of pilgrimage is a popular one in much discussion of the Christian life, from Chaucer's *Canterbury Tales*, through Bunyan's *Pilgrim's Progress* to George Herbert. The practice occupies a significant part in the spirituality of many Christians.

Pilgrimage focuses attention on what religious people do, rather than what they believe. In examining it, one encounters perceptions of religious truth as it is acted out. It raises fundamental religious questions

---

[1] From Desmond O'Grady's, *At Sea*, in *Sing me Creation*, 1977 (Dublin: Gallery Books).
[2] Cynthia Ozick 1983: 154, quoted in Wilken 1992: 110.

(Darrow 1988: 231). The Jewish Law demanded that every male should make pilgrimage to Jerusalem three times a year (Passover, Feast of Weeks, and Tabernacles: Exod 23.7; Deut 16.16). During the Second Temple period even diaspora Jews sought to observe it (Mishnah Aboth 5.4; Mishnah Tannit 1:3; Jos. *Wars* 6.9). After the destruction of the Temple in 70 AD pilgrimages to the Wailing Wall became occasions of lamentation. While in Islam also it is a sacred duty to make the pilgrimage to Mecca (Qur'an 2.196; 3.97), Christianity has never required its faithful to make pilgrimage. Nevertheless, St Jerome, in commenting on 'Let us go to his dwelling place; let us worship at his footstool!' (Psalm 132.7), says, 'The psalmist commands that we worship (Christ) in the place where his feet stood' (Ep. 46.7). However, romantic notions of pilgrimage to the Holy Land are quickly dispelled when one meets the reality of people's lives. While Jerusalem is a Holy City in the piety of the three Abrahamic religions, its political status is at the heart of the Israeli-Palestinian dispute, with each group claiming it for its capital. Pilgrimage to the Holy Land, then, is a subject fraught with complexities, religious, ecclesiastical and political.

If travel broadens the mind, does travel to sacred places broaden the spirit? (Lewis 1989). Does Christianity have a theology of sacred places, in the fashion Judaism and Islam have? John chapter 4 is presented as raising the question of the significance of place in the Christian dispensation, since Christ spoke of worship, neither on Mount Gerizim, nor Mount Zion, but in spirit and in truth.

In 379 Gregory of Nyssa wrote a letter based on his journey to Jerusalem which has been an embarrassment to supporters of pilgrimage.[3] His major critique of pilgrimage is that, in addition to the New Testament's silence on it, and the immorality involved in bringing the two sexes together, Christianity has no thoughts on places. Instead it stresses that the core of religion relates to closeness to God and neighbour. Going to places brings people no closer to God, he claims, and hence Christians should stay at home. Moreover, he claimed that the church in Cappadocia was in better shape than that in Jerusalem. Gregory would take issue with those who argue from the fact of the incarnation, and the use of bread, water, and wine, etc. to a certain scandal of particularity. Nevertheless, as we shall see, Gregory was no doctrinaire critic of the *tactile spirituality* one associates with places sanctified by Christ (or, for that matter, with the remains of martyrs, cf. PG 46.739).

Lewis puts his case rather stridently: 'The significance of the incarnation is not that God is a God of one place to the exclusion of others; it is that he is a God of all places, active in his world . . . God is

---

[3] 'On Pilgrimages', in Schaff P, and H Wace, ed. 1892: 382-383.

to be found especially in people; namely in those in need and in the gathered community of the Church . . . It follows that to set off on a journey to grow nearer to Christ is at best a complex matter. It might be that the true search is among those in need . . . In that case a pilgrimage to Israel in search of places where Christ is present, should concentrate not on Jerusalem but rather on the refugee camps and on the aid which can be given to those who are oppressed . . . Alternatively, the trail . . . may lead back to the church at home' (Lewis 1989: 390f).

He suggests that for the person sweating round the sites, the appropriate text should be, 'He is not here; he has risen' (Matt 28.6), or, 'Why do you seek the living among the dead?' (Luke 24.5). Lewis disdains the attachment to the empty tomb. Christ is in the breaking of bread and in Beirut. He abhors relics also. 'No place has a claim on God; if any place does, it is the refugee camp or the psychiatric word, but that is because of the occupants and not because of anything intrinsic in the place' (Lewis 1989: 392f). Finally, he calls for more stress on the journey than on the destination.

Clearly Lewis is pessimistic about the value of pilgrimage. Although he offers no evidence for any of his claims, he seems to presume that pilgrimage is at best a distraction from the real encounter with the Risen Christ, which is to be found among people. He does not seem sensitive to the possibility that people who go on pilgrimage may undergo a significant conversion of heart. Since Lewis carries out his discussion on purely theoretical grounds, without reference to the testimony of any pilgrim from any religion, ancient or modern, his argument is superficial. He does not distinguish between the claims of theoretical speculation, and the results of real pilgrimage. A more serious investigation of the phenomenon is called for.

Anthropological Perspectives on Pilgrimage

Pilgrimage is a significant religious enterprise in virtually every world religion.[4] While there are clear patterns of similarity in the practice of pilgrimage over a wide range of periods and places (e.g., leaving one's home, making a journey to a sacred place, for a religious purpose, etc.), modern revisionist studies of the phenomenon over a variety of cultures reveal a fundamental heterogeneity. Recent work by anthropologists of

---

[4] 'There is no great religion in the world which has not laid the gravest insistence on the sacredness of certain specified localities and enjoined on their followers the primary necessity to visit them at stated seasons and to perform with scrupulous attention the rites prescribed by tradition' (Wetherd 1947: 10, quoted in Wilken 1992: 296 n. 2).

pilgrimage protest against all attempts to predicate a unity of experience on the part of pilgrims.[5] They argue that such generalizations run in the face of the obvious diversity of perceptions and reactions, and can be seen to be a crude superimposition of a uniform, but false model of pilgrimage on the diversity of its reality.

The stimulus for the tendency in scholarship to predicate a normative universalism of the experience of pilgrimage can be traced to the formative years of social and cultural anthropology when Durkheim produced his seminal study of Australian aboriginal ritual (Durkheim 1912).[6] Under his influence, pilgrimage has been regarded as a mode of reinforcing collective values which reflect the structures of society. The opposite view has been proposed by the Turners, who argue that pilgrimage is fundamentally an *anti*-hierarchical process, which in developing an egalitarian community among the participants lays aside all pretensions to secular position. In this view pilgrimage is the ritual *par excellence* which expresses the universalism of a world religion (Turner, V and E Turner 1978). However, both theoretical considerations, and field studies in several continents do not support this view.[7]

Recent anthropological studies show up the weaknesses of such simplistic, positivist views, and rightly call attention to what actually happens within pilgrimage.

Anthropological Perspectives on Christian Pilgrimage

Effectively everywhere Christians are to be found there is a certain interest in the practice of pilgrimage.[8] If the origins of Christian pilgrimage are to be found in the geographical areas associated with Jesus, and the heroes of his Jewish predecessors, there is no shortage of more recent pilgrimage sites, whether places associated with apparitions of the Blessed Virgin Mary or associated with charismatic Christians.[9]

---

[5] This is the thrust of Eade and Sallnow, eds. 1991.
[6] See Eade and Sallnow (eds. 1991: 3f) for examples of the influence of Durkheim.
[7] See Eade and Sallnow (eds. 1991: 3f) for examples.
[8] For example, Stirrat has examined the phenomenon in Sri Lanka, in which Christianity is a minority religion in a dominant Sinhalese Buddhist culture (1991). Sallnow has investigated it in the Andes in which Christianity assumed the role of the new state religion, and virtually exterminated the imperial cults of the Inkas (Sallnow 1987, and 1991).
[9] E.g., the tested ones of Lourdes, Rue du Bac, Fatima, Knock, etc., or ones of temporary media interest, such as Medjugorje in former Yugoslavia, or Ballinspittle in Ireland. While pilgrimages associated with charismatic figures are more common in other cultures, in the west there is that of the stigmatized Capuchin friar, Padre Pio of San Giovanni Rotondo in Italy.

Some of these pilgrimage sites (especially, Lourdes) are associated with healings, and even with miracle-working. While some devotees go in the hope of obtaining healing at other sites also, there is the additional motivation of mortification present in others, where pilgrims inflict pain on themselves as a religious act (e.g., the Peruvian shrine of Senor de Wank'a, or the Sri Lanka one at Kataragama).

In a review of modern studies of pilgrimage in a variety of pilgrimages, the anthropologists Eade and Sallnow conclude, 'In most cases (of contemporary pilgrimage), the dominant motive for going on a pilgrimage is to request some favour of God or the shrine divinity in return for simply having made the journey or for engaging in ancillary devotional exercises. In many ways, they (pilgrimage shrines) represent the stock exchanges of the religious economy . . . Physical suffering and penance are exchanged for material and spiritual favours . . . ' (1991: 24). It appears to be the case that the healing powers one associates with a shrine are the dominating interest of pilgrims in many sites. As we shall see, there is little evidence to show that this is a prominent feature of pilgrimage to the Holy Land.

Sacred Places

Fundamental to the notion of pilgrimage is that of a sacred place. In many cultures the landscape itself is considered to be imbued with sacredness. Chthonian powers located in the mountains, rocks, streams, and other topographic features, etc. are held to influence human destiny.[10] Eliade speaks of sacred space as that place which has experienced an irruption of the divine. 'A sacred place is what it is because of the permanent nature of the hierophany that first consecrated it . . . The hierophany . . . goes so far as to ensure that sacredness will continue there . . . In this way the place becomes an inexhaustible source of power and sacredness and enables man, simply by entering it, to have a share in the power, to hold communion with the sacredness' (Eliade 1958: 368). Where there is a sacred place there is the possibility of breaking through from the level of earth to the level of heaven (Eliade 1958: 373). The religious man desires to be as near that space as possible. Inside is cosmos, order; outside is chaos (Eliade 1959: 20).

Eliade surveys the occurrence of the symbolism of the 'centre of the

---

[10] There is abundant evidence to show that Christian missionaries/colonizers frequently graft on to these earthly sacred sites other elements of the sacred which have their roots in the historical ministry of Jesus, e.g., through the association of the place with a shrine of the Crucified Christ, or of Mary (see Sallnow 1991 for examples in the Andes).

world' in several diverse regions. The sacred mountain, where heaven and earth meet, stands at the centre of the world. Every temple or palace is assimilated to a 'sacred mountain' and thus becomes a centre. The temple, or sacred city, through which the *Axis Mundi* passes is the junction between heaven, earth and hell (1958: 375). Eliade moves from his reflections on the general to a more specifically Christian evaluation: 'To Christians, Golgotha was the centre of the world; it was both the topmost point of the cosmic mountain and the spot where Adam was created and buried. The Saviour's blood was therefore sprinkled over Adam's skull buried at the very foot of the cross, and thus redeemed him' (Eliade 1958: 375).

Christians, of course, were not the first to situate Jerusalem at the centre of the earth. The centrality of Israel, Jerusalem and its Temple was affirmed in at least some strands of Hebrew thought. The Land of Israel was the centre of the earth (Ezek 38.12), Jerusalem was at the centre of the nations (Ezek 5.5), Mount Zion, 'the centre of the navel (*omphalos*) of the earth' (Jub 8.19).

One can also detect the status of Jerusalem as the Christian centre of the world in the *Madaba Map* (6th century mosaic in the church in Madaba, Transjordan). One can see represented very clearly Hadrian's *Cardo Maximus*, and in a prominent position at the centre on the west of the street the steps leading up to Constantine's basilica. Even the three doorways mentioned by Eusebius can be seen easily. The prominent position given to Jerusalem in the *Madaba Map* confirms the tradition which was developing within the Christian faithful, that Jerusalem was the centre of the world, and that whereas the Jews in the past had focused their attention on the temple, so now Christians focused on the Hill of Golgotha. This emphasis can be seen also in *Mappa Mundi* in Hereford Cathedral, which places Jerusalem, and the Crucifixion, at the very centre of the world. The part played by Constantine's buildings in highlighting the significance of Jerusalem cannot be over-emphasized in this process.

Eliade argues that humankind cannot live without a sacred place. Where there is no theophany to reveal it to him he constructs it for himself in terms of the laws of cosmology and geomancy. Even every family house, he claims, is conceived as being at the centre of the world. In one group of traditions, he asserts, humankind attains the 'centre of the world' without effort, while in the other it comes through difficulty (1958: 382f). He names this universal condition of humankind, 'the nostalgia for Paradise': 'The desire to be always, effortlessly, at the heart of the world, of reality, of the sacred, and, briefly, to transcend, by natural means, the human condition and regain a divine state of affairs: what a Christian would call the state of man before the Fall' (p. 383). Is this the drive which propels pilgrimage?

Sacred Events and the Holy Land

In addition to the associations of the sacred with particular places (timeless and ahistorical, which may be called 'Eliadean'), there is also the association with the place in terms of time and history (which may be called 'Durkheimian').[11] When one talks of a sacred place within the three Abrahamic faiths invariably one associates it with the manifestation of some aspect of the divinity within history, be it the history of Jews, and/or Christians, and/or Muslims. The Holy Land has a person-sacredness, prior to, and, in the view of those Jews for whom Jesus is not a person of significance, independent of Jesus. In conventional Jewish perspectives, it is the terrain chosen by God Himself as the dwelling place for his chosen people. It is already doubly sacred, and much more so than by way of the sacredness associated with static, inanimate shrines embedded in the landscape.

In a profound sense the Holy Land is especially holy for Christians because of the fact that Jesus traversed it. The terrain itself has, in the words of Gregory of Nyssa, 'signs of the Lord's sojourn in the flesh.' According to Bishop Paulinus of Nola, 'No other sentiment draws people to Jerusalem than the desire to see and touch the places where Christ was physically present, and to be able to say from their own experience, "We have gone into his tabernacle, and have worshipped in the places where his feet stood"' (*Ep.* 49.14). Gregory was reacting against the uncompromising intellectualism of a fellow bishop, Eunomius, for whom the dogmatic exactness of Christianity, couched in the language of a philosophical system was prized above all else. Gregory insisted that Christianity was not a matter of the mind only, but invited participation in sacramental practices and symbols. The terrain of the holy places 'received the footprints of Life itself' and serve to remind one that God once walked the earth. As if by way of some kind of osmosis, the pilgrim absorbs some of the holiness of the place.[12] This is strikingly true of Jerusalem, for there God manifested himself crucially, quite literally, on Golgotha. That portion of the cosmos, at least, is charged with the grandeur of God. For Christians, Jerusalem and the surrounding areas were the scene of the historical origins of their faith. Equally significant, perhaps, was the Christian belief that the Second Coming of Christ would take place in that land.

The Origins of Christian Pilgrimage

The origins of Christian pilgrimage are obscure, but certainly predate

---

[11] See the discussion in Stirrat 1984.
[12] See the excellent and nuanced discussion of what can be read as the ambiguity of Gregory's assessment of pilgrimage in Wilken 1992: 117f.

the conscious efforts of the emperor Constantine to provide a physical anchorage for the Bible, the Sacred Scriptures of the newly adopted state religion with which he hoped to unify his empire. Of the thousands of pilgrims who came to the Holy Land before the Crusades we have the records of only a few.[13]

Pre-Constantinian Pilgrims

Melito of Sardis visited the Holy Land in the middle of the 2nd century, *so as to establish accurately the books of the Old Testament*. He was in a sense, therefore, the earliest known Christian pilgrim. His purpose in going was to examine the places where these things were preached and done. He was in search of the biblical past.

We have no way of knowing how many people visited the Holy Land in the pre-Constantinian period, but we do know of some others: Alexander, a future bishop of Jerusalem, travelled from Cappadocia in the reign of Caracalla, *with the stated purpose of prayer and investigation of the sites*. Origen, a biblical scholar based at Caesarea, travelled around Palestine *seeking out the location of events recorded in the Scriptures*. Firmilianus, a Cappadocian bishop, visited Origen, and *was in the Holy Land for the sake of the Holy Places*. Pionius, a contemporary of Origen, also visited the Holy Land. Such examples as these make it clear that Palestine was already a place of Christian pilgrimage before the time of Constantine. The province of Palestine harboured the Christian origins of the pilgrims, and was also the place of the future advent. On the other hand there was the Christian view of the heavenly Jerusalem which of course ran counter to the pagan view of the significance of the

[13] Wilkinson (1977) lists, the Bordeaux Pilgrim (AD 333), Egeria (381-384), Paula, A Roman noblewoman (385), whose feats are recorded by St Jerome (*Letter to Eustochium*), Eucherius (c. 445, *Letter to Faustus*), John Rufus (c. 500, *The Life of Peter the Iberian*), the *Breviarius of Jerusalem* (early 6th cen.), Theodosius (before 518, *The Topography of the Holy Land*), Cosmas Indicopleustes (c. 547, *Christian Topography*), Procopius of Caesarea (before 558, *Buildings*), the Piacenza Pilgrim (c. 570, *Travels*), Sophronius of Jerusalem (c. 602, *Anacreontica*), Adomnan (c. 685, *The Holy Places*), Epiphanius the Monk (7/11th century, *The Holy City and the Holy Places*), Jacinthus the Presbyter (c. 750, *Pilgrimage*), Hugeburc (c. 780, *Life of St Willibald*), (c. 808, *Commemoratorium on the Churches in Jerusalem*), Dicuil (c. 825 *The Measurement of the World*), Bernard the Monk (c. 870 *A Journey to the Holy Places and Babylon*), Photius (870-877, *Question to Amphilochius*), Rudolf Glaber (1040, *History*), and Lethbald (Burgundy, 1033). Some are first hand accounts of pilgrims (e.g., the Bordeaux Pilgrim, Egeria, the Piacenza Pilgrim, Jacinthus the Presbyter, Bernard the Monk), while others are the second hand accounts of others (e.g., Jerome, Adomnan, Hugeburc, Dicuil), and others again have the character of Guide Books (*Breviarius of Jerusalem*, Theodosius, Epiphanius the Monk).

earthly city (see Eusebius on the martyrdom of Pamphilus).[14]

Constantine and the Holy Places

28 October, 312 AD, marked a turning point in the nature of the presence of the Christian community in the Holy Land, since on that day Constantine defeated his rival Maxentius at the Milvian Bridge outside Rome. He attributed his victory to the intervention of the God of the Christians. One might legitimately ask why this incident in Rome, should be so significant to the Christian community in the Holy Land.

With his victory at Chrysopolis on the Asian shore of the Bosphorus in 324, Constantine began to extend the influence of the west on the eastern part of the empire. Immediately he put an end to all persecutions against the Christians. Later in 324 he travelled as far as Antioch and possibly went as far as Palestine itself. It was probably the Council of Nicea in 325, which the emperor summoned, which brought the situation of the Holy Places to the forefront of his attention. The bishop of Jerusalem, Macarius, argued for the recognition by the Council of the status of the See of Jerusalem as rivalling that of the provincial capital, Caesarea. After the defeat of Licinius in the previous year, Constantine had written to Macarius ordering the restoration of the church's property, including the tombs of martyrs. Macarius would presumably have included in that the Holy Sepulchre which he and his congregation had believed for generations to lie beneath the temple of Venus beside the Forum of Aelia Capitolina. Subsequently, Constantine wrote to Macarius claiming as an order from God his decision to relieve the Holy Place of the burden of its pagan idol. The Temple of Venus therefore was destroyed and the site excavated. In the excavations one particular rock tomb was identified as the Holy Sepulchre.

Constantine wrote to Bishop Macarius ordering the building of an appropriately fine surrounding for the Holy Sepulchre. The church suited to honour the place of the burial of Jesus was only one of a whole series of churches which were established throughout the eastern part of the empire. The church historian, Eusebius of Caesarea (c. AD 260–340), was a participant in the dedication ceremonies of the new buildings in Jerusalem in 335. He describes the building in the third book of *Vita Constantini*. The purpose of the new building was *to focus attention on the newly discovered tomb.* And to do this, the area around the tomb was cleared and the rock cut back in such a way that the sacred spot was isolated to allow free access to the faithful, and to give the builders space in which to work.

[14] See Hunt 1984 for details.

By the second half of the century the actual tomb was completely enclosed by a church of its own, the familiar rotunda of the archaeological reconstructions. The structure seems to have been an embellishment of the Lord's tomb with an extensive courtyard before it. Presumably with the passage of time there was need for an additional building, one suitable for the faithful to congregate in for acts of worship. Therefore, Constantine built his basilica in the courtyard facing the tomb and this subsequently became known as the Martyrium. The bishop of Jerusalem was charged by the emperor with precise instructions for the construction. The building was to surpass not only every other basilica but was to be superior to every other comparable building in the empire, because, he affirms, the place deserved nothing less: 'It is right that the most marvellous place in the world should be fittingly adorned' (Eusebius, *Vita Const.* iii.31).

The other two most significant places in Palestine, the sacred cave at Bethlehem and on the Mount of Olives were also honoured with churches in the reign of Constantine, built under the supervision of his mother, Helena. Architecturally such basilicas were built within a complex which contained a courtyard open to the air, surrounded by colonnades, and adorned with fountains. The atrium, separating the sacred place from the outside world, represented for Eusebius the gradual approach of the non-believer into full faith. The atrium was a place of preparation and purification, with the waters providing cleansing, and the space being used for instruction before those baptised could approach the altar of the Lord. So the courtyard provided a place of refreshment, spiritual as well as physical, for those wishing to enter the sacred place.

The worshipper at one of Constantine's basilicas could find in the complex an echo of his own faith, having left the outside world and gradually penetrating into the sacred precincts towards the shrine which was at the heart of the basilica, which in the case of the Holy Sepulchre, of course, was the tomb. But the Golgotha buildings represented not only the spiritual temple of each individual faithful person, but also suggested the consummation of the faith of all Christians, namely the arrival at the 'new Jerusalem' announced in the Apocalypse.

While the dimensions of the Constantinian basilicas are surprisingly small, and most of them were smaller than many English village churches, there was also a forecourt and extensive atrium surrounding the buildings. In addition to providing space for admiring the buildings, the space also had to be used for accommodating the visitors, and this service of hospitality became an important function of the bishops of Jerusalem. The Holy Sepulchre precinct was ideally suited to the needs of pilgrims. There was plenty of open space in which the people could gather: Egeria notes that on the afternoon of Good Friday the large and beautiful courtyard between the Cross and the *Anastasis* was so crammed with people, that there is not even room to open a door (37.4). She had already noted that on Epiphany 'great crowds come to Jerusalem from all parts, not only monks, but lay men and women as well' (25.12).

The smallness of these basilicas, coupled with the great amount of open space surrounding them, presented a very attractive sight for visiting pilgrims who would have ample space to admire the beauty. Those who have visited the present precinct of the Haram al-Sharif (Dome of the Rock) will not need any further argument. Of the Great Church on Golgotha, Egeria later declared it to be 'beyond description'. 'It was decorated with gold, mosaic, and precious marble, as much as his [Constantine's] empire could provide, and this not only at the Great Church, but at the *Anastasis* and the Cross, and the other Jerusalem holy places as well' (25.9).

The first occasion on which Constantine's Jerusalem buildings became the centre of widespread activity was the dedication in September 335 AD. At the empire's expense bishops from all over the eastern empire were summoned, and assembled in Jerusalem (the 'new Jerusalem'), at the very spot from which their Christianity had sprung, and which was now restored as the centre of Christian faith by the emperor's own bounty. That the bishops recognised the occasion as momentous is clear from the preamble to their synodical letter: 'Having come together . . . to a great gathering which we have held for the consecration of our Saviour's Martyrium, which has been established through the service of God, King of All and of his Christ by the zeal of our emperor Constantine most beloved of God.'

Presumably, the news that the Holy Sepulchre had been discovered and that the site had been reclaimed and converted into a Christian basilica increased the number of pilgrims to the region. Perhaps the structure of the basilica complex itself suggests either the catering for pilgrims already coming, or for those whom it might attract in the future. In any place of pilgrimage there is need for a wide open space with, perhaps, a colonnade providing shelter. The erection of such buildings with imperial encouragement and ongoing support marks the transition of the Christian community from being an insecure one, to becoming a state-sponsored, publicly worshipping one.

Post-Constantinian Pilgrims

Empress Helena's journey to the Holy Land coincides with the period of the Constantinian buildings, that is after 325 AD. She was an old woman at the time and it was not long after her return that she died around the age of 80 in 329 AD. The evidence available does not allow us to speculate with any certainty about the motives for Helena's journey. We are left to rely on the public explanations put forward for it, and these are reflected also in Eusebius' *Vita Constantini*.

According to these sources her visit was motivated by *her desire to give thanks for the triumph of the Christian empire and more especially for so great a son*, the emperor, and for his pious sons, the Caesars, and she was determined to do this at the holy places in the land. The stability of the empire might also have been a matter of maternal concern because there was a palace crisis in 326 when Constantine removed members of his own family as well as others (Hunt 1984, 33).

Helena's pilgrimage, of course, was no private affair. It was made in the name of her family and at least in some sense in the name of the empire. She travelled as the Augusta traversing the provinces, receiving the trappings of royal power, dispensing money and shelter for the poor, release of prisoners, freeing of the oppressed, and the restoration of exiles, etc.

The Bordeaux Pilgrim (333)

The journey of the Bordeaux pilgrim (333 AD) was an immense one, covering some 2,200 Roman miles from Bordeaux to Constantinople, and some 1200 miles from thence to Jerusalem. He travelled by road from the Atlantic coast right up to Jerusalem, giving a detailed record of the stages and distances en route, both going and coming.[15] It is likely that he was away from home for at least a year, and a great deal of that time would have been spent travelling to and from the Holy Land. The pilgrim's account is little more than a list of places to which he attaches an incident from the Hebrew Scriptures, or from the New Testament, without any sensitivity to a hierarchy of place.[16] There is no mention of any praying, or liturgies, or of any contact with any people in the land.

[15] Geyer, P and O Cuntz. 1965: 1-26.
[16] E.g., Caesarea (the Bath of Cornelius the centurion); Jezreel (where Ahab lived and Elijah prophesied); Gerizim (Abraham's sacrifice, according to the Samaritans), and Shechem (site of Joseph's tomb). He gives more detail about Jerusalem (Pool of Bethsaida, the Bethesda of John 5.2, the pinnacle of Jesus' temptation, the ruins of the Temple, Siloam, house of Caiaphas, the hillock Golgotha, the vineyard and rock on where Judas betrayed Christ, the basilica on the Mount of Olives). In Jericho the sycamore tree which Zacchaeus climbed, and the house of Rahab, the Dead Sea, the place of Jesus' baptism, Rachel's tomb near Bethlehem, the basilica in Bethlehem, and Hebron, the tomb of Abraham, *et al*.

Egeria (381-384)

For Egeria, the physical journey, which was no different from that of any contemporary traveller, was the external factor in a journey which had as its fundamental basis the desire to visit the Holy places. This desire she speaks of with great enthusiasm in her account.[17] She is fulsome in her gratitude to the devoted bands of Christian monks who gave her group appropriate hospitality in Sinai and elsewhere. In addition to providing her group with hospitality, they showed them the biblical sites and conducted acts of worship on the spots, and gave them parting gifts to send them on their way. The modern reader and traveller can but wonder at the tenacity of Egeria and her companions who traversed the Roman empire virtually from the Atlantic to the Euphrates, having to contend with all the demands of travel along the way.

It was a feature of Egeria's pilgrimage that services of worship accompanied the visits to the Christian sites with the central place given to the reading of the appropriate biblical text. 'And it was always our practice when we managed to reach one of the places we wanted to see to have first a prayer, then a reading from the book, then to say an appropriate psalm and another prayer. By God's grace we always followed this practice whenever we were able to reach a place we wanted to see' (10.7).

Egeria's Bible was her constant travelling companion, as it was also for the younger Melania who, according to her biographer, never let it go from her hands. Accounts of early pilgrims to various places abound in evidence of severe asceticism, including abstinence from food and drink, in addition to the making of long arduous journeys on foot.

Other Early Pilgrims

The nature of the interest of other Christian pilgrims can be gauged by examining their accounts. In a letter written nineteen years after the event, St Jerome describes some elements of the pilgrimage undertaken by two Roman noblewomen, Paula and her daughter, Eustochium, in 385: 'I shall not describe her journey through Coele-Syria and Phoenicia. For I have not set out to write a draftee book about her, but am going to name only those places which are mentioned in Holy Scripture' (Letter [108] to Eustochium 8.1). Of her visit to Jerusalem he says, 'She started to go round visiting all the places with such burning

---

[17] Franceschini, A and R Weber: 1965, 29-90. English Translation in Wilkinson 1971. See also Wilkinson 1977.

enthusiasm that there was no taking her away from one unless she was hurrying to another. She fell down and worshipped before the Cross as if she could see the Lord hanging on it. On entering the Tomb of the Resurrection she kissed the stone which the angel removed from the sepulchre door; then like a thirsty man who has waited long, and at last comes to water, she faithfully kissed the very shelf on which the Lord's body had lain. Her tears and lamentations there are known to all Jerusalem – or rather to the Lord himself to whom she was praying' (9.1). At the Cave of the Saviour in Bethlehem, 'She solemnly declared in my own hearing that, with the eye of faith she saw a child wrapped in swaddling clothe, weeping in the Lord's manger, the Magi worshipping, the star shining above, the Virgin Mother, the attentive foster father; and the shepherds . . . ' (10.2).

Clearly, the genre of the letter is hagiographical. Paula's motivation, as relayed by Jerome was to be in the places of the Bible.[18] There is little reference to what she did when she came to the various sights. The only *living stones*[19] mentioned were the demented ones at the Saints' Tombs, and the monks on the way to Egypt.

In 438, Empress Eudokia paid her first visit to Jerusalem, and was present when the relics of St Stephen were deposited in his first shrine. She came back in 443 and spent the last sixteen years of her life in the city, and built a great number of churches. Her magnanimity was interpreted as a fulfilment of Psalm 51.18: 'Do good to Sion in thy good pleasure (*eudokia*); build thou the walls of Jerusalem' (Wilkinson 1977: 3).

Eucherius, bishop of Lyons (c. 434-449), writes of the situation of Jerusalem and Judaea, 'as it is known to me either by description or reading' (v. 125). In his report of pilgrims to Jerusalem he says, 'People coming into the city from the north are taken to their first holy place by the layout of the streets, and visit the Martyrium, lately built with great magnificence by Constantine. Beside this and to the west one visits the sites of Golgotha and the Anastasis. The *Anastasis* is on the site of the

---

[18] 'The whole day will be lost in talking if I go on to describe all the places through which, in her unbelievable faith, the revered Paula made her journey' (13.5). Despite this literary asceticism he refers to her visits to Sidon, Sarepta, Tyre, Acco, Megiddo, Dor, Strato's Tower, Caesarea, Antipatris, Lydda, Arimathea, Nob, Joppa, Nicopolis, Beth-horon, Aijalon, Gibeon, Gibeah, Shepherd's Field, Gaza, Hebron, Caphar Barucha, Sodom, Gomorrah, En-Gedi, Tekoa, Bethany, Bethphage, Jericho, Gilgal, the Jordan, Valley of Achor, Bethel, Shiloh, Schechem, Mt Gerizim, Well of Jacob, Nazareth, Cana, Capernaum, Mount Tabor, Succoth, etc. See extracts in Wilkinson 1977: 47-52.

[19] Palestinian Christians refer to themselves as the 'living stones' of the Land. They consider that as living Christian communities, the 'living stones', they preserve the Christian presence in the Holy Land more palpably than do the 'dead stones' of biblical antiquity and the remains of early Christian architecture.

resurrection, and Golgotha (which is between the *Anastasis* and the Martyrium) is the place of the Lord's Passion. One sees there the rock which once bore the Cross to which the Lord was fixed' (v. 126). He mentions the Temple site, the Pool of Bethesda, the Spring of Siloam, the Valley of Jehosaphat, two churches on the Mount of Olives, one sited near where the Lord taught his disciples, and the other from where he ascended into heaven (vv. 126-7).[20]

John Rufus says of Peter the Iberian's pilgrimage to Jerusalem, 'Even if it had to be by night he might have venerated the holy places, specially Golgotha and the life-giving Tomb!' He records that Peter had worshipped the Saviour in all the places . . . 'This took place to persuade those who had murmured that in all the holy places – every day perhaps, and every hour – the blessed man was spiritually offering adoration to the Lord . . . '[21]

The anonymous Pilgrim from Piacenza (c. 570) conveys better than any other writer of the period the variety of his experiences.[22]

The Persians captured Jerusalem in 614. They massacred (some) Christians and set the city on fire, and the city was plundered. Patriarch Theodosius surrendered Jerusalem to the Muslims in 638. They were very restrained in their treatment of the territories they conquered. Pilgrimage was able to resume.

In all, then, there was an abundance of practices possible for the Christian pilgrims to insulate them from the secular culture that surrounded them, and which intensified their religious sensitivies as they made their way towards the goal of the sacred places.[23] Common

---

[20] In addition he mentions Bethlehem, Jericho, the Sea of Tiberias, the Dead Sea, Hebron, Joppa, Dan and Beersheba, and Paneas.

[21] John Rufus' *The Life of Peter the Iberian* (c. 500). The original Greek text has survived only in a poor Syrian translation. See extracts in Wilkinson 1977: 57f.

[22] He travelled from Piacenza to Constantinople, Cyprus, Constantia, Antaradus, Tripoli, Byblus, Triaris, Berytus, Sidon. 'From Sidon we came to Sarepta . . . the chamber which was made for Elijah is there, and in it is the very bed on which he lay, and the marble vessel which was filled by the widow woman' (v. 159). Then Tyre, Sycamina, Ptolemais, Diocesarea, Cana, and Nazareth, Mount Tabor, Sea of Tiberias, Samaria (Neapolis), the city of Tiberias, Capernaum, Gadara, Scythopolis, Sebaste, Jordan, Jericho, Bethany, Mount of Olives, Gethsemane, and finally, Jerusalem. 'After we had prostrated ourselves and kissed the ground, we entered the Holy City and venerated the Lord's Tomb.' Then Holy Sion, the Praetorium, Siloam, Saint Stephen's Tomb, Bethlehem, Oak of Mamre, Gaza, Ascalon, Mt Gilboa, Eleutheropolis, Ascalon, Gaza, Elusa, and Sinai. Then to Egypt, the Nile, Alexandria. He had to stay in Jerusalem a long time because he was ill. Then to Joppa, Caesarea Philippi, Galilee, Damascus, Heliopolis, and eventually to Antioch the Great, and finally, Mesopotamia (vv. 171-97, in Wilkinson 1977: 79-89).

[23] With the passage of time and the growth in the number of pilgrims, catering for them became a matter of even greater significance, with the result that suitable lodgings were provided alongside the places being visited, including the Basilica in Bethlehem and at the Holy Sepulchre. By the 6th century there were *xenodochia* ('guest masters') attached to many of the principal sites visited by the pilgrims.

sense, however, guards us against regarding the rather exclusively Christian character of the pilgrimage of Egeria and others in Christian antiquity as being the norm for all pilgrims of the period. Understandably such pilgrims were imbued with strong religious sensitivities, but, as is clear in the accounts of some, they could not travel in any kind of Christian cocoon, untouched by the secular surroundings all around them.

The Purposes of Christian Pilgrimage

A pilgrimage is a journey to a *sacred place*, with a religious purpose. It is instructive to enquire into the purposes of pilgrims. However one can no longer take for granted the meaning of pilgrimage for its participants, nor even a uniform definition of the phenomenon (Eade, J and M J Sallnow, eds. 1991: 3).

The Jewish rabbi, Philo of Alexandria (d. 45 AD), provides a perspective from antiquity into the motivation for, and nature of pilgrimage. 'Countless multitudes from countless cities come, some over land, others over sea, from east and west and north and south at every feast. They take the temple for their port as a general haven and safe refuge from the bustle and great turmoil of life, and there they seek to find calm weather, and, released from the cares whose yoke has been heavy upon them from their earliest years, to enjoy a brief breathing-space in scenes of genial cheerfulness. Thus filled with comfortable hopes they devote the leisure, as is their bounden duty, to holiness and the honouring of God. Friendships are formed between those who hitherto knew not each other, and the sacrifices and libations are the occasion of reciprocity of feeling and constitute the surest pledge that all are of one mind' (*Spec. Leg.* I.69-70, the MSS insert *Of the Temple*).

We see in this extract from Philo's description of pilgrimage four elements which are regarded as being at the heart of the experience. Fundamental to all pilgrimage is a spiritual drive and aim. H B Partin's study of the phenomenon of pilgrimage detects four seminal elements. Firstly, pilgrimage involves leaving the security of one's own place, with its ritual of preparations and sense of separation. Secondly, the leaving is not for some vague meandering, or even excursion to an ordinary destination, but is a journey to a particular place, which is marked by an intensity of holiness. Thirdly, the pilgrim has her/his heart set on some personal purpose, e.g., purification, or forgiveness. Finally, in antiquity at least, such pilgrimages were always accompanied by physical difficulties, trials, or threats of failure (Partin 1967).

In our survey of early Christian pilgrimage it is clear that a major concern was to visit the places associated with the Bible. With varying degrees of enthusiasm the records we have describe how prayers were said at places associated with the ministry of Jesus, and in the case of Egeria in particular, we have detailed accounts of her participation in the liturgical ceremonies in Jerusalem.

Models of Modern Pilgrimage

No pilgrimage site matches Jerusalem as a centre for attracting people from such a wide variety of nations, and from three religions. Unlike most other places of religious pilgrimage, Jerusalem is a centre of pilgrimage for three religions, and, to add to the diversity, for the different groupings within each of these religions. The Haram esh-Sharif, sacred to Muslims, is on what the Jews call the Temple Mount. And in the central shrine of Christendom (the Holy Sepulchre) one encounters the six groups of occupants (Latin Catholics, Greek Orthodox, Armenians, Syrians, Copts, Ethiopians), each jealously guarding its rights. 'Jerusalem does not, in fact, appear so much as a holy city but as a *multitude* of holy cities' (Bowman p. 98). Moreover, pilgrims to Jerusalem engage in a great variety of practices, unlike the situation in Mecca wherein its pilgrims are put through a set routine of rituals.

Surprisingly, from the perspective of anthropologists of pilgrimage, modern pilgrims do not go to the Holy Land for a cure, such as might well motivate pilgrims to Lourdes. Neither is there any emphasis on penitential works, as one associates with Lough Derg in Ireland, or on such ascetic practices as self-flagellation and even ceremonial whippings, as one finds in some pilgrimages in the Andes (Sallnow 1991).

When we come to consider the modern phenomenon of pilgrimage to the Holy Land we enter a considerably different world from that of antiquity. Far from encountering the hazards of the journeys of old, it is possible for the modern pilgrim to 'visit the Holy Land' with such a degree of insulation from the surrounding culture that one can scarcely be described as having left one's home. Taxis to the airport, air travel with or without the sound accompanying the compulsory package of videos of dated news, sports spectaculars and comedy, air-conditioned coaches on arrival, the tight eight-day schedule under the control of the Israeli guide, religious services conducted by a spiritual director from home, all conspire to provide a different kind of experience from what obtained in antiquity. For the modern pilgrim, the experience is much cheaper, much shorter and more widely available than heretofore.

In the following brief survey of modern examples, we have no desire to reduce to one undifferentiated whole the multifarious purposes, and effects of different pilgrims from different epochs. However, patterns emerge, which reflect the different interests of different groups. Without pretending to deny the individual's experience of a pilgrimage we shall comment on typical forms of pilgrimage, and highlight one type which appears to offer a considerable development of the practice.

1 Verifying the Bible

We are indebted to F J Bliss for taking the trouble to write a day-by-day account of a pilgrimage of nine days in Palestine, which was undertaken by one hundred and twenty people, of whom twenty-two were clergymen, one being the bishop of Worcester, another Canon Tristam of Durham, and five nonconformist ministers (Bliss 1894). On Day 2, the party, having been comfortably housed, and despite the fatigue of the long journey, got down on Monday evening to what appears to have been at the core of the pilgrimage, lectures, especially those of Canon Tristam. The first lecture dealt with inscriptions, monuments, the reefs on the Mediterranean coast, and the rose of Sharon. Canon Tristam passed on to a bird's eye view of the general character of the country: 'The frame and lighting of a picture have much to do with its value. So the setting of the Bible is most important' (p. 103).

The geographical setting could deal competently with the assaults on the Bible by Higher Criticism: 'An intelligent study of the fauna of Palestine may check some of the results of the higher criticism. In Leviticus Moses gives a list of animals which he repeats thirty-eight years after in the Book of Deuteronomy, with the addition of nine new species. Why this addition? Because the first list was compiled only nine months after the children of Israel left Egypt, while the second was made after their long sojourn in the wilderness. Now, while the Canon was travelling across the Jordan he picked up all the Arabic names he could find of animals and birds, with the result that eight out of nine of these added species were found to be creatures that now exist in the desert and which only could have existed in the desert and are not found in Egypt. This change in the lists is far better accounted for by the view that Moses wrote the Pentateuch than by the theory that it was compiled by Ezra one thousand years after. The Jews were neither travellers nor naturalists' (p. 103).

The burden of the lecture at the Good Samaritan's Inn, after lunch on Day 3 was geographical, leading to the conclusion that 'The features of this part of the country have not changed from Bible times' (p. 104). Mr Bliss and Canon Tristam left the party, for a quiet day of exploration on

Day 4. Canon Tristam found the same birds and plants as on his last visit, thirteen years before. Interest was extended to pottery, and Roman traces. The next lecture dealt with matters of geology, and we are told that the Canon had himself found no less that twenty seven of the thirty eight species in the Sea of Galilee.

On Day 5 the party returned to Jerusalem, and in the evening a good audience assembled to hear the Revd Mr Kelk's lecture on 'Walks about Jerusalem'. Kelk estimated that 'there were 40,000 Jews, 8,000 Mohammedans, and 12,000 Christians in Jerusalem' at the time. However, there is no mention of having met any of them. On Day 6 the Canon lectured to half the party in Bethlehem, while those who stayed behind had 'the privilege of listening to a peripatetic lecture by the Revd Mr Hanauer upon the present Walls and Gates of Jerusalem' (p. 107). In the evening, the Revd Mr Zeller gave a learned lecture on the Druzes. On Day 7 Mr Hanauer gave his lecture on the Haram in the lecture room of Christ Church. In the evening, Mr Bliss lectured on the 'Mounds of Palestine', giving an account of his work at Tell el Hesy.

On Day 8, the bishop of Worcester preached in Christ Church on the text, 'Our feet shall stand within thy gates, O Jerusalem.' 'He spoke of the uncertainty attaching to the different sites here, and emphasized the spiritual character of Christianity' (pp. 107f). To round matters off on the Sunday, the evening sermon was given by the bishop of North Dakota, who had made a most stormy landing at Jaffa that morning. On the morning of Day 9, a small group left by land for Damascus, and the rest returned to Jaffa to embark that night. Mr Bliss informs us that they were to be lectured in Athens by Professor Mahaffy, who had already spoken to them in Cairo. The final sentence of the account of this recent pilgrimage informs us that, 'The lecturer at Rome was Archdeacon Farrar' (p. 108).

The interests of Mr Bliss, at least, are reflected in the account. Although the term *pilgrimage* is used, the account contains little that one would regard as being characteristic of that religious activity. Mr Bliss seems to regard the lectures as the core of the experience of pilgrimage. He comments, 'The enthusiasm of the pilgrims for the lectures was most gratifying to those who arranged them. In six days they listened to ten lectures and visited all the sites of Jerusalem besides' (p. 107). There is no contact with the people of the land. There are just two references to the Arabs. 'The honey is prized by the Arabs, who catch a bee, gum a tiny fragment of feather to his abdomen, let him go, and follow him to his hidden hive' (p. 104). The second refers to their building activity in Jericho (p. 105).

2 Making the Bible Come Alive

Since the Holy Land is for Jews and Christians, and to a somewhat less extent for Muslims, the land of their Sacred Scriptures, there is what we may refer to as a 'textual sacredness' about the land. Making pilgrimage to the Holy Land, therefore, involves seeing those sites, but not simply by way of merely topographical verification. Such pilgrimage primarily focuses on the 'realization' of the scenes described in the text of the Bible. In the Holy Land, 'the Bible comes alive.' In a sense, the Word becomes flesh.

Although this aspect is associated with pilgrims of the Reformation traditions, who were brought up on the Bible, it is not restricted to them. In their home parishes such pilgrims have learnt that salvation comes through Jesus Christ. The constant reading of the Bible, and especially the New Testament is a major agent of this salvation. In general they prefer to encounter the unmediated Christ in the Garden Tomb, or in Galilee, rather than in the monuments thrown up by two thousand years of devotion to his memory.

Although, in general, Catholics tend to have great regard for the sites associated with the life of Jesus they exhibit a peculiar interest in them. Catholics are less concerned with the sites themselves, than with the significance of the biblical events said to have happened at them. 'It is from the significance, not the places, that one draws inspiration, and the places serve primarily as loci where the pilgrims are better able to body forth the subjects of their meditations in their imaginations' (Bowman 1991: 114). Bowman noticed Catholics with their eyes closed during the Via Dolorosa procession. Perhaps, but, in my own hearing, one such pilgrim said during the procession on a Good Friday, 'Wouldn't you think the least they would do would be to close their shops on Good Friday!' The testimony of many Catholic pilgrims assures me that their sense of being in the very place where sacred events happened generates a profoundly moving experience, and reflects a psychology more profound than Bowman appears to presume.

3 An Orthodox Perspective

The heart of Orthodox pilgrimage is to be present in Jerusalem for the feasts. The Resurrection is celebrated as a ritual of the cosmological community of Christ. At the core of Orthodox faith is the conviction that when one stands within an Orthodox church, at home or abroad, with its walls and iconostasis replete with icons and its ceilings ornamented with stars and pictures of the Pantocrator, one is in heaven on earth, in the company of God, the Virgin Mary, and all the saints. One is on the verge of eternity.

Orthodox pilgrims, in general, are peasants, mostly elderly, having sorted out their family responsibilities. They come to the Holy Land mentally to prepare for death, to be present at the life-giving tomb. For them, salvation, whether at home or abroad, is mediated through the divine liturgy and icons. While every liturgy at home is a re-enactment of the passion, death and resurrection of Jesus Christ, the Holy Land becomes one massive icon. Such pilgrims are in no doubt that they are embarking on an adventure which they hope is going to change their lives. They set out to shake off the impurities consequent upon the Fall, and prepare for death and resurrection.

They shake off their sinful past by confession before the journey, and by having their feet washed at the port/airport of entry into the Holy Land by a Brother, and by 'baptism' in the Jordan. They enter 'paradise' itself through collective participation in the eternity imaged in the places where Christ had worked his redemptive mission. However, while each place visited effected its unique part in redemption in the past, the function of each place now is to provide entry into the entirety of the redeemed world. In that respect, at least, the specificity of each place recedes in importance when compared with the overriding function of providing access into the eternal. If the Latins use each site to emphasize a particular part of teaching associated with the site, 'the particularity of Orthodox holy places . . . is discarded as soon as it has served to bring pilgrims out of the fallen world and into the risen world manifest within the icon-dense churches built over or next to the memorialized sites: an historical moment is only distinct from others in the light of temporality – in eternity all moments are the same' (Bowman 1991: 110).

4 Meeting the *Living Stones*

Responsible tourism stresses the value of engaging with the socio-politico-cultural context of the region being visited. The major stress in the *Living Stones'* pilgrimages is the engagement with the living Christian communities in the Holy Land. The following summary of the official record gives an impression of such a Pilgrimage to Jordan, the West Bank, Israel, the West Bank and Jordan (November 2-13, 1991), undertaken by a group of 31 adults, 27 university students and two lecturers, and the two lecturers who led the group.

On Day 1, the party flew from London to Amman, arriving 15.05 local time. They had dinner and settled in at the Region Hotel. On Day 2, 'We took a bus to the Latin Catholic Cathedral for 9 a.m. Mass in Arabic with the Jordanian Christians in Amman, which was celebrated by the bishop. After Mass we introduced ourselves to the bishop and some of the leadership of the community. We then visited Dr Hanna Nassar, the deported President of Bir Zeit University in his offices.' Dr Nassar spoke about the recent history of Palestine. 'He impressed us by his obvious lack of vengeance, and the high moral character of his position: "The reason we cannot go back into history is because we are dealing with human beings, not with objects. Therefore the only viable solution to the Israeli-Palestinian problem must be a human one, two separate states."' Questions and answers followed, on the prospects for the Madrid conference, on being president-in-exile of a university, and on the circumstances under which he had been expelled. 'After our meeting with Dr Nassar we did some sightseeing in and around Amman – Roman theatre, etc. We then drove to the ruins of Jerash, one of the ten cities of the Decapolis visited by Jesus, and the most complete Graeco-Roman ruin still surviving.'

Day 3: 'We rose early to cross the bridge over the Jordan and went to Jericho . . . Then we left for Tabgha, and visited the reconstructed 4th and 6th century basilica, and viewed its enchanting mosaics, particularly that of the loaves and fishes. We briefly visited the Mount of the Beatitudes, the Church of the Primacy of Peter, and Capernaum, after which we took the boat to Tiberias, and drove straight to Nazareth, where we stayed in the Hostel of the Sisters of Nazareth.

'After supper we had a fascinating session with the Anglican priest, active in local and national politics, Archdeacon Riah Abu El-Assal. He gave us an inspiring address: "We pray for that day when the Israeli State will enjoy security, and the Palestinian people will enjoy independence, and an independent state of their own, side by side with Israel, on Palestinian soil . . . We continue to believe that only reconciled neighbours guarantee security for neighbours, and the closest neighbours for the Israelis are the Palestinians . . . You need to know about the Holy Land. It is not a Holy Land now. It will become a Holy Land when there is peace . . .

"Who are the Christians in this country? I am an Arab, but not a Muslim. I am a Palestinian, and I have not trespassed into Israel. I am an Anglican, but I am not an Englishman. I am an Israeli, but not a Jew . . . What has become of the Christian community is very serious. In Jaffa, the Anglican church had over 800 communicants every Sunday. After 1948 we were left with five people! Altogether the Christian population has gone from 35 per cent to 1.5 per cent in 1991. We have become a very small minority, and there are reasons for the dwindling of numbers. First, the wars in 1948, 1956, 1967, 1973, 1982, 1991; political pressure – we are part of the minority Arab population inside Israel and we are pressured like the rest of the Arabs.

"The State of Israel claims to be the oasis of democracy in the Middle East, and I want to say that Israel is a democracy, but a democracy for the Jews. It is not a democracy for the Arabs . . . I strongly believe that this piece of land will become part of heaven if we should witness an era of peace, a just peace. If this peace comes about, then this land will become the Holy Land. Perhaps it requires a new generation. I hope that you will become ambassadors for whatever is right, for whatever is just, for whatever leads to peace. Thank you brothers and sisters. I hope I have given you a little of my heart, and I hope that you young people will reshape the present as well as the future of the international community of which you are a part. Thank you!"' During question time Canon Riah spoke of the difficulties of his own life, and impressed upon the students the need to become aware of what is going on in other parts of the global village.

On Day 4, 'We visited the Basilica of the Annunciation, where Fr Prior said Mass with the group at 8.30. After visiting the Basilica we visited the Greek Orthodox Church of the Well. We read from Isaiah 61 and Luke 4 as we left Nazareth by bus. We by-passed Beth Shean on the way down.

'As we drove down the Jordan Valley from Nazareth to Jericho the sadness of seeing the presence of numerous settlements was relieved by the sight of a lone Japanese Buddhist monk. He was walking up the Jordan Valley in the direction of Beth Shean, a solitary figure beating his drum for peace. Fr Prior recognized the monk, since they both had been on the Walk for Peace from Jerusalem to Amman in June. Twice they had been detained and subsequently arrested. Some months after the International Peace Walk from Jerusalem to Amman (June 5-11, 1991), the Buddhist monk was still beating his drum for peace. His solitary witness was not without impact. Coming from Japan he carried none of the burden of guilt for the Jewish Holocaust with which Europeans are tainted, and which prevents them exercising their concern for the Palestinians. Even if nobody else should concern himself for peace, this solitary Japanese Buddhist would continue to beat his drum for peace for several more months.'

When we returned to Jericho we visited the ruins of the Umayyad Hisham Palace, and admired the Greek Orthodox Monastery of the Temptation of Christ from afar. We lunched in the restaurant next to the Tel, and then visited the Ancient Site of Jericho, the oldest known city in the world. 'After visiting the Tell we "swam" in the Dead Sea south of Ein Fascha. An officious Police Officer disturbed us and abused his authority. We didn't give him much change. Our final visit for the day was to Qumran, site of the Community of the Essenes where the Dead Sea Scrolls were found. We arrived at St Stephen's Gate at about 5.45 p.m.'

On Day 5, 'We went to visit our old friend, the Sufi, Sheikh Jamal under the Dome of the Rock. He addressed us, "First of all I say welcome! . . . The Palestinian leaders say 'Yes' for the peace. And I, as leader of my people, say, 'Yes' for the peace, 'No' for the war! 'No' for the suffering! This Holy Land needs real peace . . . If Mr Bush wants the peace, he can make it, as he made it in Kuwait . . . If you do not take the peace in the right time, you will lose it. And I pray from my heart for the peace . . . The people in America now see the situation after Madrid." We then visited the Dome of the Rock and the al-Aqsa Mosque.'

On Day 6, 'We took the bus to West Bank town of Ramallah to visit the Trustees' Building of the University of Bir Zeit, and then moved off in the bus to visit the campus. We encountered a roadblock of soldiers as we tried to visit Bir Zeit village. One of the leaders addressed the soldiers, "People in England will be astonished to learn that we are prevented from visiting academic colleagues in Bir Zeit University . . . It is disgraceful that we cannot do this . . . Have you told your commander that we are a delegation from an English University? We will write to our Members of Parliament . . . " One soldier replied, "You can speak to the General in Ramallah, General Eitan."' Fr Prior recited the opening verse of Psalm 1 in Hebrew, and to protest further, sang Psalm 119 in Hebrew!'

On Day 7, 'Fr Prior brought four students to St Joseph's Hospital in the morning. One had fallen from her bunk bed onto a chair, and three others were suffering stomach upsets. We were treated very well in the hospital. The remainder of the group went to meet the Armenian patriarch and visit his church. Then they went to the Mount of Olives to view the Old City, and thence to the Herodion.

'We visited the Basilica of the Nativity, and sang "Silent Night" at the Manger. Our bus took us to Deheisheh Refugee Camp. We were brought into the camp by two young inhabitants. Very soon we were approached by a column of about ten Israeli soldiers, who were in walkie-talkie communication with their commander. They insisted that they should bring us round, "to protect us". We made it clear that we did not want to give the impression that we were collaborating with the occupying forces. To our surprise, they relented, and we spent the rest of the afternoon looking at various aspects of the camp.

'We went to the Shepherd's Field where we celebrated Mass together. Then we had a meeting with the *Rapprochement* in Beit Sahour. The spokesman addressed us: "We want to tell the people what it has been like in the curfews. Explain to your people that Palestinians are not terrorists, but that we are screaming for justice. We are human beings. Animals in Europe are looked after better. Can you imagine our schools being closed? How could this happen in the 20th century? Even South Africa was never as bad as that . . . How can we celebrate Christmas with so much suffering in each family? Our children are deprived of the joy of celebrating even Christmas."'

Fr Prior recited a poem he had written on his previous visit, having seen the demolished house of a family whose father was trying to put a roof over their heads:

Beit Sahour

While shepherds watched their flocks by night
a mile away the soldiers
dynamite the inn
of the little family
whose fifteen year old, like David,
threw a stone at the Israeli Goliath
but without David's success.

For this crime against the mighty
the lowly are rendered homeless
and pitch their tent
beside the empty tomb.

The grandeur of the mother
ennobled by suffering;
the two children standing uncomprehending,
and the father with a jaded resignation
begins again to raise a covering
over the foundations.

'Later that evening, back in the Austrian Hospice we had a fascinating meeting with the Jewish activist, Gershon Baskin: "What's interesting is that the *Intifada*, more than any other political event in the history of Palestinians in this country, was a peace movement. It was a call to recognize the existence of Israel, and a call by the Palestinians to be accorded national and political rights . . . The Palestinians said effectively, 'we are facing the reality of Israel's existence, and we are calling for the implementation of UN Resolution 181. We want a Palestinian State in part of Palestine. The Israelis at that point should have been dancing in the street. But they didn't.' In 1988 I sat down and tried to write down all the issues of confrontation between Israel and the Palestinians, and I came up with a list of over thirty issues that would have to be resolved. I pared it down to seven, and I said that if we could solve these seven problems peace could come . . . Unfortunately the Israeli Peace Movement cannot influence decision makers, and therefore has a policy which is doomed to fail."'

Day 8: 'We walked through the Old City to the Western (Wailing) Wall, the Church of the Dormition, the Cenacle, and David's tomb. Unfortunately, being the Sabbath, the Chamber of the Holocaust was closed. We paused for a while outside it, and contemplated the mystery of human evil. We visited the Church of San Pietro in Gallicantu, and made our way to the Pool of Siloam. We were stopped by a roadblock of soldiers, but after some little delay we were allowed to proceed. At the Pool we had a reading from John 9, and then proceeded up the Kidron Valley to Hezekiah's Tunnel. We completed our walk to the Church of All Nations, where we arrived at about 12.45 – it was closed until 2.30. We invited the students to come back later in the afternoon, or on the following day.'

Day 9: 'We joined Archbishop Lutfi Laham and his congregation for the Greek Catholic Liturgy at the Melkite Church near Jaffa Gate, at 9 a.m. After the service we met the congregation, and had a long conversation with the Archbishop. Then we had a free day for shopping.'

Day 10: 'We rose early for the bridge crossing to Jordan. We proceeded along the Kings' Highway to Mount Nebo, from where Moses viewed 'the Promised Land'. We celebrated Mass in the Byzantine basilica. We visited Madaba with its exquisite mosaics, and then Kerak where the group visited the magnificent Crusader castle. Some were complaining of severe tummy ache. We ended the day at Petra, the lost Nabatean "rose red city half as old as time". We had dinner and overnighted at the Nabatean Hotel – the place was in bad shape.'

Day 11: 'Some went down the gorge on horses, while others walked. We explored Petra on foot. At four o'clock we left the site, and had dinner and a concert at the Nabatean Hotel, where we overnighted.'

Day 12: 'We left Petra at 6.45 a.m. and headed for Amman Airport, stopping once on the way. We flew directly from Amman, on RJ111 departing 12.15, and arrived safely at London Heathrow at 15.45. *Al-Hamdu li-llah!*'

Because of her constant contact with the Christian communities, both monastic and those centred around the bishops, and her dependence upon them, both for hospitality, instruction about the sites, and worship, Egeria may be regarded as the prototype of *Living Stones'* pilgrims to the Holy Land. For she not only visited the holy places, but she stayed with, prayed with, and was instructed by the *living stones* of the biblical lands. With her, then, the secular context of her travels gave way to a totally Christian one: holy bishop, holy places, Christian hospitality, and church festivities.

Quidquid recipitur in modo recipientis recipitur[24]

'Though we travel the world over to find the beautiful we must carry it

---

[24] This phrase from medieval philosophy (which can be rendered, *whatever is received is received in accordance with the mode of the receiver*, i.e., not that of the giver) emphasizes the critical role of the observer, and of the observer's pre-understanding before encountering a new experience.

with us or we find it not.'[25] It seems, at least to some extent, that each group coming on pilgrimage to Jerusalem, with the exception of those on a *Living Stones'* type pilgrimage, brings with it its own understanding of the sacred, and tends to return home with its fundamental predispositions confirmed.

Latecomers to the practice of pilgrimage, and somewhat reluctant, Protestant Christians tend to concentrate on the relationship between the place and the Bible.[26] Reflecting something of the reformers' disdain of the practice of pilgrimage in general,[27] they are uneasy in the presence of the elaborate liturgies one meets in the Middle East, and find the ceremonies of the Holy Sepulchre, in particular, to be too boisterous to be authentic. In the case of some, this centre of Christian veneration resembles a defiled place, full of corruption and superstition, which like the Temple in Jesus' time needs to be cleansed of its 'superstitions and fraudful degradation'.[28] In general, they prefer to encounter the unmediated Christ in the Garden Tomb, or in Galilee, rather than in the monuments thrown up by two thousand years of devotion to his memory. They prefer the landscapes and the village scenes, which make Jesus come alive. For such people, the Garden Tomb discovered by General Gordon is a God-send. Even if it has no claim to mark the place of the burial of Jesus, its tranquillity responds to the needs of their particular privatised piety.

For Orthodox pilgrims, on the other hand, the precise identification of sites is largely irrelevant. The whole land, rather than any specific part of it serves as a locus for participation in the divine activity of the liturgy. The icons on display, rather than the association of the place with the sacred events of the past, are the principal focus of attention. Catholics tend to regard sites as facilitating the 'composition of place', which helps them interiorize the particular biblical text relating to the life of Jesus.

The reality is that the significance of pilgrimage to Jerusalem means so many different things to pilgrims. The anthropologist, Glenn Bowman,

---

[25] Ralph Waldo Emerson, 1803-1882, *Essays*, xii, Art.

[26] After four years of eastern travel, Thomas Cook wrote in 1872, 'A new incentive to scriptural investigation has been created and fostered: "The Land and the Bible" have been brought into familiar juxtaposition' (Davies 1988: 148).

[27] 'All pilgrimages should be stopped,' Luther wrote (Davies 1988: vii). True Christian pilgrimage was not to Rome or Compostela, but to the prophets, the psalms and the gospels. For the 1409 Lollards' tract, *The Lanterne of Light*, there were six manners of pilgrimage: from birth to the heavenly city; going to church; visiting the poor; distributing alms; studying holy writ; and, finally, death. There is no other pilgrimage that may please God (Davies 1988: 91).

[28] Edward E Robinson, professor at Union Theological Seminary, wrote of his visit to Jerusalem in 1838: 'We counted it no loss [missing the events of Holy Week] . . . for the object of our visit was the city itself, in relation to its ancient renown and religious associations, not as seen in its present state of decay and superstitions and fraudful degradation' (1977: 239), quoted in Wilken 1992: xiii.

interprets this fact as showing that the image of the city comes from the images built up at home, rather than from encounter with the reality. 'The holy city is, in other words, a place where pilgrims who have inherited or developed certain images of a "Jerusalem" during enculturation elsewhere can embody those images and engage them as aspects of the material world' (Bowman 1991: 99). It is his contention that it is at the sites whence pilgrims set out on their searches for the centre that pilgrims learn what they desire to find. 'At the centres where they go in expectation of fulfilling that desire pilgrims experience little other than that which they already expect to encounter' (p. 121).

I contend that this is not the case of those who go on a *Living Stones'* type pilgrimage. These meet the people, and become aware of the social context in which their pilgrimage takes place. They soon discover that Palestine is not one democratic State of Israel, stretching from the Mediterranean to the Jordan, and from Mount Hermon to Eilat, as the Israeli Tourist maps imply, but, rather, consists of two distinct regions, whose inhabitants exhibit gross inequalities of living standards, and political and human rights. Such pilgrims are extricated from succumbing to the programmed pattern described by Kenneth Cragg: 'Sharp moral issues are easily submerged by outsiders in archeology or tourism, while the local Christianity is relegated to sentiment and the museum' (1992: 235). They see for themselves the extent of the belligerence of the occupation of the West Bank, and when they hear the accounts of life under occupation, or as inferiors in the Jewish state, in all the cases I have encountered they are profoundly shocked by what they find.

Living Stones pilgrims, relatively free of the thought-control propaganda of the agencies of the Israeli Tourist Board, see and hear things for themselves, and learn a great deal at first hand. They come to discover that for present-day Arab Christians in the Holy Land Golgotha is not a sad memory of a distant past, enshrined in encrustations of Byzantine and Crusader church architecture. It is part of the every day indignity and oppression which they share with all other disadvantaged peoples of the world. Their *Via Dolorosa* is no mere ritualistic procession through the narrow streets of the Old City, but the fate of being subjugated and humiliated in their own land.

This kind of responsible visiting educates pilgrims and ultimately promotes international understanding and harmony. *Living Stones'* pilgrims to the Holy Land encounter representatives of the earliest Christian communities of the region. They come to appreciate something of their life of witness to Christian values in a culture which is predominantly Muslim or Jewish. They see for themselves something of the political contexts in which Palestinian Christians live, either as second class citizens of Israel, which Israeli propagandists euphemistically call 'the only democracy in the Middle East,' or under brutal occupation in the West Bank or Gaza. *Living Stones'* pilgrims allow their moral sensibilities to be seduced neither by home-bred religious sentiment, nor by the excitement of the archaeology of an exotic land.

Encounter with the contemporary political realities of the Holy Land raises important questions for students of the Bible in particular. When one meets the Palestinians, the modern counterparts of the Hittites, the Girgashites, the Amorites, the Canaanites, the Perizzites, the Hivites, and the Jebusites, one is, on moral grounds, forced to question whether the Pentateuch continues to provide the figment of divine legitimacy for the occupation of other people's land, and their virtual *Vernichtung*. The commandment that, 'You shall destroy all the peoples that the Lord your God will give over to you, your eye shall not pity them' (Deut 7.16), and the statement that, 'The Lord your God will clear away these nations before you little by little, . . . and you shall make their name perish from under heaven' (Deut 7.22-24), are seen in a new light. In our society such sentiments, rightly, would be regarded as an incitement to racial hatred. At such points the Pentateuch shows itself to reflect racist and xenophobic·attitudes, which may well have contributed to the world-view of Dr Baruch Goldstein, and surely inform the political hermeneutics of other Jewish fundamentalists in their biblically-based justification of barbarism. Israelite self-presentation as ethnically and religiously superior appears to receive in the Bible the highest possible legitimacy in the form of divine approval. Young enquiring minds question what kind of God requires this sort of embarrassment, and what class of people needs to be constantly nourished by such xenophobia?

I am not aware of any anthropological study of the effects of such pilgrimages, but my experience of many examples of this kind assures me that *Living Stones'* pilgrims are interrogated by the experience of what they encounter. They do not simply have their prejudices refined. The pilgrims are deeply impressed by the vigour with which the *living stones* of the land witness to their faith in very trying circumstances, and by the almost embarrassing hospitality of the people in the midst of their affliction. Encountering such people in the place of their tragedy is an experience that I have no difficulty in describing as sacred. Religious dispositions, such as the admiration of virtue, moral outrage in the face of systemic sin, a determination to work for justice, and a sense of being in the company of the suffering Christ rise spontaneously to the surface of one's consciousness. One begins to appreciate that theophanies occur in the midst of the *quotidian trivialities* of the *suq*, as they do also in the formal liturgies of the churches and shrines, and on the heights of numinous mountains. In general, *Living Stones'* pilgrims encounter something altogether Other, and in the process appear to be changed profoundly.

> Sometimes, the seeker
> becomes the sought.
>
> Thereafter, the burden's
> to bear the benediction:
> as the priest his symbols,
> the poet his vision,
> woman love, the mother
> her child and mortal man
> immortality.[29]

References

Bliss, F J. 1894. 'The Recent Pilgrimage to Jerusalem', in *Palestine Exploration Fund Quarterly Statement*, April: 101–108

Bowman, G. 1991. 'Christian Ideology and the Image of a Holy Land. The place of Jerusalem Pilgrimage in the various Christianities', in Eade, J and M J Sallnow, eds. 1991: 98–121

Cragg, K. 1992. *The Arab Christian. A History of the Middle East*. London: Mowbray

Darrow, W S. 1988. 'The Harvard Way in the Study of Religion', *Harvard Theological Review* 81: 215–234

Davies, J G. 1988. *Pilgrimage, Yesterday and Today: Why, Where and How*. London: SCM

Durkheim, E. 1912. *The Elementary Forms of Religious Life*, trans. J W Swain. London: Allen & Unwin, 1964

Eade, J and M J Sallnow, eds. 1991. *Contesting the Sacred. The Anthropology of Christian Pilgrimage*. London/New York: Routledge

Eliade, M. 1958. *Patterns in Comparative Religion*, trans. Rosemary Sheed. London/New York: Sheed and Ward

———————— 1959. *The Sacred and the Profane – The Nature of Religion*, trans. New York

Franceschini, A and R Weber, ed. 1965. *Itinerarium Egeriae*, (*Corpus Christianorum Series Latina* 175: 29–90)

Geyer, P and O Cuntz. ed. 1965. *Itinerarium Burdigalense* (Corpus Christianorum Series Latina 175: 1–26).

---

[29] From Desmond O'Grady's, *Initiates*, in *Sing me Creation*, 1977 (Dublin: Gallery Books).

Hunt, E D. 1984. *Holy Land Pilgrimage in the Later Roman Empire AD 312-460.* Oxford: Clarendon Press

Lewis, C. 1989. 'On Going to Sacred Places', *Theology* vol. 92: 388-394

O'Grady, Desmond. 1977. *Sing me Creation.* Dublin: Gallery Books

Ozick, C. 1983. 'Toward a New Yiddish', *Art and Ardor.* New York

Partin, H B. 1967. *The Muslim Pilgrimage: Journey to the Centre* (PhD Dissertation presented to the University of Chicago)

Robinson, E E. 1977. *Biblical Researches in Palestine, Mount Sinai and Arabian Petraea.* New York

Sallnow, M J. 1987. *Pilgrims of the Andes: Regional Cults in Cusco.* Washington DC: Smithsonian Institution Press

————— 1991. 'Pilgrimage and Cultural Fracture in the Andes', in Eade and Sallnow, eds. 1991: 137-153)

Schaff, P and H Wace, ed. 1892. *The Nicene and Post-Nicene Fathers* (Michigan), 2nd series

Stirrat, R L. 1984. 'Catholics and the Riots in Historical Perspective', in J Manor, ed. *Sri Lanka in Change and Crisis.* London: Croom Helm

————— 1991. 'Place and Person in Sinhala Catholic Pilgrimage', in Eade and Sallnow, eds. 1991: 122-136

Turner, V and E Turner. 1978. *Image and Pilgrimage in Christian Culture: Anthropological Perspectives.* Oxford: Blackwell

Wetherd, H N. 1947. *The Four Paths of Pilgrimage.* London

Wilken, R L. 1992. *The Land called Holy. Palestine in Christian History and Thought.* Yale: University Press

Wilkinson, J. 1971. *Egeria's Travels.* London: SPCK

————— 1977. *Jerusalem Pilgrims before the Crusades.* Jerusalem: Ariel

OBLIGATIONS AND EXPECTATIONS

18
Churches of the Holy Land Obligations and Expectations: A View from the Holy Land

Agnes D Hanania

This paper reviews the background of the Christians in the Holy Land and their major concerns, and suggests some ways the churches can contribute to improve their conditions within the context of their Palestinian society and culture. The emphasis will be placed on the West Bank and the Gaza Strip (Palestine).

Christians in the Holy Land

With the establishment of the first community of Christians in Jerusalem, which dates back to Apostolic times (Acts 2.4), the first Christian Church was established. Jerusalem is the source of Christianity. The history and doctrine of the Church began there. It is from Jerusalem that Christianity spread to various parts of the Middle East and to the rest of the world (Wilkinson 1989). The roots of Arab Christians in the Holy Land go back to the early communities of Christians in the area. By the 5th century, Arab kingdoms in Syria, Jordan, Iraq, and Palestine adopted Christianity (Acts 2.11; Issa 1984: 108; Samir 1986: 26).

During the first half of the 7th century, Islam conquered the whole

Middle East and dealt with the Christians in the area with all tolerance. In the Qura'n, the Christians were mentioned quite favourably in several verses (Sura al-Ma'ida vv. 85-88). Verse 85 reads:

> And nearest among them in love
> To the Believers wilt thou
> Find those who say,
> 'We are Christians':
> Because amongst these are
> Men devoted to learning
> And men who have renounced
> The world, and they
> Are not arrogant.

In addition, when Muslims conquered the Holy Land, they gave the Christians, the 'People of the Book', in 636 AD, a covenant of protection for their persons and their possessions, known as the 'Covenant of 'Umar' (El Aref 1961: 91; Mansour 1991: 80). Since the arrival of Islam in the Holy Land right up to the present time, the relationship between Arab Christians and Arab Muslims has been one of mutual respect. What binds Christians and Muslims in the Holy Land is that they are both Arabs. Both have a common culture, a common history, a common language, and a common land.

Though different in religion, they share a common heritage (Mansour 1991: 76). Together they have participated in the social, economic, political, and cultural life of their Palestinian society. Moreover, the contributions of Arab Christians to the Arab culture as a whole have been acknowledged (Samir 1986).

Concerns of the Christians in the Holy Land

Two major concerns can be discerned with respect to the future presence of Christians in the Holy Land. These two concerns are, 1) identity and role, and 2) socio-economic conditions and emigration. While the first concern relates more to the future, the second is more immediate, but could have important implications for the future also.

1 Identity and Role

Christians in the Holy Land, as is the case of most Christians in the Middle Eastern society, should be understood within the context of their history, language, and culture. Christians in the Holy Land are mostly Palestinian Arabs. They are neither the descendants of western Christian missions who came to the Holy Land, as some western Christians assume them to be, nor are they associated with western Christian powers, which are considered by Muslims as the cause of their oppression for centuries (Habib 1986). Western Christians should realize that a difference exists between how western and eastern Christians perceive Christianity. This difference has been expressed by Schwartz:

> For most westerners, Christianity is defined in individualistic, personal and doctrinal terms. Eastern Christians tend to see themselves as a community with an ethnic or cultural background and defined traditions. Continuity is a principal factor in eastern culture, while westerners often view change as equivalent to progress. These are not contradictory values, but there is little common ground between them (1986).

That is why it is important to understand the continuity of presence and witness of Arab Christians in the Holy Land within the context of their Middle Eastern society, taking into consideration their history, their language, and their culture.

However, as the Islamic revival is calling increasingly for the integration of state and religion, concern for the future is arising among Christians. According to Habib (1986), Christians are 'trying to see how they could live in the Middle Eastern society, not on the basis of tolerance or protection by the Muslim majority, but on the basis of right and equality between all people . . . Christian communities themselves are experiencing a serious concern for continuity of presence and witness in the area.' If such a concern exists and increases, fear in the face of the future could produce among the Christians a mentality of *milla*, or closed community, a self-centred community which looks to its own welfare rather than to the welfare of all the people in its society. Such a preoccupation would be in contradiction with the teachings of Christ and the church which call Christians to serve and help others (Luke 22.26-27; Matthew 5.42 and 6.2-3).

At present, the Christians in the Holy Land participate actively in their society and give priority to national goals (Aburish 1993). Though different in religion, both Christians and Muslims struggle for their Palestinian rights to self-determination and human rights. Both participate in their society on the basis of right and equality, and share with each other the same ethos and destiny.

The question that can be raised is what can the churches in the Holy

Land do to develop among Christians and Muslims a deeper understanding of each other's religion, and of the basic human values they both share. What can the churches in the Holy Land do to support their members towards a more active participation in their society, not only for the benefit of Christians, but also for the welfare of all the Palestinian people with whom they identify, so that they can secure their human rights and live with dignity and freedom?

2 Socio-Economic Conditions and Emigration

Since the plight of the Palestinians in 1948 and 1967, the area has witnessed large group emigrations from the Holy Land. Although both Christianity and Islam regard emigration as a natural phenomenon and a human right when it is a personal choice (Mallah 1990: 97-99; Sabella 1990: 110), Palestinian emigration is considered differently. In the case of Palestinians, emigration has not been a personal choice. Both Christians and Muslims have been forced out of their land, and have been deprived of their right to live on their own land. This human injustice has resulted in exile and hard living conditions under occupation and in refugee camps, and has created, as well, deep feelings of uncertainty and insecurity about the future. Furthermore, the difficult political conditions under occupation, and the lack of funds available to Palestinian institutions have limited the opportunities for work. All these factors have combined to intensify the problem of emigration.

For the Christians in the Holy Land, emigration has become an even larger problem because of its very high percentage in relation to the total Christian population in the area. Since the later part of the 19th century up to the present, about 85 per cent of the Palestinian Christian population have emigrated; and since the 1967 war, about 20,000 Christians have emigrated. More serious are the results of some studies which indicate that about 22 per cent of the Palestinian Christian population presently living in the area expressed an interest in emigration (Khoury 1991). Regarding who intends to emigrate, a study has shown that the highest percentages were among those who hold a bachelor's degree and those who hold a secondary school leaving certificate; the lowest percentages were among those who hold doctorate degrees, and those who completed an elementary education or less. This study has shown also that the highest percentage was among the unemployed, followed by the self-employed professionals. The lowest percentage appeared among those employed in the public sector (Sabella 1991). In his study, Zughbi (1991) also indicated that four factors account for the emigration of Palestinian Christians: 1) fear and escape, 2) search for an acceptable financial income, 3) search for knowledge, which starts as a temporary emigration, and then develops into a permanent one, 4) love for adventure. According to Zughbi, the first two factors have contributed most to the number of emigrants.

While some Palestinians emigrate physically, others do so psychologically, through the use of drugs; which is another form of escape. A study conducted in the Christian Quarter of the Old City in Jerusalem indicate that 20 per cent of the Christians living in this area use drugs. These individuals tend to have bad family relationships with either parents or wife, have seven or more children in the family, and live in one or two rooms (Sayegh 1991).

These findings indicate that, in general, the reason Christians in the Holy Land emigrate, whether physically or psychologically, is because of the limited prospects for the improvement of the prevailing conditions, particularly the limited opportunities for work, which could provide them with a decent quality of life, a life which would enable them to live with their families in dignity and freedom.

The problem of emigration among Palestinian Christians is raising concern regarding the Christian presence and witness in the area. The Christians in the Holy Land represent the presence of the Church, the mother of all churches, in what is for Christians the holiest land. They are the *living stones* in the land, whose Holy Places have the most spiritual significance for Christians around the world. Christian presence and witness in the Holy Land at present is taking several forms. Besides the spiritual aspects, it is expressed through active participation in calls for social justice and peace, and through involvement in educational and social service activities, in response to the increasing needs and problems of the community.

Perhaps Christian witness in the Holy Land needs to go through a process of reflection and renewal, in order to develop a new vision, one based on the teachings of Christ and His love, taking into consideration the social and cultural context of the Christians in the Holy Land. It is important that the churches in the Holy Land, with the help of the Universal Church, should look for ways and means to encourage and guide people to stay in their land, live with the rest of their Palestinian people in dignity, and participate effectively in the development of their society.

Churches of the Holy Land: Expectations and Principles

Besides their religious and spiritual role, the churches in the Holy Land cannot be isolated from the life of their own people. They are expected to understand them, support them, and be active in guiding them towards achieving an improved quality of life where human, social, and national rights prevail. Such a role should be guided by the following principles:

1 To provide the Christians of the Holy Land with the spiritual and moral support which would enrich their lives and provide their experiences with meaningful self-rewards.

2 To encourage Palestinian Christians in the Holy Land to stay on their own land, in their homeland, and among their own Palestinian people. In addition to strengthening their national identity, this would provide a continuity of Christian presence and witness in the Land where the first Christian Church was established.

3 To support national unity among the Palestinian Arab population, by drawing on all the values that both Christianity and Islam share, and the common heritage which binds them together in this Holy Land.

4 To support the involvement and participation of the Christians in the Holy Land in their common endeavour with their Palestinian people, so that together they may achieve their political rights to self-determination on their land, develop their Palestinian society, in which peace and justice, human dignity and equality, and mutual respect among individuals will prevail.

5 To develop their relationships with the universal Christian Churches so that these churches understand better the Christians in the Holy Land, the importance of their presence, the problems they face, and their needs within the broader context of Palestinian life, problems, and needs.

6 To support and expand the services of existing educational, social, and research institutions affiliated with the churches in the Holy Land, so that they can offer these services more effectively and reach a larger number of the Palestinian people.

7 To support research studies which aim at bringing about a better understanding of the Palestinian people, and of the

Christians in the Holy Land. These studies will reveal their concerns, the conditions of their life, and suggest ways and means of improving those conditions.

To be effective and achieve their aims, the above mentioned principles ought to be considered simultaneously within the framework of Palestinian national goals and priorities. Already the churches are offering a variety of services through several educational and social institutions. These services, however, are not co-ordinated among the different churches and lack a comprehensive conceptual framework for establishing a policy to guide all such activities. Such a framework could provide more effective services where needed most. It would provide support for individuals, and would aim at helping them be:

- self-dependent, rather than dependent on others
- givers and sharers, rather than only takers
- open, rather self-centred and closed
- active, rather than passive
- motivated to learn and work, rather than indifferent
- involved, rather than withdrawn
- hopeful, rather than hopeless
- working with others, rather than being isolated
- creative, rather than being intellectually limited

The churches in the Holy Land cannot provide by themselves all the support which is needed in order to ensure the continuity of the Christian presence and witness in the Holy Land. The understanding, collaboration, and moral and financial support of the Universal Church are most necessary. This would require that needs and priorities be studied carefully, and projects be evaluated. In addition, the involvement and contribution of the communities themselves, within their means, would be necessary for more effective achievements.

In the Appendix, several suggestions for action are presented. These aim mainly at helping the Christians in the Holy Land. In addition, they aim at extending the help to all the Palestinian people living in the area.

Conclusion

This paper reviews the background of the Christians in the Holy Land, their present concerns and needs, and makes some suggestions for their support. Christians in the Holy Land wish 1) that the importance of their presence be recognized, and, 2) that support, both moral and financial, be provided to enable them stand on their feet, so that they can become gradually self-dependent and be able, in the future, to help others. The suggestions for support presented in the paper, however, cannot be realized effectively without the existence of the following factors:

1 A Conceptual Framework for Policy and Action

The needs of the Christians in the Holy Land are many. The services offered, at present, are the result of initiatives on the part of individuals or group of individuals who sensed the need for services and were willing to do something about it, even with the limited means available. The contributions of these individuals and their efforts are highly appreciated. However, for more effective results, there is a need for a comprehensive study of the conditions of the Christians in the Holy Land, and for a related conceptual framework for support, to provide the basis for policy and action. The presence of such a framework can help define priorities, and increase, expand, or redirect services for the ultimate purpose of supporting the continuity of Christian presence and witness in the Holy Land within the context of Palestinian society and culture, taking into consideration Palestinian national goals and priorities.

2 Collaboration and Co-ordination

The collaboration and co-ordination between all the parties concerned with the conditions of the Christians in the Holy Land is essential, so that all the efforts may be directed towards solving relevant issues. Initiatives in this direction between the churches in the Holy Land have already begun, a move which is highly commended. In particular, the following relationships should be supported and encouraged:

a. Closer collaboration and co-ordination between the churches in the Holy Land.

b. Closer collaboration and co-ordination between the churches in the Holy Land and the Universal Church.

c. Closer collaboration and co-ordination between the churches in the Holy Land and their communities.

d. Closer collaboration and co-ordination between the churches in the Holy Land and the Islamic leadership, to look for ways and means to improve Christian-Muslim dialogue and understanding between their faithful, who inhabit the same country.

The Christian presence and witness in the Holy Land should be of concern to all Palestinians and Christians in the world. Something can be done to improve the situation. This requires the participation, collaboration, and commitment of all relevant parties.

Appendix
Churches in the Holy Land:
Suggestions for Implementation

The suggestions presented in this section relate more to the concerns mentioned earlier. They are aimed at supporting the Christian presence in the Holy Land within the context of Palestinian society and culture. These suggestions are presented below:

I Education

1. Formal education

a. Improve the quality of teaching in the Schools

Most church-supported schools serve low to middle income students who represent the largest segment of the Palestinian people. A distinctive feature of such schools, their *raison d'être*, should be to provide quality education for the student population they serve.

However, because of the limited resources, most of these schools do not offer the quality of education they would like to offer without raising their fees beyond the means of the students they serve. Education which is meaningful must support active learning, creativity, and an awareness of community needs. Such an education should provide additional school subjects and activities not on offer in public schools, such as, music, arts and crafts, and varied sports activities. It should provide services to help students overcome personal and social problems, and guide the development of their talents and interests through the collaboration of counselling staff, faculty, and administration. In supporting the salaries of staff and teachers, and by helping to provide adequate facilities, equipment, and educational resources, many Christian families, as well as a large segment of the population could be served, particularly if this is accompanied by an expansion in the number of schools. It should be noted that these schools take low to moderate fees and serve Christian as well as Muslim students.

b. Increase the number of schools

There are many rural areas which do not have schools, and where they do, they are often elementary schools which function with unqualified teachers and inadequate facilities. By increasing the number of adequate schools, and upgrading the existing elementary schools, a wider segment of the population can be served. In addition, by doing so, more opportunities for work can be created which can help alleviate the unemployment problem.

c. Add a subject on the 'ethics of religion and culture' to the school curricula

Religious education for the young people is usually given by the schools. In Christian schools, Muslims are usually taught Muslim education, while Christians are taught Christian education. Each child has the right to learn his own religion. However, each child does not know anything about the 'other's' religion, and the common human values they both share. Often children do not know how to relate what they learn in a religion class to everyday life. The addition of a subject on ethics in the school curricula could bring young Christians and Muslims together in the classroom to discuss common issues, concerns, and values drawn from both Christianity and Islam and their common Culture. For example, how many Christian and Muslim children know that they both share human values such as humility (S. Furqan xxv:63; John 13.16) and forgiveness (S. Furqan xxv:70; Matthew 18.21-22)? How many of these children can relate, for instance, these two values to similar values drawn from their history and culture (such as in poetry, drama, painting, etc.)? How much can classroom discussions on such topics help both Christian and Muslim children understand each other better and develop stronger bonds between them?

d. Vocational schools

Vocational schools which provide quality training in a variety of technical/vocational fields are limited. There are eight vocational secondary schools and six vocational training centres in the West Bank and the Gaza Strip.

These suffer from lack of equipment and unqualified teachers. According to a study, 63 per cent of the vocational institutions did not have even a single teacher/trainer who had completed his study beyond the level of a vocational secondary school. The number of students served in these institutions was 1,473 in 1986/1987 (Mi'ari 1991). At the post secondary level, community colleges which provide vocational education are very limited also. If a political change takes place, the demand for vocational education is going to increase very much, particularly, if we consider that universities draw their students from the top 30 per cent of the number who pass the public secondary school examination.

e. Scholarships at local universities and abroad

University education is becoming very expensive. One way to encourage Christians in the Holy Land to stay in their homeland is through helping their families by providing financial support in different forms, including work scholarships and loans for the education of their children at local institutions, particularly in fields where job opportunities are expected to be available. Also, if financial support towards the cost of education is given to local educational institutions which provide quality education, both institutions and students can be served and helped. In technical and vocational areas, for which training is not available locally, scholarships abroad can help improve the quality of vocational education in the area, and consequently can benefit all the Palestinian people.

2. Non formal education

Short-term courses for training and retraining is very much needed for all the Palestinian people due to changes taking place in society. For Christians in the Holy Land, this can be a way to improve or gear their knowledge and skills to meet the demands of the job market. Some such courses can be focused on needs in agriculture, education, health, and technologies.

3. Social/educational activities for families and young people

Social and educational activities are very important means to promote personal, religious, and social values. Support for such activities would help increase youths' understanding of themselves and of others, and of their social obligations and responsibilities through participating actively in social and educational activities and carrying out related responsibilities. To be effective, however, such activities should get the support and involvement of both schools and families whose collaboration is crucial. This would require programs for parents, principals of schools, and teachers, as well as activities for youth, in collaboration with the local churches.

II Economic/business

To encourage Christians in the Holy Land to stay in their country and overcome unemployment, several options can be considered, including financial support in the form of loans without interest for individuals who want to start a new business, or want to expand and improve an existing business. The churches can use also their connections with the European Community to facilitate the export of Palestinian products. In addition, the provision of consultants can be most useful for guiding individuals towards ideas on appropriate ventures so that gradually they can become self-dependent.

III Housing

One of the difficulties facing young newly married Christians in the Holy Land is the availability of low cost housing. In the West Bank, the areas where most Christians live are concentrated in East Jerusalem and surrounding towns. In these areas the rents are increasing so rapidly that young people, with their limited income, not to mention the unemployed, barely can afford to provide for their living, and therefore find no alternative but to emigrate. The provision of low-cost housing would definitely solve an important problem. Furthermore, the provision of low-cost housing would increase the Christian presence and witness in the Holy Land. This would encourage people to stay on their land, protect the Holy Places, and preserve Christian property, and might even encourage those who emigrated to come back.

IV Health/social work

To improve the conditions of Christians in the Holy Land, their health and social conditions should be improved, particularly since low-cost health care is very limited. Support for such services, clinical as well as preventive, is needed. Already there are several health/social institutions which need support so that their services can cover a wider segment of the population, as well as provide an improved quality of service.

V Research/conferences

Research on the lives, problems, needs, attitudes and beliefs of the

Christians in the Holy Land is limited. Several activities, research studies, conferences, and publications have been undertaken by the Center for Religious and Heritage Studies in the Holy Land. These have improved Christian-Muslim dialogue, raised many thought-provoking questions, and provided some research material on several related issues. However, there is a need for much more of such activities to reach not only educated people, but also the ordinary person.

References

Aburish, Said K. 1993. *The Forgotten Faithful: The Christians of the Holy Land.* London: Quartet Books

El Aref, Aref. 1961. *A History of Jerusalem: Detailed Account of the Holy City.* Jerusalem: Andalus Library

Habib, Gabriel. 1986, October. 'Churches in the Middle East – A Continuing Witness.' *MECC Perspectives,* 4-6

Issa, Anton. 1984. 'History of the Christian Arabs in the Holy Land.' In *The Arab Christian and Moslim Traditions in the Holy Land.* 4th Conference. Tantur, Jerusalem: Ecumenical Institute for Theological Research

Khoury, Jiryis S. 1991. 'Review on Emigration.' *Al-Liqa* 3: 99-102

Mallah, Yaser. (1990). 'Meaning of Emigration in Islam.' In *The Arab Christian and Moslim Traditions in the Holy Land.* 8th Conference. Jerusalem: The Center for Religious Studies in the Holy Land

Mansour, Johny. 1991. 'Arab Civilization a Unifying Element for the Local Churches.' In *Theology and the Local Churches in the Holy Land.* 5th Conference. Jerusalem: The Center for Religious and Heritage Studies in the Holy Land

Mi'ari, Mahmud. 1991. *Vocational Education in the Occupied Territories.* Bir Zeit: University of Bir Zeit

Samir, Khalil. 1982. 'The Old Christian Arab Heritage and its Interaction with Arab Islamic Thought.' Paper presented in Arabic at the Conference of the Religious Fraternity in Cairo

Samir, Khalil. 1986, October. 'Christian Contribution to Arab Renaissance.' *MECC Perspectives,* 26-29

Sabella, Bernard. 1990. 'Meaning of Emigration in Christianity.' In *The Arab Christian and Moslim Traditions in the Holy Land.* 8th Conference. Jerusalem: The Center for Religious Studies in the Holy Land

Sabella, Bernard. 1991. 'A Study about Emigration among Christian Palestinians in the Bethlehem, Jerusalem, and Ramallah area.' *Al-Liqa* 3: 107-110

Sayegh, Michel F. 1991. 'Does our Society Suffer from the Appearance of Drug Usage?' *Al-Liqa* 3: 28-40

Schwartz, William E. 1986. 'Towards Understanding Churches in the Middle East: A Western Evangelical Perspective.' *MECC Perspectives*, 43-45

Wilkinson, John. 1989. 'Jerusalem under Rome and Byzantium 63 BC-637 AD.' In K J Asali (ed.), *Jerusalem in History*. Essex: Scorpion

Zughbi, Salim. 1991. 'Conditions of Emigrants and Relationships with their Country.' *Al-Liqa* 3: 112-114

19

Churches of the Holy Land Obligations and Expectations: A View from Outside

Hugh Wybrew

When I was asked to speak to this title I felt a great reluctance to do so. It is not easy to speak from the outside to those who live and suffer within a very difficult situation. I spent three years in Jerusalem from 1986 to 1989, and so learnt something of the Christian churches there, and something about the situation of the Palestinian people in general, and of Palestinian Christians in particular. Three years was long enough for me to realise the complexity of the situation, and to become aware of the dangers of making comments or suggestions from outside.

I have understood the title to refer to the obligations of Christians outside the situation to those in it, and to what Christians outside might reasonably expect from their sisters and brothers within it Though I speak of the latter with some diffidence, I am encouraged by the fact that most of the points which occurred to me when I was thinking about what to say have in fact been made by other contributors to this seminar. As the last speaker I can therefore perhaps perform a helpful service by drawing together in summary form a good deal that has been said in the past three days. I divide what I want to say into two parts, and begin with:

A. What the Churches of the Holy Land can rightly expect from the rest of the Christian Church

1 They can first of all rightly expect the rest of the church to recognize their existence. While at an official level the churches at large have always recognized the existence of sister churches in the Holy Land – the Orthodox, for example, the existence of the patriarchate of Jerusalem, the Anglican Communion, that of the Episcopal Church in Jerusalem and the Middle East, the Roman Catholic Church, that of the Latin patriarchate, and the Greek Catholic Church – ordinary western Christians have been only dimly aware of the existence of Arab Christianity. That situation is changing. Considerable numbers of western Christians, clergy and laity alike, take part in pilgrimages to Jerusalem and the Holy Land and are made aware of the existence of local churches. But the Arab churches in the Holy Land can rightly expect a continuing programme of education among Christians in general about their existence.

2. They have a right also to expect the church at large to be aware of the difficulties of their situation. There are difficulties arising from the political situation in the Holy Land, not least because of the deeply-rooted link between religious faith and socio-political community in the Middle East, of a kind now strange to western Christians. There are difficulties too arising from the continuous emigration of Christians from the Holy Land, largely because of the political situation, which is weakening the indigenous Christian community. Christians elsewhere need to be made aware of what is happening to churches in the land where Christianity began. Much is in fact being done: we have, for example, heard Michael Prior's lively presentation of the aims and achievements of *Living Stones*. St George's College, Jerusalem, which attracts each year many hundreds of Christians from all over the world, includes in all its courses speakers about the situation in the Holy Land. But more can be done. The point has already been made about this seminar: it is of little use if it preaches only to the converted. To be of value it must help to make the situation of Christians in the Holy Land known more widely.

3. Recognition of their existence and of their difficulties should not of course be simply theoretical, but should result in Christians from elsewhere making personal contact with their brothers and sisters in the Holy Land when they are on pilgrimage, or visiting. One of the problems of which we have heard is the reduction in the number of Arab

guides licensed by the Israeli authorities, which means that many Christian groups going to the Holy Land are guided by Israelis with no particular interest in promoting contact with local Christians. In such circumstances visiting Christians need to make more positive effort to enable such meetings to take place.

4. Acknowledging the situation of Christians in the Holy Land needs to issue in practical support. The *Intifada* has resulted in serious financial difficulties for the churches, and imposed great strains on their charitable work, not least in education and in the provision of medical services. Christians in the Holy Land can rightly expect financial support from their fellow Christians elsewhere. But although emergency help is essential, there is a no less urgent need for help in building up an economic base to enable the Palestinian Christian communities to enable the young generation to earn a living, and so feel less need to emigrate.

5. The economic situation is inseparable from the political. The spread of information and encouragement of awareness, and even emergency financial assistance, are by themselves inadequate. The point has been made already that the churches in the West should be more concerned with and involved in the peace process, and in working out the future of the country and of Jerusalem. It should be noted, however, that the churches, at least in the United Kingdom, have perhaps less political influence than outsiders might think. Religion in the West has become largely privatised. The Islamic Middle East may still think in terms of 'the Christian West'. But that is largely anachronistic. The West has become thoroughly secularised. In the 19th century religion may have been the pretext for political intervention in the Ottoman Middle East; but it would not even be used as a pretext now. There may be Christians in politics, and in Britain even bishops in the House of Lords; and the views of the churches may sometimes be sought in Europe. But they are unlikely to have a decisive voice in the formulation of policy.

B. *What the Church at large can rightly expect from Christians in the Holy Land*

1. The disunity of the Christian Church has nowhere been more sharply focused than in the Holy Land, where the historic churches have been keenly aware of their territorial and other rights and zealous in their defence. The conflicts that have regularly arisen among them have not served the Christian cause well. Several speakers at this seminar have

spoken of the need for unity among the Christians of Jerusalem and the
Holy Land. It is true that at the level of ordinary Christians a large
measure of unity already exists. There is, for example, a significant
number of inter-church marriages. It is perhaps at the level of church
leadership that the problem is more acute. Although co-operation
among the churches has greatly increased since the *Intifada* began, a great
deal needs to be done to further the work of reconciliation among them
at other levels: theological dialogue scarcely exists, and the Greek
Orthodox patriarchate has withdrawn from participation in all
ecumenical dialogues.

The church at large can rightly expect of the churches in the Holy
Land that they take seriously the Gospel imperative to unity, so essential
for Christian witness in the world. That is of course an imperative all the
churches everywhere need to heed. But in a good many places there are
local and national councils of churches, and the formation of such an
ecumenical body for Jerusalem and the Holy Land would enable all the
churches to speak with one voice on a range of practical issues. In my
experience the unofficial ecumenical bodies which do exist in Jerusalem
seem to receive most of their support from expatriate Christians.

2. There are perhaps particular reasons for taking unity seriously in the
Holy Land, home to Judaism and Islam, as well as to Christianity.
Evangelization, among both Muslims and Jews, is next to impossible
because of the political situation. Canon Riah has emphasised the
importance for the small Christian communities of practical co-
operation with Palestinian Muslims, and the need to stress what the two
faiths have in common. But Christians do have a distinctive
understanding of God and his purpose in creation and redemption, and
witness to that understanding must always be integral to the life of the
church. God, we believe, is a communion of persons united in love, and
his purpose is to unite all people and all things in that love. If, as the New
Testament insists, God in Christ is calling the whole human race into the
unity given by the Holy Spirit, witness to that faith in the Holy Land is
inseparably bound up with the quest for reconciliation and unity among
Christians there.

3. Alongside Christian witness in much of the contemporary world
goes dialogue with other world faiths. Considerable changes have taken
place in recent decades among many western Christians in their attitude
towards other faiths. The traditional assertion that Christianity alone
offers the way to salvation has been widely replaced by a recognition
that through other faiths too, people can enter into a relationship with
God. The church is only at the beginning of a new relationship with
people of other religions; but however that relationship will eventually

come to be seen, it is clear already that dialogue must replace hostile rivalry. Christians in the Holy Land are in theory well placed to promote such dialogue on behalf of the whole church. In practice past history and present politics make inter-faith dialogue more difficult in the Holy Land than almost anywhere else. So it has been encouraging to hear more than one speaker stress the need for it, as part of the process of reconciliation among the different communities of the Holy Land: Christians, it was said earlier, should open up to Muslims and try to understand their religion, and to Jews, to understand why some issues are so sensitive for them. The importance of distinguishing Jews and Judaism from Israelis and the State of Israel has also been underlined.

4. The Gospel is about forgiveness and reconciliation, between God and the human race, and among human beings. Christians everywhere are called to be a force for reconciliation in all situations of conflict. They are, sadly, sometimes themselves one of the causes of conflict. There is always a tension between being a Christian, a member of the church which is called to transcend all the natural factors that separate human beings, and being a member of a human society which tends to defend its own identity by setting itself over against other societies. This tension exists everywhere, but no church can be exempt from the obligation to. submit its human loyalties to the judgment of the Gospel. That Gospel calls Christians in the Holy Land as elsewhere to be a force for divine forgiveness and reconciliation, as well as for human justice. It has been suggested at this seminar that justice is the key to the interpretation of the Old Testament. Perhaps the key is not so much justice as the Kingdom of God, which certainly includes justice, but, even in the Old Testament, includes God's love, mercy and forgiveness. In the New Testament that Kingdom becomes a reality in human life through the suffering and death of the Word of God become human in Jesus. For Christians, justice is inseparable from God's forgiveness and reconciling love; and the call for forgiveness and reconciliation in the present situation in the Holy Land was most movingly expressed in Jean Zaru's lecture in the seminar.

5. One contribution Christians in the Holy Land could perhaps make would be to recognize that for Christian faith, place and territory have at most only a relative importance. It has been very interesting to hear different views on this subject expressed by speakers at this seminar who live in the Holy Land, close to the holy places. Some of you may know Peter Walker's book, *Holy City, Holy Places?*, a study of the divergent attitudes of Eusebius of Caesarea and Cyril of Jerusalem in the 4th century to the concept of holy places. Early Christianity had no great concern for holy places: it was much more concerned with the universal

presence of the glorified Christ in the Holy Spirit in the church as the 'place' where God was to be found. Although holy places became of great significance for Christians from the 4th century on, voices were always to be heard critical of the concept of holy places and pilgrimage to them. Cyril of Jerusalem was an enthusiastic protagonist of the concept, while Eusebius had grave reservations. Peter Walker seeks to apply his conclusion to the present situation. It is not easy to sustain theologically the traditional emphasis on the importance of Jerusalem and the Holy Land for Christianity: there is no earthly promised land for Christians. It could, he suggests, be an important part of Christian witness in the Holy Land to make clear the difference between the theological significance of the land for them as Christians, and its religious meaning for both Jews and Muslims. Bishop Kenneth has said that geography is for the sake of history, and history for the sake of meaning. There is of course an absolute political significance of the land for Palestinians as their homeland: but the land has only a relative religious significance for Palestinian Christians as Christians. The claim to the human rights of Palestinian Arabs in the Holy Land are distinct from any claims that might be made for Christian rights. Christians as such have no religious geographical claims.

6. The threatened situation of Christians in the Holy Land is not unique, nor, though it has undoubtedly been aggravated by it, is it due solely to the Israeli occupation of the West Bank: the opening lecture of this seminar revealed that Christian emigration from Palestine was significant in the first part of this century and began even earlier. It is shared by Christians throughout the Middle East. From Turkey to Egypt the continued existence of Christians is increasingly threatened, and there is an exodus of Christians, no less from Turkey, Lebanon, Iraq and Egypt than from the Holy Land. The possible extinction of Christianity in the Middle East is a matter of concern to the church everywhere, as would be a similar threat in any part of the world. The disappearance of indigenous Christian communities from the Holy Land would give rise to an additional sense of loss, given the historical and sentimental ties of Christianity there. But there should be equal general Christian concern about the decline of Christianity wherever that is occurring: Western Europe itself presents no small cause for alarm. The decline of Christianity in the Holy Land is not unique. At the same time Christians need to acknowledge the part played there in this process by the confusion of religion with social and political community, and not least, in the Middle East, by the association of Christianity with a West traditionally hostile to Islam, and oppressive towards Judaism. Paradoxically, the more the churches in the West come to the defence of Christian communities in the Middle East, the

more this association is likely to be reinforced in the minds of Islamic peoples and governments.

7. Perhaps a final point is worth making. I was very interested to read in Said Aburish's *The Forgotten Faithful* that the heads of the Orthodox, Roman Catholic and Anglican communities have urged the consulates in Jerusalem of the United States of America, Canada, Australia and other countries to stop facilitating the issue of emigration visas to members of their dwindling communities. It is of course one thing for local Christian leaders to encourage Christians to stay: it is another for Christians elsewhere to urge Christians in the Holy Land and in the Middle East in general to stay, merely for the sake of maintaining an indigenous Christian presence. The loss of ancient communities, with their cultural traditions, is always sad, wherever it occurs: it is an impoverishment of the human community. But Christians have to come to terms with the movements of history, which have already completely swept away the once flourishing Christianity of North Africa, and have left only tiny traces of the great Nestorian church, once so vigorous in the spread of the Gospel across central Asia even into China. The ecumenical patriarchate is said to have accepted that it will die out with the disappearance of the remaining Greek community in Istanbul. The churches in the Holy Land may also be destined to die. Christians will not stay, simply for the sake of staying. They will stay, if they can not only survive, but also make a reasonable life for themselves and their children. If this seminar could succeed in stimulating the churches elsewhere to give the practical help needed to create a viable economic and political basis for such continued existence, it would indeed have been worth while.

The Cumberland Lodge Declaration on Christians in the Holy Land

We, members of the Mother Church of Jerusalem, together with the other participants in the international seminar on Christians in the Holy Land, Pentecost 1993, declare the following:

We are conscious of the privilege of living, and keeping alive the Christian Faith where the Church was born.

The Christian Community in the Land of Jesus (the *Living Stones*, 1 Peter 2.5), has witnessed to our Lord in the midst of all the changing social, religious and political conditions over a period of two millennia.

We reaffirm our responsibility and constant determination on behalf of Christians throughout the world to safeguard our Sacred Heritage, along with that of Muslims and Jews.

While we, in the main, are an Arab Palestinian Christian Community, we treasure in our midst the presence of members of our Churches from a great variety of nations.

We are saddened by the ongoing reduction of the indigenous Christians in the Land of Jesus, which requires urgent attention.

We deplore the lack of access for Palestinians from the Occupied Territories to the Holy City of Jerusalem, and urge that free access to it be guaranteed for all peoples at all times.

We urge our Christian Palestinian sisters and brothers to stand firm in their ancestral home in the Land of Jesus. We expect all Palestinians who have emigrated, or were forced to leave, to come back. We request all relevant bodies to assist in their Return.

We have always welcomed the constant flow of Christian pilgrims to the Holy Land from all over the world, and we encourage them to meet and pray with the *Living Stones*.

As the Church, living in a broadly Arab and Muslim culture in the Middle East, we witness to our Christian Faith in dialogue with our sisters and brothers of the Muslim and Jewish faiths.

We share the aspirations of the Palestinian people for an end to occupation and for national independence. We therefore advocate and support a just and lasting peace in the region.

We call on the international community to respect and protect the unique historic nature of the Holy City of Jerusalem, and all the Holy Land, as being sacred to Jews, Christians and Muslims.

30 May, 1993

The Feast of Pentecost*
Michael Moxon

The tympanum over the west door of the cathedral at Vézelay in France consists of a huge and wonderful sculpture. In the centre of a great semi-circle of carved stone is the figure of Christ with His hands stretched out in blessing and surrounding Him are the Twelve Apostles. In the sculpture they are not looking at Jesus but under the influence of His blessing, the figures are all in different poses as if about to undertake some urgent task.

Surrounding this central picture are three semi-circles of stone within each of which are more carved figures consisting of men, women and animals representing the whole of creation. The effect of this tremendous work of art is utterly overwhelming. Carved by a master craftsman around the year 1140 AD the theme is that of the spreading of the Gospel message by Christ through the Apostles to all the nations of the earth.

The Gospels record the command of Christ to His disciples to preach the Gospel to all people and the promise is there, though expressed differently in each Gospel, that Jesus Himself would always be with them to inspire, guide and strengthen them in their task. However weary, dispirited or disillusioned they might become, the Spirit of their Master would always be with them. In the Acts of the Apostles just before His Ascension, the Risen Lord instructs His disciples to return to Jerusalem and wait: 'You shall receive power when the Holy Spirit has come upon you.'

* Following the conclusion of the seminar, many participants attended the service of Matins next day in the Royal Chapel, Windsor Great Park on Whitsunday, 30 May. This sermon was preached by the Revd Canon Michael Moxon, a Canon of Windsor and Chaplain in the Great Park.

Today, Pentecost or Whitsunday, we remember that gift of the Spirit and in our second lesson we heard how its coming was accompanied by remarkable events – the rushing mighty wind and the tongues of fire descending upon the heads of the Apostles. The effect upon the Apostles was apparently immediate and dynamic to such an extent that people thought they were drunk.

The Spirit of the Living God is indeed powerful. In the opening chapter of Genesis the very act of creation is ascribed to the Spirit of God moving over the face of the waters when the earth was, as the writer puts it, 'without form, and void; and darkness was over the face of the deep.' It was that same Spirit that Jesus had promised His disciples and its coming enabled them to live beyond themselves, confident that the life of the Risen Lord was in them and working through them. It was something that they wanted, or rather felt compelled to share.

That same gift of the Spirit was given to us formally at our baptism though to think that the Spirit of the Living God is restricted only to the baptised is surely a mistake. The Spirit, as Jesus said to Nicodemus in St John's Gospel, is like the wind: 'It blows where it wills and you hear the sound of it but you do not know whence it comes or wither it goes. So it goes with everyone who is born of the Spirit.' I believe that many people are inspired by the Spirit without even recognising it. That surely applies to many artists, crafts-people, and musicians whose wonderful gifts reflect the Spirit of the Creator God. The artists concerned might not see it that way but with the eye of faith we would want to affirm that whether a particular artist is a believer or not, something of God's Spirit is present in his or her work.

Nor is God's Spirit limited to the Christian Church. The church might be, perhaps should be, the body to recognise where the Spirit is at work in the world but to say that that Spirit is only to be found among Christian believers is to limit the power of the Spirit, and that is tantamount to blasphemy.

For example, I would want to affirm that the Spirit of the Living God is at work in people of other faiths and cultures. The insights of the great religions of the world and particularly the monotheistic faiths, Judaism, Islam and Christianity, have great similarities and at their best are sympathetic to each other and respect each other. A striking example of that has occurred this weekend at Cumberland Lodge where you will have gathered from the prayers, a group of Christians of different denominations and traditions from the Middle East and elsewhere have been meeting together. As, in the name of Her Majesty The Queen, I am privileged to welcome them to this Royal Chapel this morning, I know that they will not mind me mentioning the fact that part of the funding of their conference has come from Islamic sources even though there are no Muslims present at their conference. That certain Islamic leaders thought it important that some representatives of crucial Christian communities in the Middle East should meet here in the Great Park and have been prepared to give financial support to enable it to happen, is surely a sign of God's Spirit at work – that God whom Muslim and Christian alike seek to love and serve.

Again the fact that one participant said to me at dinner last evening that many of those taking part in the seminar had arrived as strangers, but having talked to each other, they now felt able to issue a declaration to which everyone could assent. This is surely another sign of God's Spirit at work. That declaration speaks of safe-guarding 'Sacred Heritages' along with Jews and Muslims and valuing the insights of other faiths. I suggest that is a fine example to all those who think that religion is only to do with bigotry and prejudice. It is also a reminder to all of us that we should be alert to the signs of God's Spirit at work in our own lives and communities. By uniting our wills and determinations with the Spirit of the Living God we release that Spirit to work in and through us, frail and weak though we may be, just as it did among those first disciples on the Feast of Pentecost.

Filled with the power of the Spirit, those first disciples were commissioned to share the Good News and preach the Gospel to all people. That was the theme of that 11th century carving at Vézelay with which I began this sermon. Is that still our task in a world in which there are many faiths, we may well ask? Perhaps we have to reassess what we mean by preaching the Gospel to all people and reflect that our Christian church has, at certain times, forced our faith upon others with terrible penalties if they did not conform. Perhaps, with great respect, the Spirit is calling us today to listen as well as to proclaim; to respect the sincerely held beliefs of others as well as share our own; to learn from the insights of other religions and see how they relate to our own faith. Maybe then, guided by people of all faiths, human beings can begin to learn to live together in harmony and peace: that peace which the Spirit of the Living God wills for everyone.

Participants

ALI, Rt Revd Bishop Michael Nazir
Secretary General CMS London (Bishop of Rochester 1994)

ABU EL-ASSAL, Mr Hanna

BARNES, Ms Gilian
Documentary film maker

BEELEY, Sir Harold
Chairman, World of Islam Festival Trust

BERGEN, Ms Kathy
Exec. Sec. ICCP (Geneva)

BUTLER, Mrs Barbara
Christians Aware

CLARK, Mr John
Partnership Secretary for the General Synod, Church of England

CRAGG, Rt Revd Bishop Kenneth
Honorary Assistant Bishop (Oxford)

CROWE, Revd Tony
Christian Action

DENNIS, Rt Revd Bishop John
Bishop of St Edmundsbury and Ipswich

DUNCAN, Mr Alistair
World of Islam Festival Trust

DUNCAN, Mrs Mariana

FARAH, Archdeacon Rafiq
Seminar Steering Committee

FARAH, Mrs Najwa

GERAISY, Mrs Adele

HAGOPIAN, Dr Harry
Middle East Council of Churches (UK), Seminar Steering Committee

HAJJAR, Mr Youssef
Director of Information Refugee Council, Oxford

HEAD, Mrs Julia
St Mary's University College, University of Surrey

HULBERT, Mr Alastair
EECCS (Brussels)

HORSMAN, Ms Roberta
World of Islam Festival Trust

HOPWOOD, Dr Derek
St Antony's College, Oxford

HUMMEL, Revd Thom
Virginia Theological Seminary

KASSIS, Dr H E
Canadian Council of Churches

MACPHERSON, Revd Duncan
St Mary's University College, University of Surrey

MIDGELEY, Revd Fr. Andrew
Rumanian Orthodox Church

MOBERLY, Sir John
Seminar Steering Committee

MOBERLY, Lady
Medical Aid for Palestinians

McDADE, Revd Dr John, SJ
Heythrop College, London

NEILSEN, Dr Jorgen
CSIC, Selly Oak Colleges

O'MAHONY, Dr Anthony
SOAS/London University

PLATTEN, Canon Stephen
Secretary for Ecumenical Affairs: Lambeth Palace

PRIOR, Revd Dr Michael CM
Head of the Dept of Theology and Religious Studies,
St Mary's University College, University of Surrey,
Seminar Steering Committee

ROSS, Revd Robin
Sec. Middle East Committee Church of Scotland

SAFIEH, Mr Afif
Palestinian diplomat

SAKKAB, Fr. Hanna
St Elias Orthodox Church, Syracuse, New York

SHAW, Revd Gordon
Gen Sec. CCBI, Seminar Steering Committee

SLAUGHTER, Mr David
World of Islam Festival Trust

SLOMP, Revd Jan
Conference of European Churches

SOUTAR, Mr Douglas
Project Officer for the Middle East, Christian Aid

STORRS, Mr Peter
Seminar Steering Committee

TAYLOR, Revd Dr William
Vicar of St Peter's Church, Ealing,
former priest in the Diocese of Jerusalem,
Seminar Steering Committee

WOODGER, Rev John
Vicar, St Mary's Church, Watford

WYBREW, Canon Hugh
Former Canon of St George's Cathedral, Jerusalem

WILKINSON, Canon John
Former Canon of St George's Cathedral, Jerusalem

Delegation from the Holy Land

AGHAZARIAN, Dr Albert
Director of Public Relations, Bir Zeit University

ABU EL-ASSAL, Archdeacon Riah
Representative: Protestant/Anglican Bishopric in Jerusalem

BARAMKI, Dr Gabriel
Vice President, Bir Zeit University

BATHISH, Monseigneur Kamal
Representative: Latin Patriarchate

GERAISY, Dr Sami
Chairman, International Christian Committee of Israel

HANANIA, Dr Agnes
Professor of Education and Psychology, Bir Zeit University

KATTAN, Dr Jeanne
Assistant Professor of English, Bethlehem University

LAHHAM, Revd Maroun
Rector of Latin Catholic Seminary, Beit Jala

MUNAYER, Mr Salim
Dean of Bethlehem Bible College

RAHEB, Revd Dr Mitri
Minister of Lutheran Christmas Church, Bethlehem

SABELLA, Dr Bernard
Professor of Sociology, Bethlehem University

SAHAGIAN, Rt Rev Archbishop David
Representative: Armenian Patriarchate

SFEIR, Dr Jacqueline
Assistant Professor of Early Childhood Education,
Bethlehem University

AL-SARRAF, Mr Faraj
Lawyer. Author of *Christianity in Gaza*

TIMOTHY, Rt Revd
Archbishop of Lydda. Representative: Greek Orthodox Patriarchate

ZARU, Mrs Jean
Religious Society of Friends, Ramallah

ZOUGHBI, Zoughbi
Middle East Council of Churches, Jerusalem